THE

COUCH

ENDORSEMENTS FOR *THE COUCH*

"As a business owner, I'm constantly trying to make my company better than it was yesterday—continually evolving and improving. Why wouldn't we want to look at our own lives and make improvements in the same way we do for our business? This book makes you analyze your own struggles and ask tough questions to improve your personal life just like you would your business. This is a great read that I highly recommend!"

—ED TRIM, PRESIDENT & CEO
(PENNINGTON & TRIM ALARM SERVICES, INC.)

"We have all heard *'experience is the best teacher.'* I completely disagree. Experience gives the test before the lesson, never teaches you the correct way—only under those circumstances can cost way more than learning from a mentor. With more than twenty years of mentoring and pastoring, Pastor Kevin Cooley mentors people away from that harmful conditioning into a new life in Christ in his new book, *The Couch.* Designed for small groups, he offers questions for believers to dig into not simply the behavior, but more so the root of why we do what we do. Don't allow your life to meander with experience as the guide. Let The Counselor put purpose in your day, step, and future with a vision of victory!"

—REV. JEFF TAYLOR, PRESIDENT & FOUNDER (TAYLOR MINISTRIES)

"If you've been looking for a book to help you find healing and freedom from pain and trauma, I highly recommend *The Couch.* Written from the heart of a pastor, Kevin Cooley gives you a step-by-step guide to meet with The Counselor and find the wholeness you need to step boldly into your future. This is a destiny-defining book that will build your faith, renew your mind, and change your life."

—ISAIAH SHOOK, CEO, TERRI SAVELLE FOY MINISTRIES

"*The Couch...* From the insights and wisdom shared in this book, you will be inspired to get up off the 'couch of life' and live a life of victory vs. living a life of the victim of the past. Each reader will glean trans-forming truths to live an overcoming, champion life. Thanks, Kevin, for sharing your heart."

—LARRY BETTENCOURT, LEAD PASTOR
(CHAMPION LIFE CHURCH IN BEAVER FALLS, PA)

"Wow, where has this resource been? Some time ago I read something that spoke to me—'The past is history, tomorrow is the future, today is a gift, that's why they call it the present.' For many Christians the past is not history, it's a prison they choose to live in now when Jesus has made a way for us to experience 'His' future for us and live in freedom. Kevin has put together one of the most practical tools I've seen in my 50 years of ministry. I highly recommend this book for both individual discipleship and as a small group study. Great Job, Kev!"

—JIM WIDEMAN, PASTOR, MENTOR, MINISTRY COACH

"After reading this book written by Pastor Kevin Cooley, from Mobile Alabama, it truly provides direction, not only for me, but for anyone who dares to pick up the book. The book is full of Godly wisdom and advice that we can use in everyday life. This is not a complicated to read and understand type book, but a book full of answers for the believer as well as those who may be struggling in areas of their lives and don't know why. This well written book is full of golden nuggets that teach how to experience true freedom and how to break away from the bondage that so easily entraps us on a daily basis."

—WADE FARRISH, ELDER (HARVEST CHURCH, MOBILE, AL)

"My friend, Kevin Cooley, has crafted a legitimate masterpiece. The Couch tackles some of the most critical components to spiritual growth, renewal, and revival. It is clear, creative, & clever. Kevin not only un-veils years of wisdom, but timeless truths that will transform your life. I promise, promise, promise that this book will stay close to you for years to come. Did I tell you it's a masterpiece? Well, yes, it is. Every word carefully written and prayerfully published. A masterpiece."

—TODD R BISHOP, PASTOR, CHURCH UNLEASHED, LONG ISLAND, NY;
AUTHOR, LEADERSHIP UNLEASHED, LEVERAGING TENSION,
& THE HUMAN RIGHT

"My husband, Kevin Cooley, I often say is the 'real writer' in the family. Our boys don't fall far from the tree, either. They got their dad's writing abilities. *The Couch* is a book you will want to devour when you pick it up like I did. Kevin asked me to proof it, and I kept saying over and over as I read it, 'Wow! This is sooooo good! This is going to help scores of people!' I felt like a broken record. As I made it through chapter after chapter, supposedly proofing it, it kept ministering to me. I finally chose to just read it for myself. Trust me when I say this is cheap but valuable therapy from The Counselor. What's so cool is I know this man better than anyone on the planet and I'm telling you: he lives this stuff! Kevin has led our family to have a life that works. That's the name of our podcast that releases the third Thursday of every month at midnight, A Life That Works! And that's exactly what you will have more and more of as you apply what you learn from *The Couch*."

—ADRIENNE COOLEY, AUTHOR OF *HAPPY ANYWAY*, *LOVE ANYWAY*, AND *BELIEVE ANYWAY*; SPEAKER, PASTOR'S WIFE, FRIEND, AND MOM

"Kevin Cooley is truly a one-of-a-kind unique individual, leading over 300 churches in India and still making time to pastor a church, here on U.S. soil. If anyone knows about the baggage of expectations, what a U.S. Pastor should look like and do… Kevin does. I am so thankful to know that there are still people who have a heart for whatever the Lord says. If Kevin was able to shed the weight of others' expectations, from his past, I know his NEW book, *The Couch* will show you the way to do that, too!"

—NICOLE CRANK – HOST OF "THE NICOLE CRANK SHOW," BEST-SELLING AUTHOR, SPEAKER, AND SENIOR CO-PASTOR OF FAITHCHURCH.COM

"Life is a collection of seasons and cycles. The seasons are in God's hands. The cycles are in yours. This book will train you how to break the bad cycles that are stunting your growth and frustrating your soul. It will train you how to break out of patterns that are holding you back so that you are free from the weights and sins that are keeping you from running your race. We have all wrestled with the frustration of wanting to see change happen in these cycles, but this book will show you that you can change and give you the strategies on how!"

—PASTOR JOEL SIMS, SENIOR PASTOR OF WORD OF LIFE CHURCH)

"Pastor Kevin Cooley is a mentor, personal friend, and father in the faith for a burgeoning move of God across the nation of India and beyond. I've had the great privilege of working alongside Pastor Kevin for over two decades and the profound impact he has had on my life is due in great part to the message found in this book. Pastor Kevin seeks to lead the body of Christ into true freedom. His faith-filled approach leaves no room for bondage to remain. I'm sure you and anyone else you know will be blessed by the truths found in this book just as I have."

—MIKE VAN BUSKIRK

"In *The Couch – 7 Sessions with the Counselor*, Kevin delves into the depths of the human soul, offering a profound journey of self-discovery and spiritual growth. Through biblical insights and personal reflections, he fearlessly explores the path to freedom from the twisted and destructive patterns that hold us captive. […] As a reader, I found *The Couch* to be a liberating journey. Kevin's candid insights and scriptural wisdom create a powerful combination that encourages lasting change. This book is an excellent resource for both individual study and group discussions, and it has the potential to touch countless lives and lead readers to a deeper understanding of God's love and grace."

—JOSH ROBERTS, INTERNATIONAL FAMILY CHURCH

7 SESSIONS
WITH THE COUNSELOR

THE

COUCH

KEVIN W COOLEY

FOREWORD BY PASTOR DAVID CRANK

SCRIPTURE REFERENCES

DEDICATION

*I dedicate this book to the people of Harvest Church, and the
loving, hardworking pastors of local churches everywhere.*

I wrote this book for the people of Harvest Church where I have enjoyed the honor of serving as their Pastor for half of my life. I reluc-
tantly answered the call to pastor Harvest, but it has been one of the
great joys of my life. Over the years I have found myself in counseling sessions helping people work through some of the painful pitfalls
and unexpected curveballs of life. We have enjoyed great victories
together and we have mourned losses together. But above all, we
have grown and learned together. Out of those experiences, and with
a great desire to continue helping "set at liberty them that are bruised"
I have written this roadmap to freedom. The chapters reflect many of
the issues that people have come to me looking for relief. My hope is
that you too will find freedom, and discover your destiny, and that
you will be healed of your past so you can step into your bright future.
If you're ever in the beautiful village of Mobile, Alabama, stop in to
Harvest Church to worship with us, and remember: No Perfect People
Allowed.

Your Future is Bright!
Pastor Kevin

TABLE OF CONTENTS

FOREWORD

Ever feel like you're tripping over the same stupid problems, again and again? A few sessions with THE Counselor will do us good. Get comfortable on *The Couch* with Kevin Cooley and learn how to finally get rid of those twisted beliefs that have been holding us back.

It's time to lose the shame and end the blame! God will never do for us what we can do for ourselves. So... what are we waiting for? Take a seat on The Couch. The freedom you've been searching for is just a few pages away. The Counselor awaits.

—DAVID CRANK, AUTHOR, SPEAKER, SENIOR PASTOR
(FAITHCHURCH.COM)

PROLOGUE

IN CONCLUSION...

No, the line above is not a typo. Statistics show that many people who start a book will not finish it. I don't believe you're *that* person, nonetheless I've put a major practical application in the beginning of this book, just in case you, or someone you know, needs **immediate relief** from what is harassing them.

WORK IT OUT

We All Have Issues. Dr. Henry Cloud often begins his seminars by asking, "Does anyone NOT have any issues? Please stand up. I want everyone to see what denial looks like." Have you ever had to "work it out"? Our issues must be faced openly and honestly. Maybe you have met someone and said to yourself, "*They* **have issues!***" Perhaps you've looked at your spouse and said it aloud. "You **definitely** have some issues!" Conversely, you might have looked at yourself in the mirror, said the same and realized it was true. "**I have issues.**" Be honest...

> *"...work out your own salvation with fear and trembling,*
> *for it is God who works in you, both to will and to work for*
> *his good pleasure." Philippians 2:12b–13 (ESV)*

The apostle, Paul, makes it clear we should all "work out our salvation." Don't mistake the phrase to mean something that it doesn't. There is only One Way to salvation: repentance of sin and faith in the Lord Jesus Christ. We cannot earn it through "works."

However, one of the proofs of God's graciousness towards us is that He allows us to customize our lifestyle and create a world that fits our personality... likes and dislikes...enabling us to fill our life with the people we enjoy. We tend to leave how we feel about ourselves out of this equation. You can be one of those people you enjoy! You can like yourself!

As a Christ-Follower, the very Life of God is resident within you. You can learn, from the tutelage of The Counselor, to "work it out." God will allow you to have as much of His abundant life as you choose, but it is a cooperative effort.

What is diminishing your level of freedom? God delivered the Israelites from Egypt, but it was a different process to get Egypt out of Israel. I want to help you engage in that process. The truths in this book will help you identify the enemies of your soul, so that you can not only discover your destiny, but actually enjoy it!

Are you ready?

Let's begin…

-1-
KILL YOUR AMALEKITE BEFORE IT KILLS YOU!

1

KILL YOUR AMALEKITE BEFORE IT KILLS YOU!

Question: How many therapists does it take to change a lightbulb?
Answer: Just one. But it's very expensive, it takes a long time, and the lightbulb has to want to change.

How to Kill What's Been Killing You

Amalek is an interesting word. In history it refers to a warlike, sneaky group of people that dogged Israel during their travel to the Promised Land. Over time their name has become synonymous with the carnal nature and works of the flesh.

Contrary to what some teach, our struggle is with our own flesh…just as much as, if not even more than, the devil and his evil spirits. In fact, we only have four, real enemies:

1. Sin
2. Selfishness
3. Sickness
4. Satan

Yes, we "wrestle not against flesh and blood," (see Ephesian 6:12) but our enemy seeks entrance through our thought-life and through the desires of our own flesh. This book is about specific truths that, if applied, will devastate any darkness that may be lurking in the recesses of your soul. James, who served as the Pastor of the local church in Jerusalem around the middle of the first century AD, tells us in James 1:21 (NKJV) to:

"Therefore lay aside all filthiness and overflow of wicked-ness, and receive with meekness the implanted word, which is able to save your souls."

Our souls are made up of three major parts: our mind (thinkers), our will (choosers) and our emotion (feelers). Some people have a broken "chooser," while someone else may have a defective "feeler." But the one thing we all have in common is that we are each uniquely screwed up in our own special way. Don't misunderstand me: IN CHRIST WE ARE PERFECT! But that doesn't mean we can't still have baggage, and most of us do. Remember, if you don't have any issues, please send us your photo so we can see what denial looks like. ;-)

Our objective, however, is not to point out problems, but to help you actually get past your past. In other words, you can't walk freely into your tomorrow if you are still bound up in your yesterday. It is imperative that Christians live in truth. And you are not powerless to do so. Why? It is a scriptural command, not just an option. Jesus said,

"You shall know the truth and the truth shall make you free." John 8:32. (NKJV)

The most powerful thing God has given you is your ability to make decisions. No matter what circumstance you may find yourself in, you have the ability to respond. I call it Response-Ability or the ability to choose your response.

Partial Obedience is Rebellion

Saul's first mission from God, as Israel's first and new king, was to annihilate an entire people-group — the Amalekites. "Why?" (You may ask.) "I thought God was good!?!" **Even in God's judgment He**

is merciful. The Amalekites were an irreconcilably wicked people. They offered their babies as burnt offerings to the dark deity, Molek. They fashioned a hollow, bronze statue in Molek's image, filled it with wood to fuel a fire, and when it heated to a glowing, red-hot state, they tossed their children onto its outstretched hands and watched them sizzle to death.

Jehovah, who is the God of Israel, seems to have chosen clemency for future generations by putting a stop to this wicked worship, but this people-group would not cease the dark practice. So the gracious God of Heaven, in His mercy, chose to intervene.

DESTINY DELAYED IS THE DEVIL'S DELIGHT

God desired that the Israelites enter the promised land peacefully. Yet, it was the Amalekites who refused to allow Israel to pass, undisturbed, through Amalekite land as they were leaving the bondage of Egypt.

If the Amalekites represent the sinful strongholds of the flesh, then it is comparative to see how our flesh can hinder us from entering into our personal "Promised Land" of destiny. It is our flesh that will abort our future if we allow it to. And…if we don't deal with our flesh… our flesh will deal with us. If we don't subdue our flesh, it will subdue us. Often the enemy's entry point into our life is through our mind. Thoughts come. It's important to think about what we think about.

SAUL HAD NO EXCUSES

God had many reasons for removing this people-group from the planet. But it all started when King Saul failed to execute God's will, and, as we are about to see, his decision came back to haunt him. Neglecting God's plan is always regrettable. Destiny delayed is the devil's delight.

Saul was a remarkable man. He stood head and shoulders above everyone. He was chosen by God as Israel's first king. In the early days of his reign, he was a man of great humility, but at some point, during his rule, Saul changed into an egomaniac.

The Bible reveals that Saul, instead of performing God's plan, adjusted it to his own liking. **He kept the King of the Amalekites alive!** To keep a king alive as a servant in your court was like having a living trophy. At the root of this sin, like most, is **pride!** And pride always has a better idea. Pride always thinks its plan is better than God's. Here we have a clear display of Saul's vanity. He valued his own image and reputation above complete obedience to the known plan of God. And if King Saul teaches us anything, it's that, in God's eternal economy, partial obedience is equivalent to rebellion. Saul had gradually moved beyond *sin*—missing the mark—or making a mistake. He had even moved past *transgression* by going beyond the known boundaries and parameters God had established.

Sadly, Saul, once so full of promise, had moved into *iniquity*, an inward desire or bent toward evil. Something in Saul's psyche, perhaps by his upbringing or some traumatic event in his past, had twisted his inward motivations and distorted his moral compass.

Iniquity, either created by pain or inherited through lineage, is a serious thing that must be soundly dealt a deathblow! Left unchecked, it will devour you and cause you never to step into your maximum potential. And this is why Jesus came—that we may have life and have it more abundantly. Total and complete victory is entirely possible and available.

Years later, on the battlefield, King Saul was destroyed. And can you guess who claimed the credit for his demise? An Amalekite. Let's read the story now, found in 2 Samuel 1:1–16 (NKJV).

> *Now it came to pass after the death of Saul, when David had returned from the slaughter of the Amalekites, and David had stayed two days in Ziklag, on the third day, behold, it happened that a man came from Saul's camp with his clothes torn and dust on his head. So it was, when he came to David, that he fell to the ground and prostrated himself. And David said to him, "Where have*

you come from?" So he said to him, "I have escaped from the camp of Israel." Then David said to him, "How did the matter go? Please tell me." And he answered, "The people have fled from the battle, many of the people are fallen and dead, and Saul and Jonathan his son are dead also." So David said to the young man who told him, "How do you know that Saul and Jonathan his son are dead?" Then the young man who told him said, "As I happened by chance to be on Mount Gilboa, there was Saul, leaning on his spear; and indeed the chariots and horsemen followed hard after him. Now when he looked behind him, he saw me and called to me. And I answered, 'Here I am.' And he said to me, 'Who are you?' So I answered him, 'I am an Amalekite.' He said to me again, 'Please stand over me and kill me, for anguish has come upon me, but my life still remains in me.' So I stood over him and killed him, because I was sure that he could not live after he had fallen. And I took the crown that was on his head and the bracelet that was on his arm, and have brought them here to my lord." Therefore David took hold of his own clothes and tore them, and so did all the men who were with him. And they mourned and wept and fasted until evening for Saul and for Jonathan his son, for the people of the Lord and for the house of Israel, because they had fallen by the sword. Then David said to the young man who told him, "Where are you from?" And he answered, "I am the son of an alien, an Amalekite." So David said to him, "How was it you were not afraid to put forth your hand to destroy the Lord's anointed?" Then David called one of the young men and said, "Go near, and execute him!" And he struck him so that he died. So David said to him, "Your blood is on your own head, for your own mouth has testified against you, saying, 'I have killed the Lord's anointed.'"

So there you have it. You can kill your dysfunction—or it may circle back and kill you. "But I was born this way," you may argue. Of course you were! We were all born this way: sinful. And this is precisely why Jesus said,

> *"Most assuredly, I say to you, unless one is born again, he cannot see the kingdom of God." John 3:3 (NKJV)*

DRAGGING AROUND A DEAD CORPSE

Even the great, holy, apostle, Paul, had issues. That's why he cried out in Romans 7:24 (NKJV), "O wretched man that I am! Who will deliver me from this body of death?" Tradition teaches us that if someone had committed a homicide, part of their punishment was having their victim chained to their ankle. They would have to literally drag the dead corpse around as it decayed. It allowed everyone to know exactly what they were: a murderer. It was a constant reminder of their painful, embarrassing past. Metaphorically, many people today are dragging the dead corpse of their stinking past around with them everywhere they go. It can infect every relationship they try to cultivate and everything they endeavor to do.

Before he was a Christ-Follower, Paul was a sadistic murderer of Christians. He hunted Christians and could be correctly labeled today as a serial-killer. Some say he likened himself to a "wild boar of a man" who killed for the pleasure of it. See Titus 3:3–7 (CEB).

After Paul was born-again, he still had to face temptations, regrets, and the "bent" he had before he was saved. Can you relate? I would venture to say, any "issues" or "struggles" you are facing today are, in some way, connected to sinful temptations you yielded to previously. That has been my personal experience as well. But there is a Way made to freedom. Let's jump right into getting some relief! Years ago, the Lord revealed this process to me, and I simply call it "The 5 R's."

How Did Paul Get Past His Past (The 5 R's)

The Bible reveals FIVE principles that must be practiced for continuous, victorious, Christian living:

I. **Recognize**— MY sin put Jesus on the cross! Situational ethics lead to death; ungodly alliances destroy destiny. Sin and demonic activity is like fungus: it grows in the dark. But when The Light shines upon them, they lose their power. Bring your issues out into the light... the open!

    a. Walk in the Light

        *1 John 1:7 (NKJV), 'If we walk in the **light** as He is in the light, we have fellowship with one another, and the blood of Jesus Christ His Son cleanses us from all sin."*

    b. Expose it, otherwise known as accountability. You can never have **intimacy** until you have **honesty.** Accountability helps you encounter the value of vulnerability.

        Proverbs 28:13,18 (NKJV) "He who covers his sins will not prosper, but whoever confesses and forsakes them will have mercy... [18]Whoever lives blamelessly (honestly) will be saved. But he who is perverse (dishonest) in his ways will suddenly fall."

    c. You can't deal with it on your own. If you want to change your life, change your friends. Join a small group at your church. We need the right people in our life to bring our struggles into the light and stay there.

    It can be extremely liberating to bring the pain, addiction, mistake, or abuse out into the open with the right person. Confession is indeed good for the soul. Admit it and quit it.

II. **Repent— Change the way you think.** The term "repent" comes from an old British military word meaning, "About Face!" When

8

you repent, you have chosen to reverse your decision about the sin that is stealing your crown! You are actively deciding that unforgiveness, lust, lying, or addiction is not only unacceptable to your Lord, but also to yourself. You deserve a better way to live.

    a.   King Saul showed us that partial obedience is rebellion and disconnects us from God's flow of Divine favor.

> *"If I regard iniquity in my heart the Lord will not hear me." Psalm 66:18 (NKJV)*

    b.   James 1:21–22 (NKJV) exhorts us,

> *"Therefore lay aside all filthiness and overflow of wickedness, and receive with meekness the implanted word, which is able to save your souls. ²²But be doers of the word, and not hearers only, deceiving yourselves."*

    c.   Repentance has a transforming effect on our lives.

> *"And do not be conformed to this world but be **transformed** by the renewing of your mind..."*
> *Romans 12:2 (NKJV)*

Thinking differently changes everything.

    d.   This requires **"Taking responsibility."** You've got to own it. Early on, I taught my two sons this concept. "That's what real men do: take responsibility.*"*

III.   ***Renounce***— give it up. Refuse to allow iniquity any access into your life any longer. Formally declare your resignation. Refuse to follow and obey this bondage. Vanquish it from your life. Use your authority in Christ, call it by name, and command it to leave your life, in Jesus' Name!

    a.   **Your greatest weakness will keep you from your greatest promise.** Sampson's lust for women stole his strength. Moses' anger kept him from entering the Promised Land.

King Saul's pride forfeited his royalty. You are not what others call you, rather you are what you answer to. Answer to Grace as it beckons you to RENOUNCE your sin. No longer allow it to have dominion over you. What you did or what was done to you is not who you are. **Your identity is in Christ.**

b. This is the time when you exercise your authority and command the unwanted rulers that have controlled you to exit your life. The Name of Jesus is above every name, and demons must respond to that Name.

> *"Therefore God also has highly exalted Him and given Him the name which is above every name, that at the name of Jesus every knee should bow, of those in heaven, and of those on earth, and of those under the earth, and that every tongue should confess that Jesus Christ is Lord, to the glory of God the Father."*
> *Philippians 2:9–11 (NKJV)*

c. **Renouncing something means no longer having anything to do with it.** Renouncing could include destroying items that have aided in your sinful behavior.

> *"And many who had believed came confessing and telling their deeds. Also many of those who had practiced magic brought their books together and burned them in the sight of all. And they counted up the value of them, and it totaled fifty thousand pieces of silver. So the word of the Lord grew mightily and prevailed."*
> *Acts 19:18–20 (NKJV)*

d. **Your authority does not depend on your ability, it depends on His power.** When you command the stronghold of the devil to go, in Jesus' Name, it HAS to go, according to the rules of conquest.

e. **Repentance never produces shame.** Condemnation produces shame, and shame comes from Satan. Conviction says, "You made a mistake." While condemnation says, "You ARE a mistake." I love the comforting words of 2 Corinthians 7:11 (NKJV),

> *"For observe this very thing, that you sorrowed in a godly manner: What diligence it produced in you, what clearing of yourselves, what indignation, what fear, what vehement desire, what zeal, what vindication! In all things you proved yourselves to be clear in this matter."*

IV. **Replace it.** Replace iniquities and incorrect deeds with God's **Word,** God's **Spirit,** God's **People,** God's **Presence,** and godly **Practices.**

a. **Receive a fresh INFILLING of the Holy Spirit.** Why? Because Jesus teaches us in Matthew 12:43–45 (NKJV),

> *"When an unclean spirit goes out of a man, he goes through dry places, seeking rest, and finds none. Then he says, 'I will return to my house from which I came.' And when he comes, he finds it empty, swept, and put in order. Then he goes and takes with him seven other spirits more wicked than himself, and they enter and dwell there; and the last state of that man is worse than the first."*

You must fill that void with Life Himself! And there will be no space for the enemy to come back to. It is vital to fill the place, the stronghold hell had in you, with the Presence of God.

b. **Satan is too weak to take a place in your life.** The only way he can gain access is if you give it to him. Do not give the devil a room for habitation in your life. Create or include

11

yourself in atmospheres that are conducive for God's Kingdom. Get around God's people. Guard yourself against unresolved conflict. Ephesians 4:26–27 (NKJV) points out,

*"Be angry, and do not sin: Do not let the sun go down on
your wrath, nor give place to the devil."*

   c. **Ask Jesus to fill you with His Holy Spirit.** Stop and do
that right now.

*Luke 11:9–13 (NKJV), "So I say to you, ask, and it **will
be given** to you; seek, and you **will find**; knock, and it
will be opened to you. ¹⁰For **everyone** who asks receives,
and he who seeks finds, and to him who knocks it will be
opened. ¹¹If a son asks for bread from any father among
you, will he give him a stone? Or if he asks for a fish, will
he give him a serpent instead of a fish? ¹²Or if he asks for
an egg, will he offer him a scorpion? ¹³If you then, being
evil, know how to give good gifts to your children, **how
much more** will your heavenly Father give the Holy
Spirit to those who **ask** Him!"* (emphasis mine)

   d. So, what are you waiting for? You have not because you
ASK not. Or as I say at my church, **"Get your 'Ask' in
gear!"**

V.   **Return— to your First Love.**

*"...you have persevered and have patience, and have la-
bored for My name's sake and have not become weary.
⁴Nevertheless I have this against you, that you have left
your first love. ⁵Remember therefore from where you
have fallen; repent and do the first works..."*
Revelation 2:3–5 (NKJV)

a. **Remember**— Recall where you've fallen from. In other words, remember to Whom you are returning: Love Himself! God doesn't have any love: He IS Love! And remember that living for God is much better than just living for yourself. God's plan is so much better than yours.

b. **Repent**— go back to the top where you belong. "Pent" means "the top" like the "penthouse." Realize, in Christ, you are over it. You're above it now because you are seated with Jesus in heavenly places in Christ.

c. **Repeat**— do the things you used to do when you were right with God. Act as though you are justified, "Just-as-if-I'd-never-sinned." Because as far as God is concerned—you haven't. How would a good, guilt-free, righteous person act? Do those things because that is who you are.

SOMEBODY'S KNOCKIN'...

"Behold, I stand at the door and knock. If anyone hears My voice and opens the door, I will come in to him and dine with him, and he with Me. [21] *To him who overcomes I will grant to sit with Me on My throne, as I also overcame and sat down with My Father on His throne."*
Revelation 3:20-21 (NKJV)

Salvation is past, present, and future: We have been saved; we are being saved; and we shall be saved. (That reminds me of a bad joke: The Past, the Present and the Future walked into a bar. It was "in tense.")

Sozo, the Greek word for salvation, is amazing! Dr. C.I. Schofield called it "…the all-inclusive Word of the Gospel." I am saved from past sin. I am being saved from present sin and, should I repent, I will find myself saved from future sin. Rev. P.C. Nelson, who was acclaimed as the foremost Greek scholar of his day, defined **sozo** as "…deliverance from past, present, and future sin, sickness, poverty, and calamity."

I'm not telling you to "get over it." I am actually telling you that you already have gotten over it. You have been "raised up together, and` been made to sit with Him in the heavenly places in Christ." Ephesians 2:6 (NASB) When? Right now! Friend, you have already been made free from your past. You have just as much right to come into the Throne Room of Almighty God as He has to sit upon His own throne! Jesus has made a way for us… He IS the Way for us.

There's no way I can know what traumatic thing happened to you. I am sorry for whatever abuse you have endured, and my heart goes out to you. There's no way any of us can change the regrettable things we have done to others. We cannot alter our past, but we can bring our past to the altar. I don't know what you've done or who you have done it to, but that's just it: it's not about what you have done. It's about what Jesus has done for you. He didn't just suffer on the cross **for** you, but **as** you. He took your place. He is our substitute. You *are* over it. You can go free. Whom The Son Sets Free Is Free Indeed.

Olly-Olly-Oxen-Free

When I was a kid growing up in South Jackson, Mississippi we would play hide-and-seek. I was a master. I was seldom found. Many times, I hid so magnificently that they gave up on finding me! Once they left me there for what seemed like hours. (It was probably 15 minutes.). I had hidden too well.

Have you hidden too well? So well that no one can find you? If the lights are on, but nobody's home then it's time to come out of hiding.

Come Out, Come Out, Wherever You Are

"Olly-Olly-oxen-free" is a catchphrase used by kids to indicate that the game is over, and it is now safe to come out of hiding. That's what the Holy Spirit, the Great Counselor, is whispering to you right now: "Come out Come out wherever you are! You are safe. You don't have to hide anymore. You can go free."

Are you ready to stop playing games?

Are you tired of hiding?

If You're Tired of Hiding...

Confess this Prayer Out Loud:

Dear Jesus, I confess and reaffirm that You are the Lord of my life.

I **Recognize** my sin. It is what put You on the cross to die. I bring my misdeeds and mistakes out into the Light of Your love. I confess I have been wrong, and I refuse to hide it or make excuses. I **Repent** of this bent toward wrongdoing and evil. I change my mind about it and declare it is no longer acceptable. I turn away from _____ (call the sin by name here) and refuse to yield to its influence any longer. I **Renounce** _____ (call your sin by name here). I say you no longer have any place in my life!

I resign. Sin, I will not cooperate with you ever again! I banish you and vanquish you from my life, home, body, family, and lineage! I command you to exit my life in Jesus' Name! I close the door to you—be gone! I cast you out! And Lord Jesus, I now **Replace** _____ (call name of sin here) with God's Love, God's people, God's Word, God's Presence, God's Power and Godly Practices.

I declare, in Christ, I am over this issue, and moving forward into the Abundant Life that Jesus purchased for me with His Holy, Sinless Blood. I **Return** to You, Jesus, as my First Love. I may not be perfect now, but I am now perfectly Yours. I give God's Word and God's Spirit first place in every area of my life. If I mess up, I will not give-up. I will trust the Holy Spirit to pick me up, In Jesus' Name — Amen.

PERSONAL NOTE: I believe your results and relief are to be immediately discernible.

But let me also encourage you that though Freedom comes immediately and completely, it is also a progression that comes in layers. And, paradoxically speaking, Salvation, though instant, is a lifelong process.

So, don't get off "The Couch" yet. Continue on in this journey and keep "working it out." The best is yet to come. And now that we have this foundation for freedom laid...

"The Counselor will see you now..."

QUESTIONS FOR SMALL GROUPS OR PERSONAL REFLECTION:

1. In what area am I, like King Saul, partially obeying God?

2. Is there an iniquity or "bent" where I see a pattern of struggle?

3. Do I recognize and understand that if I don't "Kill my Amelakite" that it will kill me? And am I willing to deal with my "issues" before they deal with me? Do I honestly want to change and be free? Why?

4. Have I applied the "5 R's" to my issue? If not, why? If yes, what changes have I experienced so far?

5. List 3 potential accountability partners and prayerfully contact one today and Join a Small Group at your local church.

-2-
FROM A VICIOUS CYCLE TO A VICTORIOUS CYCLE

2

FROM A VICIOUS CYCLE TO A VICTORIOUS CYCLE

"Holy Spirit, in what specific ways does my personal style of doing things alienate others that have a different temperament than mine?"

Have you ever been on "The Couch"? Ever paid some stranger $135 per hour to tell them all your junk? I'm gonna save you some money today. (Please remember that when sending an offering or giving several copies of this book as Christmas, graduation, or wedding presents.)

POTENTIAL IS HELD HOSTAGE BY BELIEFS

We've all experienced pain in our lives, so how do we get past our past? If you're more than three years old, you've experienced something relationally that you did not enjoy. The devil comes up with his perspective on what happened to you, and he loves re-telling the stories of the past in a way that stirs up pain in the present. In fact, the devil loves to help us re-experience pains of the past perpetually. Are you familiar at all with what I'm talking about?

The problem isn't the pain though. It is the message that's attached to the pain. And sometimes, long after the sting is gone, the root of the pain is still there, on repeat, and it creates the imprint of a faulty belief system. Then, eventually we start living out of that false belief system. Your God-given potential is either held hostage or liberated by your beliefs. When you operate from within a faulty belief system, it skews your whole life, causing it to stray out of alignment which, in turn, creates more pain. It's a vicious cycle. Later in this chapter, I'm going to give you the tools to get out of this vicious cycle and get into, what I call, "The Victorious Cycle".

THE GREAT DIVIDE

The great dividing line of the Bible is located in the Book of John, meaning that you can answer the question: "Does God let bad things happen to good people." Or the additional query: "Does God make people sick?" The answer is a definitive "NO." But let's explore a bit further. Is it the devil or do we just live in a fallen world? Here's the undeterred truth in John 10:10 (NKJV). It says very clearly," the thief comes only to steal, kill and destroy." In reality, that's all he does. The only reason the devil shows up in our lives is for those reasons. That's it! Some good advice is: "Don't make any deals with the devil." Unless you're really smart like this one guy...

He was playing golf and wanted to win so badly.

All of a sudden, a stranger appeared and said "Hey! If I let you birdie on this hole, would you give up 1/3 of your sex life?"

The man thought for a second. *If I birdie this hole, I'll be in the lead.*

And he replied, "Deal!"

Poof! The stranger disappeared and the man birdied on that hole. He makes the turn at the nine and was still in the lead by one, but the guy he was playing was really good and always beat him.

The stranger appears again and says, "If I help you eagle on this hole, will you give up another 1/3 of your sex life?"

And the man says, "Yeah! Deal!"

He eagles the hole and has a two-stroke lead.

They're coming around on the 18th and he's only one stroke in the lead and the stranger appears again and says, "If I guarantee that you win this round of golf and you have bragging rights to your buddy, will you give up the other 1/3 of your sex life?"

The man says, "I'll do it."

And he wins the match!

Then he asks the stranger, "Who are you?"

The stranger says, "I'm the devil. Gotcha!"

Then the devil asks the man, "What's your name?"

And the man replies, "My name is Father O'Malley. Gotcha!"

AUGMENT OR DIMINISH

So, in-spite of this humorous antidote, the thief truly does come only to steal, kill, and destroy. But here's the good news that's the kicker. Jesus says in John 10:10 (NJKV), "But I Am come that you may have *life* and that you may have it *more abundantly.*" Jesus comes, not to **diminish** your life, but to **augment** it. Many people think, *"If I serve God, I will be stuck and won't have any fun!"* No! The reason He comes is that you may have *life.* The NIV says, "that you may have it to the full." A full, satisfied, fulfilling existence! He might add 33.3% to your sex life! I'm not going to get into any testimonies—just gonna keep moving along here. But I will tell you it pays to serve God, in every way! His life can bless all areas of your life. Can you pause and say "Amen" right here?

Parenthetically, let me add this: Did you know that God's plan is better than yours? In fact, God likes His plan more than he likes your plan. Some of us have some good ideas but His plan is great! Ask King Saul. I'm sure he would now agree that God's plan is better.

HOW TO GET PAST YOUR PAST

Let's talk about how to stop the devil from digging up the past and how to be free to accomplish what God wants in our future. Satan always uses negative circumstances and he's not very nice. Most of us were raised to be gracious, so if we are berating someone and see that they're down, a lot of us will back away and say," Alright, I'm gonna give you a reprieve. I'm not gonna kick you when you're down." But how many of you have experienced the devil kicking you when you are down? He is not human and does not back up or back off. He will spit on you too. He's mean. He's the devil. In fact, when you take the letter "d" off of devil, you've got "evil." He's the epitome of evil. He's vile and he hates you. He wants to steal from you. He wants to kill you! And he wants to destroy your destiny, your life, and your dreams.

We, as "nice people", may back away. But not the devil! When you're down, that's when he really presses in and tries to go for the jugular! He pounces when we're vulnerable. He likes it when you're down: he thinks you're an easy target. So don't think he's gonna give you any mercy when life gets tough. That's when he turns up the pressure, locks down the screws and creates even more pressure in your life. But I'm here to tell you how to defeat him every time that happens. And I did say when, not now and again. The trials of life come to us all.

The reason the devil is so dangerous is because he operates in stealth. In fact, he's in stealth-mode much of the time. He knows we have authority over him; that's why he's sneaky. If he could trick you or sneak in without you knowing it's him, you, as a Christian can't or won't think to use your authority, so you grant him access to your life. Wouldn't it be nice, though, when he shows up if you knew it was the devil every time? Unfortunately, he doesn't show up in a red suit with horns and a pitchfork, knock on your door and say "Hi! I'm Monte D. Lucifer and I'm here to 'complicate' your life. May I come in for a little while and chat?" We'd be like h...! "Heavens no! Of course not!" But because he operates in stealth, we don't always realize it's him working, until he has negotiated our life situations into a vulnerable position.

THE DEVIL IS A TRICKSTER

Let me tell you about a couple of tricks of the devil. He tries to make us think that we're fighting each other. In reality we may not be doing so at all. In fact, as I mentioned before, in Ephesians 6:12 (NKJV), we are guaranteed that, "we wrestle not against flesh and blood."

People are not our problem. We are really wrestling "against princi-palities and powers and the rulers of this present darkness." Our battle lies in the realm of the spirit. Behind every thought there's a spirit. Our job is to discern which spirit is involved.

A few years ago there was a popular song that said, "It started with a whisper!" Many of our struggles are inflamed by a whisper too. Here's two of the devil's favorite disguises. He's a whisperer… You've heard of the Dog Whisperer, or the Horse Whisperer? Those are good things. But these types of whispers are not a good thing. Satan whispers to remind you of the hurt and pain of your past. But util you are healed of your past you cannot step into your future.

He whispers to our mind that the pain, the faulty belief, is our own doing. We're the ones who came up with this scenario or that problem. We're the ones who decided to go headlong into something, when all the while, it was the devil tempting us through the lusts of our flesh or soul.

Let me show how the devil operates. He's the guy that would be standing on the side of the temptation saying, "Come on man! Eve-rybody's doing it! You're gonna love this! It's gonna be so fun! This is awesome! Nobody will know. You know you want to do it! And you deserve it."

As soon as you enter into temptation and commit the sin, then the devil immediately jumps to the other side as The Accuser of the brethren saying, "I can't believe you did that! You're an idiot! What a loser! How can you call yourself a Christian? Don't even try talking to God because He's not gonna have time for you now because of what you did! You're not worthy to come into God's Presence!"

And this is how the devil operates. He's mean! And he tries to convince you that you are the evil one!

Here's another tactic Satan employs. Sometimes he tries to con-vince us that God is mean and speaking to us. Often, in our moments of defeat, the devil comes and suggests," God did this to you!"

Or here's an even trickier one. If there is something that you want to do, but it's not God's will. He will tell you," Yeah! This is the

Lord! Go ahead and do that!" And if you haven't renewed your mind with God's Word, you can't tell the difference between the voices speaking to you. *Is it the devil's voice? Is it God's voice? Is it your own voice? Is it your spouse's voice? Is it the opinions of others?* Recall that I told you there's a a spirit behind every thought. We must discern which spirit it is. There are a lot of voices out there, but there's an easy way to discern which voice is talking to you. We're gonna get to that in just a minute; I'm gonna keep you holding on a bit longer.

Let's go to a scripture first. It is 2 Corinthians 11: 2–3 (NKJV).

> *"For I am jealous for you with godly jealousy. For I have betrothed you to one husband that I may present you as a chaste virgin to Christ. But I fear, lest somehow, as the serpent deceived Eve by his craftiness, so your minds may be corrupted from the simplicity that is in Christ Jesus."*

That word *deceive* means to swindle.

THE SWINDLER

In the 8th grade I played the villain in the school play. My goal was to swindle Dudley Do-right out of the deed to the ranch by trickery. That's what the devil does. He's tricky. The word *deceive* adds another word— "subtle trickery." It reminds me of a time I was in New Orleans with my son, Garrison. We were getting a passport renewed because we were going out of the country on a mission trip.

This guy walked up to me and said," Man, I bet you $5.00 I know where you got them shoes."

And I thought for a minute. *There's no way he knows where I got them. I'm from Mobile, and I bought these shoes in Tulsa. There's no way he can know that.*

I said, "Alright man! Where'd I get these shoes?"

He said, "You got them on your feet! Give me my $5.00!"

That's why I don't bet.

I gave the brother $5.00, and said, "You got me, dude! You got

25

me!"

Subtle trickery! Never negotiate with the devil. Just read him the Bible.

Do You Boo

Let's go to verses 13,

> *"For such are false apostles, deceitful workers, transform-*
> *ing themselves into apostles of Christ."*
> *2 Corinthians 11:13–14 (NKJV)*

Some people are tricky and subtle, are they not? This verse says you've even got to watch out for some religious people or for certain "ministers"! Because they're false apostles. False pastors. False workers, transforming themselves. In other words, they're posers. You can't make yourself a pastor or an apostle of God. Only Jesus does that! We should quit trying to be something we're not: Do You Boo.

In verse 14 we are told,

> *"No wonder! For Satan himself transforms himself into an*
> *angel of light."*

In other words, sometimes the devil makes himself look good! You know the old saying, "If it's too good to be true, it probably is." Well, I'm here to tell you; if it's too good to be true, it probably is. The devil takes advantage of us by using our lusts, desires and what we want in regard to our unsanctified desires. But if you take those desires and submit them to Jesus and get those desires sanctified, then, God says in Psalm 37:4 (NKJV),

> *"He shall give you the desires of your heart."*

Isn't that a good plan? You still get what you want. You still get the desires of your heart. You're just submitting those desires to the Lordship of Jesus. Because the things God wants for you will bless you. The things the devil tries to give you have more than strings attached. There are hooks attached too. And if he gets you hooked, he's not gonna cut you loose; you're gonna require deliverance.

Let's look at 2 Corinthians 2:10–13 (NKJV).

> *"Now whom you forgive anything, I also forgive.* [That's a pretty good deal too.] *For if indeed I have forgiven anything, I have forgiven that one for your sakes in the presence of Christ, lest Satan should take advantage of us for we are not ignorant of his devices."*

Your enemy, Satan, has tailor-made plans designed to derail your life. These are called demonic schemes. Satan's schemes include getting you so upset with somebody that you won't forgive them. The devil knows if he can get you into unforgiveness or bitterness towards another person, then he's got you hooked! **But we are not ignorant of his schemes**. Paul essentially says here, *"I know somebody did you wrong, but go* ahead *and forgive them so that the enemy doesn't get a foothold into your life."*

Let's go to Genesis 3:7 (NKJV).

> *"The eyes of both of them (Adam and Eve) were opened and they knew that they were naked."*

Obviously, they were naked before, but they just didn't know it. Why? Because they were surrounded by the glory of God. I like what one pastor who teaches on marriage a lot calls it: *gloriously naked!* When you're a Christ-follower and you get married and you're making out with your wife—that's gloriously naked. Jesus restored everything Adam and Eve lost! I just gave you a good reason to serve Jesus. It's called *gloriously naked!* You should serve God if for no other reason.

Now, I need to warn you, you don't get gloriously naked until you get married. It's an incentive program that God has going on. Then, the story continues in Genesis 3:7 (NKJV),

*"Any they knew that they were naked and they sewed fig
leaves together and made themselves coverings."*

This represents what religion tries to help you do: cover up your
own mistakes. But religion can't fix your problem.

THE WORLD'S FIRST RELIGION

I call this *fig-leaf-ology*—aka, religion. In verse 8, of Genesis 3
(NKJV), we can catch a glimpse of the first couple and their responses.

*"And they heard the sound [voice] of the Lord God in the
garden in the cool of the day [wind] and Adam and his
wife hid themselves from the presence of God among the
trees of the garden."*

The trees of the garden were meant to bless them, but now they're
hiding amongst the blessings trying to stay away from the Presence
of God. (Now that's another sermon that I don't have time to preach,
but when your blessings keep you away from the Blesser then you
have lost your way.) Verse 9 lets us know what happened next.

*"Then the Lord called unto Adam and said to him, 'Where
are you?'"*

Now, quick little theological training here. In the Bible, when
God asks a question, it's not because *He* doesn't know the answer.
Furthermore, when God asks *you* a question, it is not because He
doesn't know the answer—it's because *you* don't know the answer.
Here's a paraphrase to continue the tale.

"Adam, where are you?"

And Adam was probably thinking, *"I'm not sure. I used to know
but now I'm kinda… lost."* And indeed, he was.

Adam said, "I heard your voice in the garden and I was afraid
because I was naked and I hid myself."

And God replied, "Who told you that you were naked? Have you eaten from the tree which I commanded you that you should not eat?"

And the man responded, "The woman you gave to be with me, she gave me of the tree, and I ate."

You better marry the right person, or they will eat you out of house and home? (Sorry! I couldn't resist!)

Keep in mind also, before the devil defeats you, he has to disarm you. A little trivia question: What were the first recorded words of Satan in all of human history? They were: "Hath God said?" The first words that the devil ever spoke (that we have recorded) involved questioning the Word of God. If the devil can dispose you of your sword, only then can he defeat you. Your sword is God's Word. And if he can get you to doubt God's Word, instead of believe God's Word, then he's got you at an extreme disadvantage. God's Word is the weapon that leads to our success. The devil wants your Bible on your coffee table. That's fine with him—just so long as you don't read it. He doesn't mind if you have the Bible app on your phone so long as you never open it. Or, if you do open it, you're so distracted by social media that you're not paying attention to it anyway. And the devil doesn't even care if you believe God's Word as long as you keep your mouth shut and never speak it.

Your Bible is more than important. In fact, at our church we have Bible reading plans in the form of a bookmark. If the devil is kicking your butt, it could be because you're not reading your Bible, meditating the scripture and speaking God's Word out of your mouth. You may be thinking, *"Come on! Seriously? You really believe that that ancient book can help me?"* But it's not an old, ancient book—it's an Eternal Book. And by the way, you don't read your Bible as much as the Bible reads you. Imagine reading something and suddenly be like, "Whoa! Wow! Are you kidding me? This is exactly what I needed. How did You know? Oh, never mind."

God knows everything about us. He can position us within His Word where it feeds us exactly what we need. And what might that be? He's more than capable of giving us the special tool or weapon we need to do warfare against the enemy of our souls in that moment

—in that exact circumstance. Maybe you don't need a sword. Maybe you need a Holy Ghost Ninja throwing star! Hit the devil right between the eyes, man (or woman)! It's all in The Book. Don't forget, the devil's first words to man were to question God's Word. If he can get you to doubt it then you will live without it.

We must also notice, at this point, what the man and his wife began to **think**. After they sinned and after they questioned God's Word, they began to contemplate new ideas such as, "*Something is wrong with me.*" And guess what? That's because The Liar, the Pain Perpetuator, was there whispering, "Yeh! You're weird. Something *is* wrong with you! You're messed up! Something's not right about you. You're a little off." That type of **thought** never comes from God! Ever! And never will. Furthermore, it is guaranteed to be the devil. And I'll tell you why. Because we don't think that kind of stuff about ourselves, all by ourselves. Just the basic human need for survival and human self-preservation doesn't allow us to think those kinds of things. Those thoughts always come from the dark side. They always come from the enemy of your soul. So if you have a pervasive, ongoing thoughts such as, "I am damaged goods. Something is wrong with me. I'm just different from everybody else. I'm not normal. I'm dysfunctional. I'm broken. I may even be evil." Those thoughts come from your enemy, Satan. If you were on the couch of counseling today, I'd just tell you to quit listening to those thoughts and decide to stop believing that pack of lies. And now you're saying, "Well, how do I quit thinking those things?" I'm going to tell you.

WORST DAY EVER!

Ever had a bad day? Ever had a day where you were like, "Yep! I am definitely a sinner! I'm messed up." Ever had an even worse day? A day where you said to yourself, "I wonder if I'm actually beyond being a sinner? I wonder if I'm a psychopath or a narcissist or if am evil?" Ever been there? Seriously. You are not alone. Many people have. Some have even thought, *"Not only am I an evil individual, but I'm so evil, perhaps, I'm even demon possessed! I've got company."*

30

Listen carefully please and let me just tell you the truth. No thought like that can ever come from God—ever. God never announced, "You're demon possessed!" On your absolute worst day, He is still your greatest fan. On your most evil day, He is thinking good thoughts about you. In fact, because Jesus came and died on the cross for our sins, He doesn't think any bad thoughts about you at all…ever. You're His favorite! Jeremiah 29:11 (NIV) tells us exactly what God is thinking about us all.

> *"'For I know the plans I have for you,' declares the Lord, plans to prosper you and not to harm you, plans to give you hope and a future.'"*

In other words, God says, "I know My Own thoughts. I think good thoughts about you!" You may still be thinking, *"Yeah, but I'm an evil scumbag. I'm a worm. I've committed adultery. I've been divorced three times. I've stolen money. And I'm an addict. I kicked the dog!"* (Just fill in the blank.) God's like, "I love **you**. You are My Favorite. Come to Me. Let me give you a hug. Come here: Drawn close to Me! My goodness will draw you to change."

And while He's hugging you, He'll be cleaning you up a little bit at a time. He loves you and on your worst day, He's your best friend. He is not gonna kick you when you're down. He is the One Who is going to help you get up. He is our Glory and the Lifter! He is your Creator and your Redeemer. He is The Counselor. He is your Advocate.

IDEAS OF DEFEAT ORIGINATE WITH SATAN

In the Book of Matthew, Chapter 16, has an "Aha" moment. God spoke to Peter. Remember the story where Jesus said," Who do men say that I am?" And they answered, "Some say John the Baptist. Some say Elijah." Then He asks Peter, "Who do you say I am?" And Peter spoke by the Spirit of God and answered, "You are the Christ; the Son of the Living God." And Jesus basically replied, "Good job! You didn't figure this out by yourself. God revealed it to you. You just heard from God, Peter." I'm certain that Peter was like, "I heard from God. Yeah!"

But then Jesus said," I'm going to be turned over to the Pharisees and the Romans and they are going to crucify me." And maybe Peter thought, *"Hey! I know how to hear from God. That can't be true."* And the Bible says Peter **rebuked Jesus** saying, "No you are not! You're not gonna die!" (How many of you know it's never a good idea to rebuke Jesus? Just saying.)

And here's what happened. **Jesus didn't rebuke Peter**. He turned around and said, "Get behind me, Satan." Peter went from hearing from God to hearing from Satan in the space of a few verses. Why did that happen? Because Peter is an unknown person: a fisherman. Jesus comes along; calls him to be His disciple; brings him out of obscurity to being one of the most important men in human history. And then Jesus says, "I've been your best friend. I've been your mentor. I've been your Rabbi. But now I'm going to die and be taken out of your life."

Of course, Peter didn't want that to happen. He didn't hesitate as he said, "No! No! No! That is not gonna happen." And because Peter wanted this so badly, he thought sure it must be God! *Just because we want something doesn't mean it's God's will.* That's why Jesus turned around but didn't rebuke Peter. Instead, He rebuked the spirit that was whispering in Peter's ear. He said to the real culprit, "Get behind me Satan." Behind every thought there is a spirit.

Consider this warning that the devil will try to use other people who are close to us to get us off-track. We better recognize it. We better address it. And if they won't change, we might need to filter them out of our lives.

Allow me to say this in a pastoral way. Not everybody deserves to be in your life. What I love about the scenario with Jesus and Peter is that Jesus kept Peter in His life, but also, Peter changed and adjusted. Humility will do that. Peter eventually came around, so much so that he became one of the greatest apostles in human history. However, if people don't stop listening to certain spirits, then they disqualify themselves to be a voice in our lives.

So like Jesus, address the spirit behind the thought, not just the person sharing it.

THOUGHTS ARE SEEDS

In times of crisis the devil almost always speaks. Let me say it a more accurate way. In times of crisis, he busies himself planting thoughts. Here is an example from Ephesians 4:26 (NKJV)

"Be angry and do not sin."

(It's okay to be angry as long as you don't sin.)

"And do not let the sun go down on your wrath, nor give place to the devil."

Allow me to clarify this key truth: The devil is so weak he cannot assume a place in your life; you have to give it to him. God simply says not to do that. Do not allow it.

Here's one way people give place to the devil: Yield to anger. That's okay. It happens. The trouble comes when we don't deal with that anger in a godly way. If you're married, and you have a fight with your spouse, please do not go to bed on that anger. When you wake up in the morning, you're now facing aged anger. You've more than likely gone from simple anger to toxic anger and then can move on from toxic anger to wrath. What has occurred in the spirit-realm during this time? You have just given a foothold to your arch-nemesis, Satan. Some things in life are better when they are aged, such as cheese and wine, but never does this apply to anger.

Now you must get him out. It is not hard to get him out, but you never had to let him in from the start. Here's what you do. Let's say you have a great marriage. Then you have a fight, and you go to bed. Next, the Pain Perpetuator comes and whispers a thought in your ear. He puts his spin on the argument, and you wake up different than when you went to bed. You may start to think, "*Maybe I need a new woman.*" Or, "*Maybe I married the wrong man.*" Why? **The thought that has been planted in your mind has begun to take root.** You didn't come up with that idea by yourself. It was planted there by your enemy. Anger has begun to age.

Remember what Jesus said about a man who sows wheat in his field? He goes to bed and the enemy comes and sows tares or weeds. The enemy, the devil, plants thoughts and they become like those weeds. God is not going to tell you that you married the wrong man or you married the wrong woman. Once you chose them for marriage, they became Mr. Right or Mrs. Right and it's your job to bless, love and heal them. Certainly, in extreme circumstances, when a spouse is unwilling to live for God or to work on the marriage or they abandon the marriage or become abusive—those are different scenarios. Those are extreme cases and a bit rare, but they do happen.

WEEDS IN THE GARDEN OF MY MIND

As a young adult my primary thoughts did not take into consideration Satan's influence in my thought life. I didn't recognize it was the devil whispering lies to me and trying to plant seeds of failure. "*I won't succeed because eventually I'll just give up or fail to remain consistent.*" I had seen a pattern in my life where I would do really well and excel at something, then I would either get bored, lose interest or would fail to continue to be disciplined. I lived with an ongoing thought pattern, "*Okay, you can stop now. You're not going to go any further anyway. Just quit before you embarrass yourself and everyone sees you for the fake you really are.*" I was completely unaware that the devil was afraid of my success—just like he is of yours.

Another thought I had as a young adult was, "*If people really knew me, they would reject me.*" I really doubt that I'm alone. I believe a lot of us have probably had similar thoughts. Allow me to share a few more so I can include everyone with me. "*You know, you're really not very smart. You might be clever. You might have people fooled for a while but once they get to know you, they'll see that you are not a very bright guy. You're such a fraud."* There was also, *"God loves other people more than He loves me."* (CERTAINLY NOT TRUE AS WE HAVE DISCUSSED. I'm actually His favorite, BUT so are you.)

I've also experienced foreboding thoughts such as, *'Something bad is going to happen. I don't know when, but everything's going too good. Something bad is going to happen; either to me, my wife, my kids, or to my church or ministry. Something bad is going happen. It's just a matter of time...."* If the devil can get you to **believe** just one of those thoughts, guess what's going happen? Something bad! But when we **recognize** that it's him—and that's key—and then reject those thoughts and follow through by **replacing** them with The Seed of God's Word, then Satan's schemes *cannot* come to fruition in our lives, because something greater will then be growing and displacing it.

Don't Let Satan Slide Up in Your DM's

Fear is a liar. It's never just the pain caused by a negative experience. It's also the message that Satan attaches to the fear and the pain. So, whatever happened to you, and I'm sincerely sorry that it did, whether it was... abuse (verbal, sexual, or physical). Whether it was divorce, abandonment as a child, poverty, failure, ridicule, bullying, etc. Whether it is addiction and you're trying to medicate some pain on your own; I'm here to tell you that you don't have to medicate anymore. Jesus has healed the pain, and also the source of it! You don't need the addiction. You don't need the bad habit. You don't need the toxic relationship. HE has supplied ALL your need. Your healing is already taken care of. Your next step is to learn to receive the healing and to walk in it.

Uprooting Toxic Thoughts

There are three things we can employ to destroy the devil's lies that ruin lives:

1. **Expose the devil's lies**. Are you familiar with the phrase, "Liar, Liar, pants on fire"? Satan wants you to suffer silently because once the lie comes into the light, it loses its power. Satan puts shame around everything you do so that you will hide it inside a cloak of darkness or deception. Of course, he will put fear around our actions so that we won't come out and confront them. But sin and fungus both have something in common: they grow in the dark. But as soon as you expose sin to the light, the fungus-like lie begins to die. Lies lose ground in the soil of our mind. That is what the sweet conviction of the Holy Spirit does: He leads us into the liberating light of God's Truth and Love and crowds out the crop of lies from Hell. Then our lives begin to yield the peaceable fruit of the Spirit! Jesus said it this way John 8:32 (NKJV):

> *"You shall know the truth and the truth shall make you free."*

The Holy Spirit is the Spirit of Truth. The situation or subject doesn't matter. If you can be honest and truthful with God about it, you will be exposing Satan's lies. Consequently, you regain the power you previously gave away, and begin to take back the ground yielded to darkness.

DEFINING MOMENTS

Can you recall a time when something unfortunate occurred in your life? "Life" happens to us all. No one is spared. And during such times of tragedy or pain is when Satan insinuates his lies into our consciousness. I would like for you to think of at least one such thing that happened in your own life. Some of you may say, "I've got a list!" Maybe your parents got divorced when you were a kid or one of your parents was killed at a young age or you were molested by a neighbor or…fill in the blank. In that moment of pain, the devil came and attached a message or meaning to that event. And when you believed that lie, it became the source and fountain of perpetual pain and dysfunction in your life. But here's the good news: these defining moments do not have to define you! Once that lie has been exposed, space is created for the Holy Spirit to come in and convey Jesus, The Truth, to our heart and mind. The Counselor transmits Christ into that space, and He discloses the reality of Sonship to your soul. In other words, you "know The Truth, and He makes you free."

EXERCISE

Quiet your mind. Now ask The Counselor, the Holy Spirit, "Is there anything You would like to talk to me about?" When He brings something to your remembrance (a thought or memory may bubble-up to your mind; or a picture of a present or past circumstance), ask Him, "What lie of the enemy did I believe as a result of that 'defining moment'?" Now, I want you to ask God, "Okay, if *that* was the lie I believed, Holy Spirit, what then is The Truth?" Remember, what does the truth do? It makes you FREE!

Write 3 Lies That You Recognize You Have Believed, and Then Write The Truth Beside Them:

1)

2)

3)

---

2. **Expel any word that does not agree with God's.** The ultimate Battle-Royale was fought between Satan and Jesus in the wilderness when Jesus was tempted. And what did Jesus say every time? **It is written...** He knew what was written and He spoke the

scripture against the devil as a weapon. No, not with actual swords. This battle wasn't fought with natural weapons; it was fought with words and thoughts. And that is the battlefield where we must win the fight today and every day. Be a champion in your thought-life and you will be a champion in all of life.

THE POWER OF A SINGLE THOUGHT

Satan took the entire human race captive with one thought in the Garden of Eden. Do you know what that thought was? *"God is holding out on you! He gave you this whole garden and said you can't eat off this one tree? You know why God is holding out on you? He doesn't want you to be like Him."* The truth was that they were already like Him. They were made in God's Image. And the fact remains, God wants us to be like Him still. Mankind is God's highest form of creation. God's goal is to guide you into being conformed to the Image of His Son, Jesus. So next time you look in a mirror remember: you look like your Daddy.

God gave Adam and Eve the entire garden. He said, "This one tree is mine." I think that tree represents what is called The Tithe. And Satan rebuffed, "God wants you to give 10% of your money to the church? What kind of God do you serve? I'll let you have it all." See, God is not holding out on us, friends. But He does want to be First. Because when He is first in your life then He can bless the rest of your life. And if you expose and expel the lie that God is holding something back from you, then you will begin to walk in your Divine Destiny. And it's not just about 10% of your money. It applies to everything. *So, God doesn't want me to have sex before marriage? God's holding out on me!* No, He's trying to protect you from gonorrhea, clap, herpes, aids, unwanted pregnancy, STD's, trauma, drama, and pain. It's the same reason I didn't let my kids drive my car when they were six.

"I do it on Xbox all the time, Dad. Give me the keys!"

"Uh, no."

Why? Because they didn't have a license. If we drive without proper certification, we will get hurt and hurt others. Consequently, we need a license to get married. If we proceed improperly, without wise instruction, we're going to needlessly hurt ourselves and others. Now, I'm using the term "married," but, conversely—if we shack up without a license, we're gonna hurt ourselves and other people as well. The fallout does have a radius. One individual is not the only person these types of actions hurt. The wages of sin is still death (Romans 6:23 NKJV). When you sin, stuff dies. It's like spraying Round-Up on your garden. But Jesus came to give us Abundant Life.

> *"The free gift of God is eternal life in Christ Jesus our Lord." Romans 6:23b (NKJV)*

BOUNDARIES CREATE SAFETY, ORDER, FOCUS AND POWER

God doesn't want me to have fun. He doesn't want me to drink. He's such a prude. God is a teetotaler. Well, first of all, Jesus turned water into wine, so I don't know about all that. But it is a proven fact that when you put boundaries on something it creates safety, order, focus and power. Do you know what a swamp is? It's a river without discipline. It could be a powerful flow of water, but it lacks the focus and boundaries to guide it in the proper direction. When you have discipline and boundaries in your life, it creates focus, flow, productivity, power, and life. Otherwise, your life becomes just like a swamp that is filled with unprofitable vermin and stagnation. Again, it isn't about The Tithe, it is about keeping Christ first and at the center of EVERY part of our life. He is the Lord of all—or not at all. He requires first place. He will not settle for being second priority. Whatever or Whoever is First orders the rest.

God is not trying to take something from you. He is trying to add potency to your life. This is one of the first verses I memorized (and this is how I remembered where it was:10-4 Good Buddy).

> *For the weapons of our warfare are not carnal but mighty in God for pulling down strongholds; casting down arguments and every high thing that exalts itself against the*

knowledge of God, bringing every thought into captivity to
the obedience of Christ. And being ready to punish all dis-
obedience when your obedience is fulfilled.
II Corinthians 10:4–6 (NKJV)

Take captive every *thought*. That word *captive* means to take a spear and place it at someone's throat. So that's what you're to do with every thought that comes into your head. You take God's Word and place it at the throat of every thought and demand, "Where are you from? Do you match the Word of God or not?" If it doesn't match The Word of God, then slit its throat. This is how we take every thought captive. For example, we don't have to say everything that comes to our minds. My aunt used to say," I got so mad I was gonna give that person a piece of my mind. And then I realized I couldn't afford it." Keep the contents of your mind for yourself. And don't accept that you have to say everything. Just because it comes to your head doesn't mean it needs to come out of your mouth. Expel any word that does not agree with God. Then get into His Word (the Bible) and find a better thought that produces safety, order, focus, life, peace, and power. Where the mind goes the life follows.

List Your 3 Dominate Thoughts Here and a Scripture
to Either Support or Disrupt that Thought:

1.

2.

3.

THE FINAL INGREDIENT

Express your agreement with God's Word. Say it out loud. Repeat what God has already said about you. Jesus came to earth, was born of a virgin, lived a sinless life, died in our place that we could live a sin-free life too.

When I was fifteen years old, I experienced a dark depression. That wasn't normal for me. I was a fairly happy guy, but I experienced a lot of rejection when I started living for Christ. All my friends abandoned me. I went from Mr. Popular to Mr. Weirdo at school. I didn't realize it at the time, but God was delivering me from popularity, also known as the need to receive approval by other people. It was like He was saying, *"I'm going to teach you to need to be obedient to Me more than being accepted by people so that you can be blessed instead of popular."* I can now testify that blessed is much better than popular. I can obey God and not care who likes it or who doesn't like it. I'm not doing it for them; I'm doing it for Him. I'm delivered from popularity and addicted to obedience. When you obey The Word and Spirit of God it will not always make you popular with people. But popularity is a cheap substitute for being powerful.

During that time in my life, it was dark. I was lonely. I had grown accustomed to the company and acceptance of the crowd. I soon developed the habit of walking around our local mall, essentially trying to be around people artificially.

I had a tremendous spiritual hunger. I would read my Bible every night. I'd sit up, sometimes until 2:00 in the morning, and read through large portions of scripture. I didn't know where to read, so I just started at Genesis. I went through Leviticus and all that weird stuff. Then, I finally I got to Samuel and Kings. I loved all the stories! I read the whole Bible. God's Word started seeping into those dark, lonely places and the Light began to warm my soul. But it also began to expose Satan's lies. I began to expel any word that didn't agree with God. As I expressed my agreement with God's Word, the lies of the enemy began to wither in The Light.

One day, when I was riding down the road – on an aside, my pickup truck was enough reason to get depressed – I was in this deep, dark funk. All of a sudden, I remembered something I had read the night before: King David was dealing with depression too. Perhaps he was going down the road in his royal chariot feeling depressed and started shouting, "Why are you downcast oh my soul!?! Put your hope in God!" I remembered other things that he had said. I started shouting the Word of God, all by myself, in my little truck. "Why are you downcast oh my soul!?! Put your hope in God!" I started declaring," Bless the Lord, oh my soul!" Your soul is your mind (thinker), your will (chooser) and emotions (feelers). "Bless the Lord, oh my soul and all that is within me! Bless His holy name! And forget not all His benefits: He forgives all my iniquity. He heals all my diseases." During that dreary day, I shouted out God's Word. "The joy of Lord is my strength!" I did this for about 10 minutes or so and then realized I was laughing. I thought, "*I feel pretty good. That was better than getting drunk with my old friends. That was awesome! And no hangover!*" I learned that speaking God's Word, out loud, could change my state of being. And every time that dark depression tried to come back on me, I said, "Oh No you don't! The joy of the Lord is my strength." And I spoke God's Word aloud.

When I started practicing the art and discipline of taking every thought captive, the devil started backing off. I bet he was like, "Man, you scare me! You sound like Jesus." Did you know you can scare the devil? He is a fear-based creature that lurks in the shadows of darkness, deceit, and depression. When the Light of God's Word begins to spill out of the overflow of your heart in the form of words, it exposes the devil as the weak poser that he actually is.

But you've got to practice the three things we just discussed. You have got to do the 3 E's.

- **Expose** the devil's lies.
- **Expel** any word that does not agree with God's.
- And **Express** your agreement with God.

So today, I want you to take these three, simple, practical tools and vigilantly put them to use. The Truth vanquishes your mind's foe and makes you free, indeed! But YOU must wield it.

List 3 Scriptures That You Will Begin to Declare on the Regular:

1.

2.

3.

How to Get off the Crazy-Train

My phone rang and at the other end of the line was my friend who was lost and calling from a payphone. (Kids, ask your grandparents what a payphone is. And no—it did not take photographs.) Anyway, in an exasperated tone, my friend all but shouted, "I can't find your house!" What do you suppose my reply was?

"Where are you?"

Of course, he didn't know because he was lost! I asked him to describe his surroundings. After another payphone pitstop or two we finally got him to the house.

Now let me circle back around to a particular thought because it contains a key to getting off the crazy train. In fact, the exit ramp off the Vicious-Cycle onto the Victorious-Cycle begins with this question: "Where are you?"

There are lots of good reasons why God asked Adam this question in the garden of Eden, and not the least of them was because Adam did not know where he was. He was lost! The first step to getting found is identifying where you are.

Where are *you*? Admitting that you don't know or aren't sure is perfectly acceptable. Just begin to describe your surroundings to The Counselor. Tell Him what you see, how you feel, and He will help you identify where you really are. Ask The Counselor to help you answer that question and you have initiated the process of getting out of the Vicious-Cycle and finding the Victorious-Cycle.

From this point on, riding the Crazy-Train is a choice. I just told you how to hop off and alter your train-of-thought. (See what I did there?) Let the prayer below help you to head into a better direction. Pray it out loud.

PRAY THIS:

Father, I come before your throne of Grace today in the Name of Jesus. I am making the decision today to expose Satan's lie and to not live in the shadow of defeat any longer. Holy Spirit, you are my Great Counselor. If there is any lie that I have erroneously believed, would you bring Your Light to it? Would you cause it to rise up and help me to recognize any lies of the enemy that I've incorporated into my life? Maybe I have believed wrong thoughts and ideas for decades, but today I pray that you would help me to see all. Holy Spirit, after you show me, will you tell me The Truth? I know The truth makes me free, so tell me the truth today and minister to the deepest hurts. I invite you to do your work of healing in my life and soul. I declare, "No more perpetual pain; I now expect perpetual peace! Jesus is my Prince of Peace! I declare I'm off the 'Crazy Train' and into a new, Victorious-Cycle!"

I thank you for it, Lord. I believe I receive it now, in Jesus' Name.

FROM A VICIOUS CYCLE TO A VICTORIOUS CYCLE

Now say this:

"Holy Spirit, expose any lie that I have believed."

Wait for a moment and let The Counselor, the Holy Spirit, show you any lies of the enemy that you've believed. Once He's revealed the enemy's lie to you, ask,

"Holy Spirit, what is the truth? Would you speak your truth to my heart now?"

Just listen to what He is saying to you. Be still and know that He is God. You're now off the Crazy-Train. Welcome to the Victorious-Cycle!

QUESTIONS FOR SMALL GROUPS AND PERSONAL REFLECTION:

1. If our Salvation exists in past, present, and future tense, what practically does it look like as we "are being saved?"

2. Scripture exhorts us to "be filled with the Spirit." Why is it imperative to constantly be filled? And how do we engage in that process?

3. Our actions and beliefs are based on our responses to shame, fear, and control. What shame in your life has brought you to fear and how have you to allowed it to control you?

4. Satan took the entire human race captive with a thought in the Garden of Eden: *"God is holding out on you! He gave you this whole garden and said you can't eat of this one tree!?! You know why God is holding out on you? He doesn't want you to be like Him."* But they were already like God. They were made in God's Image. What Lie have you believed that has caused you to question God's good intentions toward you?

5. Now that "the lie" has been exposed, what is The Truth for that situation according to God, and how would believing God's Word change the trajectory you've been on?

6. 2 Corinthians 10:4–6 (NKJV): Instructs us to "take captive every thought." The word "captive" means to take a spear and place at to someone's throat. Have you done these three things: **Exposed** the devil's lies? **Expelled** any word that does not agree with God's Word? **Expressed** your agreement with God? If yes, explain. If not, take a moment and do it now.

-3-
THE BLAME GAME

3

THE BLAME GAME

Church services offer many things. It can be a time to worship or an occasion to receive encouragement. I don't know if you've been to a professional counselor before but having done so causes me to think church services also offer a kind of group therapy. Most counselors cost around $125–$250 per hour (at the time of this writing), so attending church gives everyone a group-rate. The even-better-news is that Jesus has already paid the bill. That's quite a bargain, wouldn't you agree?

When we come together The Ultimate Therapist, Himself, the Holy Spirit, is with us.

The Bible calls Him "The Counselor." The late Reverend John G. Lake reportedly loved to declare, "The greatest thing of all is that God is with us!"

Jesus said,

> *"It is to your advantage that I go away; for if I do not go away, the Helper (The Counselor) will not come to you; but if I depart, I will send Him to you." John 16:7 (NKJV)*

This is really a funny description of what was to come because Jesus was basically saying, "I'm leaving so I can send you a full-time therapist because you people are really messed up!"

An obvious paraphrase, but Jesus knew the same things I've been witnessing over several years, while pastoring people. No matter our ethnicity, or socio-economic status, we all have at least one thing in common. We are all uniquely screwed up in our own special way. In other words, we are ALL in need of a full-time counselor. And Jesus provided even this for each of us.

So, as you read these words, lift your expectations. Anticipate tapping into some of that good, Holy Spirit therapy. We all need it. If you don't need it, please remember to look in the mirror so you know what denial looks like. LOL

It's Not the Pain

We've all experienced pain in our past. Disappointments in life. Rejection in relationships. Tragic loss. Human errors. In the previous chapter we've learned how, along with the "help" of the enemy of our souls, we incorrectly interpreted what those messages mean. It's not the pain that causes the damages. It's the enemy's interpretation attached to that pain.

We suffer unnecessarily because of the faulty "tapes" that play in our heads; things that we review time and again because of what we have gone through. In other words, we tend to meditate and ruminate on the wrong things.

Many of the thoughts we entertain aren't always true. The most vital truth about the devil we must know is that he is a liar. John 8:44 (NLV) shows us this. For you are the children of your father the devil, and you love to do the evil things he does. He was a murderer from the beginning. He has always hated the truth because there is no truth in him. When he lies, it is consistent with his character; for he is a liar and the father of lies.

Deception is satan's native tongue. He expertly leads us on, and when we believe his lies, we begin to live in dysfunction that can become a primary source of perpetual pain in our lives. We begin to affirm those lies with our own declarations, thus living self-fulling and destructive prophecies, now reaffirmed by our experiences.

After reading the previous chapter, I hope you have insight into the particular lie that may have had you bound for some time. The lie you have been believing for so long no longer has to define your experience as a person. My prayer is that you allowed the Holy Spirit to come in and reveal the truth that "Sets us Free," as promised in John 8:32 (NKJV).

> *"And you shall know the truth and the truth shall make you free."*

FORBIDDEN DESIRE

The Blame Game is something that crops up in all relationships. In Genesis 3, we see that this started in the very first relationship in human history. The story is built around forbidden desire. It seems completely human that we desire the forbidden. Consider placing a child in a room full of Xboxes, play stations, smart phones, and all manner of other cool toys that a kid would like. Then tell the child, "You can play with all of this, but don't play with the little red, rubber ball." What do you think the mind of the child going to fixate on? That red, rubber ball. They're going to be thinking about the forbidden thing, including why they can't have it, and perhaps, all the reasons they should. We all have a red, rubber ball in our life. For Adam and Eve, it was an apple…an actual red ball.

SATAN'S FIRST RECORDED WORDS

Please allow me to remind us of the scenario in Genesis 3:1 (KJV), where the devil speaks, through the serpent, to the woman, "Hath God indeed said?" These are the first recorded words attributed to the devil.

The first thing satan did was question God's Word.

> *"But you may eat of the fruit of any tree but the fruit of the tree in the midst of the garden, God said, you shall not eat of it, nor touch it lest you die." Genesis 3:3 (NKJV)*

> *"And the serpent said to the woman, 'You will not surely*

die, for God knows in the day that you eat of it your eyes
will be opened and you will be like God, knowing good and
evil.'" Genesis 3:4 (NKJV)

God didn't want Mankind to know evil. Our Lord wanted us to know only good. Early on, the devil twisted this truth by selling humanity the idea that God was withholding something from them. As we discussed in the previous chapter, God is not withholding anything from us. He's given us all things we need for life and godliness. Furthermore, He has given all things richly to enjoy.

"So when the woman saw that the tree was good for food,
that it was pleasant to the eyes and a tree desirable to
make one wise, she took of its fruit and ate. She also gave
to her husband with her." (Genesis 3:6)

Adam was right there with her the whole time! We blame Eve, but it wasn't just her fault (we will get into Adam's version of The Blame Game later).

NEGATIVELY NAKED

In that moment the eyes of both Adam and Ever were opened. They suddenly understood the difference between right and wrong... and they knew that they were naked. They had always been nude. They just didn't know it. It's called being gloriously naked. They actually had the glory of God upon them. His glory surrounded them. In fact, glory was the environment in which they lived. And they were so remarkably conscious of the glory that they had no awareness of their nakedness. My hope is that you will enter in to such an awareness of God's presence in your life that you will no longer live out of the consciousness of your shortcomings and faults.

I believe the Holy Spirit would have me point out again, this state of being *gloriously naked* is restored when you come clean before Him with honesty and repentance, and when you get married. If you get naked before you get married, it may be temporarily pleasant, but it is not glorious. But when you get married and get naked with your spouse, that's glorious nakedness! God has given full restoration to Mankind. Believe me, it's worth waiting for. The Bible says in Genesis 2:25 (NKJV), "They were both naked and not ashamed!" And when you are "in Christ" God's glory returns to reside upon your life and your soul.

To my single readers, being gloriously naked is worth waiting for because the other stuff is a cheap substitute. It's like artificial sweeteners. You think it's sweet, but it has an aftertaste…and then, over time, it can kill you.

Religion Is a Cover-up

> *"The eyes of both of them were opened and they knew they were naked. They sewed fig leaves together and made themselves coverings." Genesis 3:7 (NKJV)*

This is what religion does: it tries to cover up sin. Let me state this plainly. Religion is insufficient for the job at hand because the conscience needs to be cleaned. Religion can not do that. Only Love can release the cleansing needed.

> *"And they heard the sound of the Lord walking in the garden in the cool of the day." Genesis 3:8 (NKJV)*

The phrase "cool of the day" refers to what is happening in the spirit realm. Adam and Eve had the ability to walk in both realities. They could walk in the natural, the terrestrial realm, but they could also walk in the supernatural, or the spirit realm. Jesus retrieved that for us through His work of Redemption. (Plus, Jesus completely negated, humiliated, and obliterated satan. I like reminding folks of that fact.)

> *"Then the Lord called to Adam and said 'Where are you?'" Genesis 3:9 (NKJV)*

Let me emphasize here The Law of First Mention. When God asks a question, it is not because *He* doesn't know the answer. It's because *we* don't know the answer.

So, God asked, "Adam, where are you?" Adam did not know where he was. He was lost. This question was not to humiliate him, but to help Adam locate himself and realize he needed assistance.

The good news, the essence of this story is that anyone who is lost can be found. Jesus came to seek and save all the lost. Death, hell, and the grave failed to hold Him down. If, like Adam, you don't know where you are, God is asking, "Where are *you*?" Genesis 3:9b (NKJV) You will hear that same question, in various forms, repeated in your life until you answer Him or until you die.

> *"Adam responded, 'I heard Your Voice in the garden and I was afraid.'" Genesis 3:10 (NKJV).*

This is what happens when you're not right with God. You hear God's voice, but you're apt to be afraid; God scares you.

WHAT HAD HAPPENED WAS...

The verse continues, "Because I was naked, and I hid myself." When we are in sin, we have a natural tendency to hide from God. Note the response of God to Adam's statement, "And God said, 'Who told you that you were naked?'" God knew immediately what had happened. And this caused the Lord to ask another therapeutic question, "Have you eaten from the tree from which I commanded that you should not eat?" (Or "Did you play with that little, red, rubber ball?")

INTRODUCING THE BLAME GAME.

"And the man said..." Are you ready? It starts right here. The first feelings and emotions in human relationships and marriage after "the fall" were fear and shame. The result was hiding... from God and from one another. Many marriages and human relationships are still plagued with these symptoms today. The first symptom of broken-ness in Adam and Eve's relationship was the response of blame.

"Adam says, 'The woman YOU gave me, to be with me; she gave me of the tree and I ate.'" Genesis 3:12 (NKJV).

This is a double Blame Game: not only did Adam blame the woman he blamed God for giving him the woman in the first place, forgetting that ALL of God's gifts are good! Have you forgotten that your spouse is a good thing?

Just asking.

COULD GOD REALLY BE YOUR PROBLEM?

A major key to unlocking your freedom is to stop blaming God for your present problems, your past dilemmas, and your current pain. He will never do for you what you can do for yourself. Own it. Spit the apple out. Take responsibility (response-ability) and stop playing games. The Blame Game has no winners. Ever.

DID GOD MAKE A MISTAKE?

It's like that guy who said, "I thought I was wrong, but I was mistaken." Adam was implying God had failed. Essentially, he was saying, "God, this is really YOUR fault. You gave her to me; she gave me the fruit."

I like God. He's a very secure Person. Instead of defending Himself, He just simply turned to the woman and said, "What is this that you've done?" (What part did you play in all of this?)

The woman basically said, "The devil made me do it. The serpent deceived me, and I ate." She blamed the poor 'ole devil. And folks have been blaming either him or God ever since.

"So the Lord spoke to the serpent, prophesied"— this is the NKT (New Kevin Translation…aka my paraphrase)—"I'm gonna send my Son, Jesus. He's gonna kick your butt and we're gonna take care of this business. Yeah—you will kill Him. But He will defeat the grave, be the first man to enter into death and kill it, rise from the dead and restore everything you just took away from my kids. You messed with the wrong family, devil!"

In this moment, God the Father, was prophesying satan's demise. And whatever tragedy or perilous circumstance has befallen you, God has already prophesied the devil's demise and your total restoration! I noticed something interesting as I was studying to write this chapter. Adam and Eve lived in total paradise. Perfection. They were physically perfect, emotionally whole, and spiritually alive. They existed in a perfect environment, ran around gloriously naked in a lovely garden…and yet they still had marriage problems. In fact, God was the perfect parent that gave his children the world. Literally! Yet they still rebelled and made poor choices.

They lived in paradise for three chapters, approximately 33.5 years by some estimations. That was all the perfection they could handle before messing things up for the rest of us. But rest assured, had they not, one of us would have. So don't go blaming them.

LET THE GAMES BEGIN

Imagine God interviewing Adam and Eve.

"So, what happened? You didn't eat of the forbidden fruit, did you?"

They immediately start The Blame Game.

Not only are we born with an inclination to sin, but also with the inclination to blame others for our own shortcomings. Few earthlings take responsibility for their sin. Theologians call this human characteristic "sin transference." You and I call it The Blame Game.

Blame says, "I'm not okay, and it's your fault." Most counseling sessions are about somebody who is not even in the room! (Ask me how I know.) Pastors spend much of our counseling time discussing someone who is not even present. All too often it's, "…what *they* did to me."

For the record, I get it. Life happens. And I know firsthand that people can be mean. Even Christians. Sheep bite! I have the scars to prove it. Counselors often make a statement that opens the door for a tough question. "I hear you and I'm sorry that happened. What is your part in this? What part of this can you own?" When your part is revealed, often a path to healing is opened and cleared before you. It is then we know what you can change. You must choose healing or hurt, life or death, and victimization or victory.

> *"But the path of the just is like the shining sun, that shines*
> *ever brighter unto the perfect day. The way of the wicked is*
> *like darkness; they do not know what makes them stumble."*
> Proverbs 4:18–19 (NKJV)

SIGNS OF BEING A BLAMER

Allow me to say this section does not necessarily encompass all the signs indicating a Blamer frame of mind. Instead, I've isolated the ones I see most often. My approach is sort of like a Jeff Foxworthy comedy line, but it is no joke: You might be a Blamer if:

1. **You Are Defensive**. Are you easy to approach, or are you prickly? In your relationships, are you easy to be entreated, or are you defensive? Do your partner or friends think, *"I can easily converse with my loved one or friend about this."* Or do they think, *"Choose your battles; I'm not even going to bring this up because it will turn into a fight?"* Perhaps you have been there. My wife and I have a great relationship, but we've been through seasons where it wasn't so great. The Blame Game was usually a big part of those difficult seasons. I can think of two major seasons in our marriage of thirty years at the time of this writing that were not so good. One of them lasted almost a year, and one lasted over six months.

I jokingly say, "We've been happily married twenty-eight years...twenty-eight out of thirty isn't bad."

Usually this blame thing, being defensive and wanting to defend oneself, only serves to stir up more strife. In short, if you're defensive, you might be a blamer. It's a soft answer that turns away wrath.

2. **You Have a Critical Spirit.** Ergo, you always see what everybody else is doing wrong, but fail to see your own faults. Jesus said it this way:

> *"And why worry about a speck in the eye of a brother*
> *when you have a board in your own?* [4]*Should you say,*
> *'Friend, let me help you get that speck out of your eye,'*
> *when you can't even see because of the board in your*
> *own?* [5]*Hypocrite! First get rid of the board. Then you can*
> *see to help your brother."* See Matthew 7:3–5 (NLT)

When someone comes to you, talking about the speck in your eye, you may rest assured they probably have a 2 X 4 in their own. Many times, people want to talk about your splinter to keep the attention off the telephone-pole sticking out of their own eye-socket.

I'm a Southerner. We have many phrases and colloquialisms that are peculiar to our culture. One of these is the description of some ministers as being "a clothes-line preacher." These are the individuals that want to beat you up about everything. You leave church bruised not blessed. Please don't misunderstand me. There is a time when men of God must declare truth boldly and confront sin strongly. But these "ministers" don't feed the sheep, they beat the sheep and even bleed the sheep. Let's be "ministers of reconciliation" not humiliation.

"You're all a bunch of hell-bound, fornicating, reprobate sinners dressing in a manner that draws illicit attention. You need to repent. You're a bunch of backslidden buzzards!"

I agree with you. That's why I wouldn't go to that church either! A lot of "clothes-line preachers" hammer on the stuff they, themselves, may be guilty of. Perhaps they feel so personally guilty that they have to find relief somehow, so they beat up their parishioners. And this type of behavior isn't exclusive to preachers. Family members, politicians and "friends" can behave like this too.

Criticism, by the way, is not a fruit of the spirit. But the way some people practice it you would think it's a virtue.

"I have the gift of discernment, and I discern that you're all jacked up."

Come on! That's why Jesus came! We are ALL jacked up, albeit you don't have to remain that way. I know this is an unpleasant thought. But, if you are critical, you might be a blamer.

3. **You Have a Victim Mentality.** If you are a victim all the time and every time, you might be a blamer. *"Can you believe what my boss did to me?"*

One of the lamest lines is, *"You make me so angry!"* Wow! If somebody can **make** you angry, then they really have a lot of power over you. Guess where that power came from? You gave it to them. Take it back. If somebody can "make you" do anything, then they are your master. But not if you don't allow them to be. Again, it's your decision. Choose life. Don't give your power away. Jesus gave it to you—so use it. It's your response-ability.

If someone else is always your problem, or the cause of your problem, you're probably the problem. Don't be a blamer. When you choose to blame, you're choosing powerlessness. If you're always blaming, you are choosing to be a victim. Decide today to be a Victor!

Personal Confession: I've had to deal with this issue. The problem was that I had not been aware of this insidious snare. How long had I been living this way and needlessly causing the people I love around me to suffer? Anyway, I was recently on The Couch having a session with The Counselor. (We all need these on a regular basis.). He helped me discover why I often process rejection through anger. In my line of work, people come and people go. Thankfully more have come than gone. But as a Pastor, when someone leaves your church (and your life) it's difficult not to take it personally. And it has historically been painful for me almost every time someone exits. Often, it seems to me, some of these people have defiled the virtues of loyalty, faithfulness, and perseverance that long-term relationships require. And this angers me!

But the Holy Spirit, my Therapist, helped liberate me from this long-term, low-grade bitterness.

"Kevin, you feel they have broken principles, and it hurts, so you are mad. But this is the time you set the <u>Principles</u> of Christ aside and operate as The <u>Person</u> of Christ. HE is never a victim; He is always the Victor. Because Love never fails."

May I just say that I've been a lot less disappointed with people since that Divine coaching session. It's hard to stay hurt and mad at someone you pray for. Now my objective is to allow the Person of Christ to be the *filter* for my behavior instead of the Principles of Christ to be the *filter* for others. Both have their place, but it's only Love that never fails. God help me "error" on the side of Love. Lord knows, He does that for me.

Extra Baggage is Always Heavy and Costs Extra

Something extra and awful comes along with blaming. Blamers very often experience deep anxiety, and its presence lingers. Anxiety is now among the top health threats globally! Blamers also often suffer from interrupted sleep patterns. They have trouble falling asleep or staying asleep, or even sleep all the time. Because they feel that they have no power, they are always anxious.

"It's somebody's fault, other than mine. I'm a victim!"

When you're always the victim, you're always looking over your shoulder. And if you're always looking back, you struggle continually to see where you're going. You're as nervous as a cat on a hot tin roof. Blamers approach relationships as a consumer. Blamers are always taking, but they seldom give and never own anything. Why? They have forsaken their response-ability.

Tough Medicine

Most children hated taking medicine, but they learned to do so. I'm about to hand out a dose of tough medicine, but it is highly effective. If you're going to overcome The Blame Game, you must swallow this pill: Responsibility. You must **take** responsibility.

Blamers and those with a victim mentality often target happy people and powerful people. They want to leech off these individuals.

These strong, personable individuals have what the blamers want, but are incapable of possessing. They want happiness, yet they're never happy. They want power, yet they're never powerful. Why? Because they never do what successful people do. They never take responsibility for their actions and their choices. It's always somebody else's fault. Powerful people take responsibility for their own lives. Even the Bible exhorts us to "choose you this day whom you will serve." See Joshua 24:15 (NKJV).

Jack Canfield, best-selling author of "Chicken Soup for the Soul," stated in his book, *The Success Principles*, "If you want to be successful, you have to take 100% responsibility for everything that you experience in your life. This includes the level of your achievements, the results you produce, the quality of your relationships, the state of your health and physical fitness, your income, your debts, your feelings—everything!"

Don't Wait for Others

If you're struggling in this area, let me give you a little positive pep-talk. Stop waiting for everybody else to change. Instead, change YOU. Nothing changes until you change. Take back the power. Take back *your* power. Take ownership of your life. After all, it only belongs to you.

Partners in Crime

One of the partners of blame is "control." There is an ensuing chapter in this book for control-freaks but allow me to give you a little fore-taste now. Control is the act of always trying to fix everybody...everybody but yourself. It can look like codependence. It can also seem as if we are always bailing somebody out. But if we have to bail out the same person over and over and over again, there exists a pattern that needs to be broken off *our lives*.

We all have to be bailed out from time to time; that's what friendships, relationships, and marriages are for. However, repeatedly bailing out the same person indicates that we are enabling wrong behavior. We must require others to take responsibility for their own choices and let them bail themselves out. Else they will never learn and grow. And you will always be stuck.

What I Taught My Sons

Since my two boys (now young men) were knee-high to a grasshopper, I've told them, "If you ever do something dumb and get put in jail, save your phone-call for somebody who is going to come get you out, because it ain't gonna be me. I'll leave your butt in jail. If you do the crime, you'll do the time. Now, I'll still love you unconditionally. I'll still come and visit you, but I'm not going to be one of those parents who will always come and bail you out of trouble. If you get in trouble, you are indeed in trouble."

I also taught them, "If you get in trouble at school, you need to know that when you get home, you're in trouble again." That might be one of the reasons that I have two amazing young men for sons. They are not perfect, but they love Jesus, His church, their Momma, each other, and me. We have a relationship. I don't just love my sons. I actually like them too! They're not afraid of me, no more than I'm afraid of God. I respect God, and I know what not to say to Him. I also know I can say a lot to God because I know He loves me. We're in a relationship and relationships require genuine honesty. I'm thankful I have that with my family too.

Control says, "*I'm going to fix **you**, then **I** will be okay.*" That kind of thinking is messed up. At some point, if you really love someone, you must let them be okay or not be okay on their own. Realize control is an illusion. There is a God—and you are NOT Him. This is also a huge part of loving yourself. In fact, not even God controls everyone. If He could, He would make every one get saved, support the local church, and live right.

Control is a Form of Idolatry

Control also says, "*Hey! Worship all my great ideas. After all, I don't have any bad ones, ever."* That attitude is idolatry—the worship of one's own ideas and opinions.

God is not trying to get you to obey all His rules. That thought alone can set you free. Even He is not a control freak. He has Laws in place to govern life and the universe. Cooperate with them and they will bless you. Break them and the consequences will be forthcoming (gravity, for example). Once again, it is your choice. But cultivate a relationship with Him, and you will eventually come to know how amiable He can be.

WE'VE ALL PROVEN THIS ONE

We've all thoroughly proven we can't obey all the rules. God's goal isn't to get you to conform and obey the rules. God's goal is to form a relationship with us. This truth brings up the age-old question: *"Then why in the H-E-double-hockey-sticks did God put that stupid tree in the middle of the Garden of Eden in the first place?!?"* And that is a fair question.

Here's the simple answer to a very complex question. God wanted our relationship with Him to be our own decision. It is the same reason He says,

> *"Bring all the tithe into the storehouse."*
> *Malachi 3:10 (NKJV)*

You don't *have* to tithe. It's a choice. The command to tithe is kind of like the tree in the garden all over again. "Tithe" is a Hebrew word. It means "tenth" or, "ten percent." Every time you take the first ten percent of your income and consume it on your own needs and desires, instead of bringing it back to God, you're metaphorically and quite literally back at that tree again. You are unknowingly asking, "Hath God said?" Or "What is God holding back from me?"

Do you really *have* to tithe? No, you don't have to; but you can if you want to. And there's always a blessing in honoring The Lord, His direction, and placing Him first. Life is about choices. God is trustworthy. And He wants to be first in your life, so He can bless the rest of your life.

How Love Rolls

God has never once ever tried to control you. Ever. And He never will. Again, that's why He put the two trees in the garden. If He had not put the Tree of the Knowledge of Good and Evil *and* the Tree of Life in the Garden, then He would have been controlling you by the absence of choice. You would have had no alternative, except to do what He said, to live the way He dictated. But that is not how Love rolls. Love is a decision. Because He placed that tree in the garden, now you have freedom to choose… a decision to make. He's not controlling you. Your destiny is in your own hands, so to speak. The choice is yours. (Choose Life.)

Extreme Predestination Errors

Some say, "Everything happens for a reason." True. Sometimes that "reason" is because people are dumb! Not everything that happens is supposed to happen or intended by God. This truth, along with the reality that God has given us a free will, shoots a hole in some of the doctrines of "whatever God wants is what is going to happen." God is Sovereign and His Will truly shall come to pass, in Jesus Name. In other words, His eternal purpose shall be fulfilled.

But you don't have to play a part in God's purpose. You can if you want to. It's best if you do. I know I am because God said, "I've set before you life and death." It is like He's saying, "Pssst! Hey! HINT: Choose life!" (Deuteronomy 30:19, paraphrase). It's kind of like when your teacher walks by as you're filling in one of the answers on a test. She clears her throat and tries to get your attention so she can point you to the correct answer, or at least send a signal that the current choice that you are considering isn't correct. The Counselor, the Holy Spirit, will help you make right choices. That's a good deal, is it not? He is a sure guide through this life. We must learn to listen and cultivate our connection with Him.

Rules without relationship breed rebellion. That's why God

doesn't want you to obey the rules. He wants you to be in a relationship with Him. Helicopter-Moms can illustrate this. They do not really help their kids when they are always hovering. We must all learn to choose well. I'm reminded of an old saying, "You don't prepare the road for the kid; you prepare the kid for the road." (Or something like that.) Don't prepare the road for the kid because... you're not that good. You are not God. You cannot go out in front of your child and make sure the way is prepared and every pothole is filled in, but you can prepare the kid so they can navigate the road properly with the help of The Counselor, the Holy Spirit. They have acquired this skill because you have taught them to abide in and live by the principles you've taught them from God's Word, and to develop their own relationships with The Holy Spirit.

THE ROOT OF CONTROL

The root of control is fear. God doesn't control us because He doesn't fear anything, nor does He motivate with fear. When we partner with the spirit of fear, we invite intimidation and manipulation to the party, and they don't let anybody have fun. Because control comes from fear, it creates a culture of suspicion. This aspect creates an environment where we don't trust anyone else either.

Some control others by withholding their love. Their attitude seems to be, *"I'm not going to let you hurt me, because I'm not going to love you. If I don't love you, you can't hurt me."* But a loveless life is not an abundant life.

Some build walls to control. People do different things in an effort to try to maintain control due to their fear. There is still good news here.

> *"God has not given us a spirit of fear, but He has given us*
> *a spirit of love, power, and a sound mind."*
> *2 Timothy 1:7 (NKJV)*

As you're reading this, say aloud, "I do not have a spirit of fear. I have a spirit of love. I have a spirit of power. I have a sound mind.

I'm not crazy! I have a sound, disciplined mind! My mind has been renewed to the place of right thinking—in sync with God's Word. I have the mind of Christ. I think like Jesus. I think the thoughts of God!"

Have you ever worked for a controlling boss? Are you a controlling boss? Did you have controlling parents? Are you a controlling parent? What's the opposite of control? Freedom. To Yield. Serving. What's the opposite of blame? Responsibility. And the result? Power!

THE PATHWAY TO POWER

Do you want more power in your life? If you can't be responsible for anyone else, who can you be responsible for? Yourself! You can't always control what happens *to* you, but you can control what happens *in* you. You are not powerless. You are powerful. The choices you make can be good choices, Godly choices. Powerful people take responsibility for their life by taking responsibility for their choices. On any given day our number one job is to control our attitudes, thoughts, and actions.

Stuff happens, right? Life happens. Flat tires happen. I had a flat tire when I went to a soccer tournament in Orange Beach, AL. The tire picked up a screw. I wasn't happy about it, but I kept a good attitude and God provided a good 'ole Southern boy to fix it for me. He only charged me $15.00, instead of having to buy a new $200.00 tire. Hallelujah! I kept my attitude right. My wife slept through the whole thing. She was over on the passenger side "ZZZZZZ-ing." The peace of God was all over her, possibly because I didn't allow the situation to upset me! Yep, life happens; work happens; family happens; bills happen; in-laws happen; out-laws happen, but we don't have to let a freak-out happen. We don't have to melt down. We don't have to get caught up in the vortex and the spin cycle of crazy.

TAZ AND BUGS

Maybe you remember the Tasmanian Devil and Bugs Bunny? These were the cartoons I watched in the '70's and '80's. (Kids, ask your grandparents.) Anyway, like Bugs, you can stay cool, calm, and collected even when you have a Tasmanian Devil standing right in front of you. You can be at peace when someone is manifesting their bad-tempered impatience and spinning out of control.

Don't get caught up in their crazy cycle. Just say, "Eh, what's up, Doc? You can keep your crazy over there, but this is the Peace Zone... the Shalom Zone is right here where I am."

The Tasmanian Devil is out there. Some of you work with him. Some of you are married to him. Taz is the attendant at the gas station, or the check-out lady, or the person who calls saying you owe them money. Or it could be that guy in traffic that keeps using sign-language to tell you that "you're number one!" He is everywhere, but you don't have to get caught up. Stay in your own Victorious Cycle! Remember, your spiritual shoes are made of God's Peace. You can walk in that peace, even if you have to walk through hell itself. In fact, the Psalmist announced,

> *"Yea though I walk through the Valley of the Shadow of Death, I will fear no evil!" Psalm 23:4 (NJKV)*

Those are some high-quality shoes.

You're not responsible for what's going on inside of another individual. You don't have to fix them. Let me set you free from that responsibility. That is not your job, because you're not Jesus. You're not The Counselor. The only person you have to be responsible for is the one sitting in your chair. I'm not saying we shouldn't be loving or compassionate. I am saying we shouldn't try to fix everybody, because then we will need to be fixed.

CONNECTION PROTECTION

My top goal in relationships is continually building and protecting connections. My wife is really good at this. She will say, "I want us to connect; we haven't connected today."

For a long time, I would usually respond, "What are you talking about? 'We haven't connected?' I've worked all day and I got home late because life happened... church happened...sheep happened. The Tasmanian Devil showed up for counseling, and I'm tired. What do you mean, we haven't connected?"

Now, I'm finally starting to get it. We must protect our connection. We protect our connection by constantly building our connection. And when we protect and build our connection it actually provides protection.

That's exactly the same thing God is trying to protect in your relationship with Him. So, you messed up; you blew it. Welcome to the human race. Don't run and hide from God. Go to God and say, "Hey! Let's connect." Protect your connection with God. It will protect you.

PROTECTION OF THE CONNECTION IS YOUR PRIORITY

Say aloud, "I'll protect the connection." Then, take some time to read 1 Corinthians 13:4–8. Concentrate on the section describing love's attributes, "Love is patient, love is kind, etc." Insert your name in place of love. For instance, I will say aloud, "Kevin is patient. Kevin is kind. Kevin does not keep a record of wrongs done to him." When I get to the end I'll say, "Kevin never fails." That's a big one. But put your name in there. When we walk in love we do not fail. It may look like failure, but in the long run we will see a victory!

Practice this with your spouse. Involve your friends, your relatives, your parents, and even your kids in strengthening yourself through this methodology. Protect your connections. Just like the branch needs to stay vitally connected to the Vine, we have to stay connected to the right people and protected from the wrong people. After all, your life is a collection of connections. Life is made of time and relationships.

PLAY THE RIGHT CARD

Here's a practical application to end this section. There are two cards, metaphorically, that you can play in any relationship. Whichever card you play, God will play the other one.

THE COUCH

You hold the Love Card and the Change Card. Here's how it works: Think of someone you're in a relationship with. When you think, *"If they would just change in this area,"* and you go to work trying to change them in that area, God says, *"I'll play the Love Card. You try to change them, and I will just love them."* The high road is the love way. If you choose to merely love them, God says, *"Ok, if you are going to love them then I Am going to change them."*

Jesus is the King of Hearts. So always play the Love Card. Love Never Fails. He has a perfect record. Undefeated. You see, you can love anyone, but you cannot change anyone. That decision belongs to them. Even God can't change some people. They have to embrace it. But He has a much better chance of changing them than we do, so love them. Pray for them. Let God conduct the change campaign. I like His chances way better than mine anyway.

Let me quote a wise, elder brother in my church here:

> "When we are dissatisfied with another person, we have ONLY three options:
> 1. Change that person or situation with which we are dissatisfied.
> 2. Get rid of the person, place, or thing… (oft times this is illegal).
> 3. Change our attitude toward the person, place, or situation.
>
> Those are the ONLY three options. Number three always works, but sadly we most often go on disappointedly looking for that fuzzy, feel-good, fourth option, which just doesn't exist."

The Bible says,

> *"There is no fear in love. Perfect love casts out fear, because fear involves torment. But he who fears has not been made perfect (or mature) in love. Perfect love (mature love) casts out all fear." 1 John 4:18 (NKJV)*

68

SH!%@* HAPPENS

Sometimes it feels like life has "happened" to you. I get that. I don't know what's happened to you, personally, but let me tell you the story of a young girl in India who was sold into the sex trade because she angered her elder brother. He got mad at her, so he sold her as a sex slave. She was victimized for a long time by the sick, human-trafficking industry. But in the midst of that dark, demonic trade, Jesus found her. He loved her. He did what Jesus always does: He saved her. Someone came to the village where she lived to preach the gospel. She listened from a distance, but prayed the prayer of salvation when the missionary concluded.

OUR RESPONSE-ABILITY

Even as she was working in the sex trade, she said, "Jesus, because you have forgiven me, I can choose to forgive my brother. I had no control over what he did to me, but I do have control over how I respond." Then, in her heart, she forgave him. After this, a series of events occurred whereby she was literally, physically set-free from actual slavery. But here's what I want you to take note of: even while she was a captive, she was free, because she chose to respond with love and forgiveness.

I hope the challenges in your life wasn't something like that, but even if it was, God never leaves anyone without the ability to respond. We have Response-Ability. Every human has been granted this ability by our Creator. Allow me to encourage you to respond in Faith and Love. You always have a choice. Choose Love; Choose Life. Choose Freedom; Choose Jesus. Play the Love-Card. Love NEVER Fails.

WHAT'S THE OPPOSITE OF LOVE?

Most say hate. But actually, it's fear. Why do people hate other people just because they are a different color or culture? They fear them.

What does Perfect Love do? Cast out hate? No. It casts out fear.

Fear causes hate. And hate shrivels the soul. It reduces us to pettiness and shrinks our hearts. But Love enlarges our spirits with the revelation that "if God is for me, it doesn't matter who is against me." Romans 8:31 (NKJV) Love has an abundance-mentality. Fear has a scarcity-mentality.

There's no greater example of what I'm talking about than Jesus, Himself. Murdered, publicly executed, hung naked on a cross, ridiculed, and shamed, Jesus was literally buried in a borrowed tomb. But He consciously rose above all of that. He rose above the pain. He rose above the hate. He rose above the fear of being abandoned in the grave by His Father, God. Ultimately, He rose over death itself! How? Not by blaming, but by making a determination to yield to the Love of God. He knew God, His Father, loved Him. That's how He rose above it all. He played the Love Card. Let this sink in. While in the midst of experiencing agonizing pain caused by the cruel people in front of Him, spitting in His face, mocking Him, He prayed,

"Father, forgive them. They know not what they do."
Luke 23:34 (NKJV)

He did not wait for the pain to stop before He initiated the process of forgiveness. He knew the Power of Love so well that He forgave them while it still hurt.

Because Jesus rose above this tragic circumstance of life, we can rise above it all, too. When He arose, so also did we! How? Love. Never. Fails. And if Love is the dominant force in your life, you will never fail either. This is our greatest Response-Ability: Love Anyway. (Shameless plug: My wife wrote a beautiful book called, *Love Anyway*. You can order this amazing devotional at AdrienneCooley.com)

QUESTIONS FOR SMALL GROUPS AND PERSONAL REFLECTION:

1. Who are you waiting for to change, so you can stop being a victim? Where can you use your response-ability and take your power back?

2. In what ways are you more focused on "keeping the rules" with God and in what ways are you developing your relationship with Him?

3. What choices have you made or are you currently working to "choose life" when it comes to your relationships with both God and others?

4. Don't try to fix everybody, because then you will need to be fixed. Who are you trying to fix that only God can fix? How will you adjust regarding this issue?

5. Who, if anyone, do you need to forgive, even while it still hurts?

71

-4-
CONTROL FREAKS

4

CONTROL FREAKS

Misunderstandings happen. They are common, and may even be considered to be routine, in all of our interactions. Misunderstandings can be especially common in marriage. (So I hear.) ;-) I have even seen misunderstandings erupt through the misinterpretation of Scripture. Genesis 3:16 (NET) offers great insight. "I will greatly increase your labor pains. You will want to dominate your husband, but he will dominate you."

The old King James Translation is much nicer, "...your desire will be for your husband." When I first read this passage, as a newly married man, I thought, "I'm glad that's in there. God says she's gonna desire me. This is awesome."

And then I realized it wasn't that kind of desire He was talking about. God was actually saying, "Because you disobeyed my Word by thinking you knew better than I did, your wife will constantly express that she knows better than you."

Basically, God was declaring an eternally unresolved conflict and a power struggle in relationships that are outside of God's Kingdom. He said, and I paraphrase again, "Ladies, you're going to want to dominate and control your husband, but he's going to be the designated leader."

As Pastor, author and Founder of Marriage Today, Jimmy Evans says, "This creates a fight with no decided winner." Does this describe your marriage? I believe it describes a lot of the human race! Couples struggle, and people-groups fight in on-going conflict where there can be no clear winner. Why? Because these are relationships that are outside of God's Kingdom or outside of the way of successfully conducting oneself.

Relationships inside God's kingdom work better. That is one of the reasons I have a godly pride in my church. Our church is very culturally, ethnically, and generationally diverse. I see people deliberately working at improving their relationships. It takes intentional effort and applying Kingdom-principles.

Take An Internal Survey

Were you raised in a home where one parent was clearly dominant or controlling? Do you believe that dominance had a negative impact on your parents' marriage? Did that dominance have a negative impact on your family in general? I've never had many folks answer "no" to those questions. The desire for control and dominance are features of the fall of mankind. They are not features or principles of Christ's Kingdom.

Why do people work so hard at control and dominance in the world? Because people don't know Jesus. They haven't met Love. Even so, I have to ask a similar question: Why is there so much effort put into control and dominance even by God's people? These people are saved, but they haven't renewed their minds to God's ways of thinking and operating.

Authority -vs- Control and Dominance

Authority exists in the earth to control the sin nature and regulate human behavior for the common good. That's why we have law enforcement. Imperfect humans are doing the job of law enforcement, so they are going to make mistakes. However, the Bible instructs us that we are to pray for those who are in authority. Should we riot, loot, and throw things at people who are in authority? Clearly the answer, from a biblical perspective, is no. (And if you're living your life from some other perspective then you may have just discovered your problem.) This may be happening in our society, but that doesn't mean they are right. Have you ever heard someone say, "Well at least we can pray."? The Bible says the MOST we can do is pray.

THE MOST WE CAN DO

No, prayer is not the least you can do. It is the MOST you can do! Your relationship and standing with God cause your requests to carry a special weight with Him. When you're talking to Almighty God, as He's sitting on His throne ruling the universe, remember you're His favorite child. He takes note when you approach Him saying, "Abba Daddy."

His response is like, "What do you want baby?"

Your response is, "Would you please help with this situation in Charlotte, N.C., or in St. Louis, MO, or L.A., New York, Rome, or India?" Or wherever you need Him.

God's reply is, "Yeah, baby. I'm gonna get right on that because I love you and because you asked. After all, you're my favorite."

RULING ON EARTH

We want God's Word, so we can apply those principles to our lives. Let's study Mark 10:42–44 (NKJV),

> *"But Jesus called them to himself and said, 'You know that those who are considered rulers over the nations lord it over them and their great ones exercise authority over them yet it shall not be so among you. But whoever desires to become great among you shall be your servant and whoever of you desires to be first shall be slave or servant of all.'"*

Let me paraphrase this: If you use the authoritarian model that the world uses then you will miss My Kingdom. Being a servant-leader is God's way of ruling. If you plan to rule God's way, then you have to be a servant, not a master. Being a man, by the way, does not give you the right to dominate and control women, or anyone for that matter. Rather, it gives you a Divine responsibility (Response-Ability) to love and serve them.

I have a reminder that pops up on my phone once a week that asks, "Cooley! (That's me.) Are you being the chief-servant in your home?" I make myself open that reminder. I am diligent to read the question and answer it honestly each time. There have been times I wish it had said, "Cooley! Are you being the Chief of your home?" The problem is… that's not my job. My job is to be the Chief Servant. In my case that means I better be washing dishes as much as anybody, even cooking meals and taking out the trash and speaking kindly to my wife and kids and dog.

My wife and I both work. She is no longer a stay-at-home mom. She did an incredible job raising our two sons for the first 16 to 18 years of their life, but now she's an ordained minister of the gospel just like I am. She has her own ministry. She has a great speaking gift, and she's an amazing writer, published author, leader, and manager. So, we help each other out. We try to out serve one another. (She usually wins.)

One of our date nights (that we do once about every six to eight weeks) is to go to the wholesale store, Sam's Club, together. We like it! We have fun. And her top love language is "acts of service," so I score major points.

We tell each other, "It's Sam's night!"

We're like a couple of little kids. It's crazy! (See what happens when you get older? You get excited about going to Sam's.) They have samples there, and who doesn't like free stuff? This is kind of embarrassing, but when our kids were little, one said, "Daddy, I'm hungry. Can we go to Sam's?" That may have been a sign we went there too often, and we may or may not have abused the samples. (For the record we are now COSTCO people.)

THE CONTROL CAUSE

What causes people to become control freaks? In the Scripture it's called a "Jezebel spirit." Did you watch Sanford and Son when you were a kid like I did? Fred would call Aunt Esther, "You old Jezebel!" I want to offer a caveat right now. This is not a knock against women.

In over 33 years of ministry, I've learned that most folks, including Christians, are good people. And some are knuckleheads. I've dealt with a few people who have this controlling or "Jezebel spirit," and most of them have actually been men. Obviously, women can have it as well because it draws its name from a woman, named Jezebel, in the Bible. But I want to make it clear. This is not a problem or issue that is exclusive to women. Anyone can be a Control-Freak. You might currently be abused by this evil influence and you're not aware of it. You might just live with a sickening feeling because of a certain relationship. So, how do you get free from this controlling, "Jezebel spirit"?

There is great insight in 1 Peter 3:7–9 (NKJV),

> *"Husbands, likewise dwell with them* [your wife] *with understanding."*

I will not kid you. This is a tall order. I do not want you to underestimate your situation. Furthermore, "understanding" requires research. Let each man study his own special, unique, one-of-a-kind wife.

I'M REMINDED OF A STORY

A guy was walking on the beach one day, praying and meditating when Jesus appeared to him in a vision and said, "You've been such a faithful servant. Because of this faithfulness I want to answer any one prayer and give you any one thing you want. I want to bless you."

The man said, "Well, Lord, I've always wanted to go to Hawaii, but I'm afraid of flying. Could you build me a bridge to Hawaii?"

Jesus said, "Come on; I could do it but the resources, the time, the manpower would be quite a lot. It's a bit of a selfish request. Isn't there anything else you would want instead?"

The man reflected for a moment before saying, "Well, as you know, Lord, I'm on my third marriage. I need help in that area. Can you help me understand women?"

Jesus smiled and replied, "Would you like that bridge to be four lanes or two lanes?" (Cue the laughter. Obviously, this is just a joke. Don't allow yourself to be offended, but if you were easily offended you wouldn't have made it this far into the book. So, congratulations!)

A WEIGHTY SITUATION

I understand the scripture here is weighty. "Husbands, dwell with them (your wife) with understanding." We are commanded to do this, so it must be possible! But I submit to you that it takes intentionality.

Peter then goes on to tell husbands *how* to understand their wives. If you're a male reader, are you ready? Do you have your pens and highlighters out? (This alone is worth the price of this book.) This is how you understand your woman, "Dwell with them with understanding, giving honor to your wife as the weaker vessel."

LET ME CLARIFY SOMETHING

She is not weak, although the Bible does say, "...*as the weaker vessel*." Most women, generally speaking, are physically weaker than men. There are exceptions, of course. However, intellectually, and emotionally, most women are far stronger than men, again, generally speaking. To the men who think women are weak... I was in the room both times when my wife gave birth to our two boys. A new respect was also birthed that day as I watched what she endured in that process, and I'm forever grateful to her.

Living with a wife according to understanding produces profound spiritual results. Peter continues, "As being heirs together of the grace of life, so your prayers may not be hindered."

Many years ago, while ministering in Amsterdam, a missionary-friend spoke prophetically to me and my wife saying, "The more 'together' you are the more grace for life there will be!" I endeavor to honor her as my peer and equal in both our home and our ministry. One of my goals in life is to help her reach her full potential as a daughter of the Most High God. And I'm convinced I will stand before God one day to give an account of how I encouraged and stewarded the tremendous gift I call my wife.

Some men think, *"Prayer doesn't work."* Others sincerely ask, "How come my prayers don't get answered?" It is simple. You treat your wife like a second-class citizen. But, an atmosphere of honor accelerates faith, like lighter fluid accelerates fire.

The way Jesus treats HIS wife ought to be a reflection of how you treat your mate. If you learn how to treat your wife like Jesus treats His, you'd get more of your prayers answered too. I guarantee it will help, perhaps in other areas of your life as well. (Yep, dishonor is also why many men are sexually frustrated in marriage too.) God's Word works!

AGREEMENT IS EXPONENTIAL

Things get exponentially better when you come together and pray. When two or more pray in His Name, Jesus said, "I will be there in the midst of them." Matthew 18:20 (NKJV) The ancient prophet, Amos, asked, "Can two walk together, unless they are agreed?" The power of agreement is described as exponential because one can put a thousand to flight and two can put ten thousand to flight (Read Deuteronomy 32:30). When you come together in agreement, with your spouse or friend, you are ten times more powerful than you are by yourself! Some believers do themselves a great disservice by not properly stewarding their most sacred relationship. Learn how to honor your spouse.

The Apostle Peter continues in 1 Peter 3:8–9 (NKJV),

"Finally, all of you be of one mind, have compassion for

one another; love as brothers; be tenderhearted, courteous. Not returning evil for evil; Reviling for reviling but on the contrary, blessing knowing that you were called to this that you may inherit a blessing."

Men, try understanding her differences, instead of trying to control her and make her like you. She is not like you. That's why you married her. Unity does not require uniformity. If you're exactly alike, then one of you is unnecessary.

Women are awesome. Women are strong. Women are tough. Women are pretty. Women may usually be physically weaker than men, but I believe God made them physically weaker so they wouldn't rule the whole universe!

The Fall of Mankind Changed Everything

Did you know that there was no reference to Adam being over Eve until *after* the fall and their expulsion from the Garden of Eden? When they were in God's garden, God's Kingdom, they were complete peers and equals. Only after the fall did God come and give instructions concerning the new rules of order about relationships. And this had to be done because when you have multiple people who want to be in charge, chaos is usually the outcome.

Now, please note that every time God speaks of authority in scripture, He cautions us to use it correctly. We are always warned not to misuse it in a dominating manner, but to use it in a relational manner to serve and protect. Rules without Relationship breed Rebellion.

Stop Barking

Let me paraphrase an example from Ephesians 6:4 (NKJV),

> *"Fathers, do not provoke your children to wrath..."*

Provoke means to "bark at" or name-call. God says don't do that. Don't yell or bark at your kids. In the deep, southern portion of the USA, we'd say, "Don't holler at 'em y'all."

It is especially important to remember this: Each time you speak to your child you are indirectly training your child how to react relationally, and barking in relationships does not lead to harmonious, loving, peaceful, productive, kind, enjoyable times together. No person in their right mind enjoys being yelled out. My wife grew up in a home where her dad was…loud. When we first got married, she tried to bark at me. She'd be in the middle of barking, and I would turn and walk out of the room. That left her having an argument with herself.

She would get really mad and yell, "Don't walk out on me!".

I would reply, "You're not going to speak to me like that." Note that I didn't bark back. (Didn't say I wasn't tempted to.)

I did that to my wife in one instance and I didn't see her for two weeks…and after the second week I could see her a little bit out of my right eye. (That's not true, just kidding again.)

My dad told a joke at his work once. "I tell you what. I had my wife down on her knees begging the other day."

The guy he worked with said, "Wow! Really? How'd you do that?"

Dad said, "She was down on her knees begging, saying, 'You come out from under that bed and fight like a man!'"

But in all seriousness, within a relationship, you don't have to allow yourself to be treated in an ungodly or unkind way.

My wife says, "Train people how to treat you." And once again, she is right.

NEVER RETALIATE

Never retaliate by behaving in a rude, unkind way. The Bible says,

> "…do not return railing for railing." 1 Peter 3:9 (KJV)

It goes on to explain that we are actually called by God to pass out blessings! And if we attend to this ministry, we should inherit a blessing. Sounds like an attractive offer.

The arguments with my wife I've described above were in our

younger days. I did things she didn't like too.

Now that we've been married for about thirty years at the time of this writing, she has learned to say, "You're not going to treat *me* like that." And she is right again. We do have to train people how to treat us.

My response is (almost) always, "Yes ma'am."

Why? Because she knows how she wants to be treated, better than I know how she wants to be treated. And I have got to learn to be humble and teachable so I can "dwell with her according to understanding." She helps me "understand" how she wants to be treated.

Sometimes I have to reply to her, "You're right. I'm sorry. Give me a minute to get my act together." And she graciously does.

SILENCE IS NOT ALWAYS GOLDEN

Back in those younger days, I wasn't a yeller, but would go into silent mode. I'd just not talk for three days. That's not fun for anyone.

Praise God. I don't do that anymore; I've grown up. Now I just don't talk to her for one day. (I'm kidding!) My wife has told me I can be very immature for my age. At my age, I take that as a compliment.

Non-relational authority is not Christ-like. In other words, when you try to use the sheer strength of your personality to get somebody to do what *you* want them to do, you're being a Control-Freak, like Jezebel was. May I invite you to consider using the Fruit of the Spirit to motivate people? That creates a safe atmosphere and safety is one of the key elements to a healthy, organizational culture.

GOD REFUSES TYRANNY

If anybody could be a dominator, it would be God. Who has more power or a stronger personality than Him? Yet, God has never dominated or manipulated you or anyone else for one day of your entire life. He is humble, loving, gentle, and kind. He's a relational God. He wants to connect with you on a personal level. Even He is not a Control-Freak.

The animal kingdom reflects built-in dominance. There's the lead dog, the queen bee and the alpha male. You know what they say about the lead dog? If you're not it, your view never changes. But in the human race, there is no built-in dominance.

Why? Because in Genesis 1:26 (KJV), God said, "Let *Us* make man in *Our* image." In the Godhead, there's no lead dog or queen bee because The Godhead functions in total submission one to another. They honor one another. They have relational authority with each other, and that's why it works. Isn't that an amazing, paradoxical concept? There is order, honor and love, and they are co-eternal and co-equals. Family.

A ROUTINELY INCORRECT THOUGHT

You may say, "But God the Father, He's the top dog, right?" The Holy Spirit and The Son, give preeminence to Him. But God the Father had no problem with allowing Jesus to be the Savior of the World, the King of kings, the Lord of lords. The Holy Spirit displays great humility through a life that says, "I'm going to talk about, reveal and point people to Jesus. I'll spend my time, and my primary focus, telling everybody how great Jesus is." Jesus displays great humility with a life that testifies, "I'm going to send you another Comforter like Me—the Holy Spirit because He's awesome… He's The Comforter and The Counselor! In My earthly ministry I could do nothing without Him!" They completely honor One Another. There is a magnificent deference one to the other. And they are magnanimous!

If your home was like that it would be like heaven on earth! Think of how great our country would be if we had godly leaders, we could elect to office who understand these Kingdom Concepts intentionally creating an atmosphere of honor in our nation!

THREE LEVELS OF UNGODLY CONTROL

The ancient queen, Jezebel, was synonymous with control because she used a full measure and arsenal of controlling methods: manipulation, domination, and intimidation.

CONTROL FREAKS

You might be a Control-Freak if you use…

MANIPULATION

It is the gateway to control. Revelation 2:18–20 (NKJV) says,

> *"To the angel of the church of Thyatira"*

(The angel, by the way, is probably the pastor. I remind my congregation often that their pastor is an angel).

> *"These things, says the Son of God, who has eyes like a flame of fire and His feet are like fine brass. He says, 'I know your works. Your love, your service, your faith, your patience. And, as for your works, the last are more than the first. Nevertheless, I have a few things against you, because you allow that woman, Jezebel, who calls herself a prophetess to teach and seduce my servants to commit sexual immorality, eating things sacrificed to idols. I gave her time and space to repent of her sexual immorality and she did not repent. Indeed, I will cast her into a sick bed and those who commit adultery with her into great tribulation unless they repent of their deeds; and I will kill her children with death and all the churches will know I am He who searches the minds and the hearts. And I will give to each one of you according to your works."*

Now that's a heavy-duty scripture, isn't it?

STRANGE NAME, GREAT MAN

God will always raise up people to do his work. He has always done so and is doing so today. During this time, when Jezebel ruled as queen, God elevated a man named Jehu to do God's work.
2 Kings 9:30 (NKJV),

> *"Now when Jehu was come to Jezreel, Jezebel heard it."*

What did she do? She put paint on her eyes, adorned her head, looked through the window and batted her eyelashes at Jehu. What was she trying to do? She was trying to manipulate Jehu because she knew he was coming to kill her. She thought, *"I'll seduce him. It has always worked. I'll bat my eyes and give him the duck-face."*

HER GO-TO STRATEGY WAS MANIPULATION

What does manipulate mean? Here's the definition: to control unfairly or unscrupulously. You can do it sexually, with money, with self-pity, self-harm, jealously, deceit, fear, guilt, shame and even prophecy!

Yes, there are some people who will try to manipulate you through a prophetic word. Such speech is not a prophetic word, it's a pathetic word. Preachers have easily manipulated people. They're some of the worst. Several years ago, I told the story about how someone had given me a Rolex watch. It was a beautiful, $10,000 watch. That thing was gorgeous. Long story short, I was on a mission trip in Asia, and it was stolen. I was just heartsick about it, of course.

Anyway, I told the story of the lesson I learned through that unfortunate experience and for the next two weeks I had church members try to give me their watches. The first person came up with a watch and I thought, *"That's so nice."* I was just about to receive it and it dawned on me—the Holy Spirit is our Helper—their giving wasn't being led by the Spirit of God. They were feeling sorry for me because my watch had been stolen. They loved me as their pastor. (Remember, I'm an angel after-all.) ;-)

While I appreciated that, I told every single one of them, "I appreciate it, but I don't feel like I'm supposed to receive that gift."

I felt they were being motivated because of the story I had told and I refused to manipulate people's emotions for personal benefit.

DON'T "MILK" SITUATIONS

Some preachers tell stories and then they milk it. They drain the congregation like a dairy farmer drains his cows. They encourage people,

"Give me all your watches." The problem is that we are not farmers, we are shepherds! As leaders, we have to be careful of how and why we share things. God weighs motives.

In 2 Samuel 23:15 (my paraphrase), we read how King David was in the middle of a battle when he said, "Oh, that I had a drink of the water from the well in my hometown, Bethlehem. I love that water."

So, his mighty men fought through the Philistines; got some of their leader's favorite water and brought it back to King David. In that moment he must have realized the same thing I realized about the watches.

David said, "I cannot drink this water."

He valued the people that the Lord had made him steward of over his own personal wants and desires. He poured that precious water out to God as a drink offering because he knew how powerful his words were as a leader. On that day he decided, *I'll never use my words to* manipulate my men to get my own desires met. I'm going to use my words to lead my men to *get God's desires met.*

We all have to beware of control and manipulation. I don't need a watch today. But I am a little short on cash, though. I'm kidding!!! In all seriousness, manipulation is a sin and it is unrighteous. It's like marijuana: a gateway to far worse things. Manipulation is the dark doorway to control.

You might also be a Control-Freak if you use...

INTIMIDATION

Some people try to lead by intimidation. Jezebel tried this with Elijah. Elijah was a great prophet that had just killed 450 false prophets of Baal. Yet Jezebel sent a message that scared him so badly, this once bold man of God simply ran away.

Amazingly, what 450 men couldn't do, one Control-Freak, by the name of Jezebel, did. Note that I don't mean one woman. I mean one person anointed by darkness with the spirit of manipulation and control. I use the term anointed because these individuals are flowing under the influence of an evil spirit, whether consciously or unbe-knownst.

IDENTIFYING JEZEBEL'S WORKS

How do you know if a person has this influence working in their life? It's not so much what happens when you're with them, it's what hap-pens when you're not. Let me give you an example of what I mean. When you think of offending this person do you become terrified? *Oh my, what are they going to say? What are they going to think? What are they going to do?* They may send someone to you with a message that has a profound impact on you.

Some people just convey fear or intimidation. How? They walk with that dark spirit. When you give yourself over to intimidating people, you're yielding to that controlling spirit. Don't yield. We are not led by intimidation. We're led by the Spirit of God. Follow peace; not fear.

REFUSING INTIMIDATION

I attended a soccer match a few years ago now. After the game we were waiting for my oldest son. His team had won, and they were in the process of leaving the field. Well, the fans of the other team that lost were not happy. I understand. I'm not happy when our team loses, either, however, they were getting violent about it. They wanted to fight some of our fellow students, and that sort of thing.

As we waited, a big ole steroid-filled redneck decided he was go-ing to take out his frustration on little ole me.

He said, "I'm gonna punch your teeth down your throat."

My youngest son was standing right beside me. Honestly, I was wondering who this angry man was talking to. I looked behind me because I hadn't done anything.

Then he screamed, "I'm gonna snap your f#@!g neck!"

My son urged me, "Come on, Dad. Let's go."

But I thought, *"I will not be intimidated. I'll leave if the Spirit of God leads me to, but not because an angry man intimidates me to."*

Instead, I asked, "Are you talking to me, sir?"

He said, "That's right; you heard me. I'll choke you out, and I'll snap your blanking-neck!"

I said, "Well, if that's what you need to do to feel better about yourself, you're welcome to try."

I stood and smiled at him with an expression that read, "*I just might be a little crazier than you are. You might be possessed with something, but so am I. And greater is He that's in me than he that's in that's in you.*"

I've never been a fighting kind of guy. I'm a lover; but I'm not going to be intimidated by some evil spirit working in somebody. So, I just stood there and looked at him. The man started visibly shaking. He wasn't leaving, and I wasn't either, but I wasn't shaking. I was just thinking, "*Holy Spirit, what would you like me to do in this moment?*"

I know the voice of God. The Holy Spirit said, "If he comes at you, throat punch him." So, we had a stare down.

After a few moments he said to his wife, "I'm shaking. I don't know why."

I thought, "*That's the anointing, buddy. It will not be a fair fight if you come at me.*"

Now you might be thinking, "*The Bible says turn the other cheek.*" That's if you're preaching the gospel, not being threatened at a soccer game by a bully! If you try to steal my milk money, I'm not obligated to turn my other cheek.

As he was talking to his wife, I walked around him about ten yards over to where a deputy sheriff was standing and said, "Sir, the man over there just threatened my life."

He said, "He did? What did he say?"

I told the deputy what he said. Several kids from the school verified my statement by saying, "We heard him."

So, the deputy went over and said "Sir, you're going to have to leave the property."

The man said, "It wasn't me! Why do I have to leave?"

"Sir," the deputy stated, "you can leave one of two ways."

As you can guess, he left! I "won" because I'm not going to be intimidated, and I sided in with civil authority. Later that same season, at a different game, that same man was again escorted off the property by police for trying to intimidate other parents and players. The gentleman had all the signs of having developed a mental illness, but it may have started when he was a boy being intimidated and controlled by someone else. Then he began to yield to it.

Looking back, I have had my moments. Once I was passing out Gospel tracts in India to children in a neighborhood. Four men wearing turbans came out in the middle of the street. It was like a Western, but it was an Eastern, because we were in India. Pardon the pun, but I couldn't resist. They all had machetes. So, I asked, *"Okay, Holy Spirit, what do you want me to do?"* The verse that came up in my heart that time was Hebrews 12:1c, where the apostle Paul said, "...let us run the race set before you..." So, I took off like a shot. I was gone! Yep, I ran. You have to be led by the Spirit of God, and I felt led to run. And that's a true story!

Accompanying me that day was a friend, named Antonio, from New Orleans. He is a six-foot tall, African American, brother. Antonio is a good-looking guy, great communicator, and a wonderful preacher.

When we got back to the hotel, Antonio said, "I didn't know white people could run that fast!" He further said, "I didn't think I was going to catch you!"

I replied with a big smile, "I was highly motivated!"

INTIMIDATING PEOPLE WIN BY THREATS

If you choose motivation through intimidation, you are yielding to the wrong spirit. Or, when you give yourself over to intimidating people, you yield to this dark spirit.

People operating under the influence of this spirit will say, "If you cross me, you're gonna pay! If you displease me, I'll divorce you! I'll beat you! I'll reject you! I'll withdraw from you! I'll harm you! I'll withhold from you what you need and want."

They will use your past against you. They will threaten, "If you don't do what I want you to do, I'll expose you!"

God NEVER does this. Love covers; fear threatens to expose and intimidates, and often with vibrato too.

Some threaten to withhold affection from the other. "If you don't do what I want you to do, I will stop meeting your need. If you don't do what I want you to do, then I will have an affair on you!"

This spirit thrives on the attitude of, "I'll one-up you." That's a spirit of intimidation, which is the spirit of Jezebel, who was a Control-Freak, and a false prophetess. That spirit is not from God. The spirit of satan is intimidation and retaliation and the Spirit of Christ is Grace and Forgiveness.

How do you respond to somebody like that? Graciously. You remove yourself from the situation. You may have to ultimately withdraw from the relationship if they do not change. If you realize that you have been resorting to this ungodly tactic, animated by this wrong spirit, you are on dangerous ground. Your next step is to stop right now and repeat the steps to freedom revealed in the beginning of this book in Chapter One: Recognize. Repent. Renounce. Replace. Return.

You might also be a Control-Freak if you use...

DOMINATION

Domination is the third of the three levels of ungodly control. It is the ultimate manifestation of the Jezebel spirit. Jezebel had military power and she murdered God's prophets because she lusted for control and dominion. Jezebel sent her military after Elijah because she could.

Dominators use power to exert control. They try to gain the upper hand financially, physically, politically, or personally. Now generally—and I guess this is a stereotypical statement, so bear with me—men *dominate,* and women *manipulate.* Please note I did say stereotypically. When you control—or try to control anyone—you have usurped the role of God in that person's life. You've declared yourself to be God to that individual. This a very dangerous sin. The Lord doesn't like it at all because **He** is God, and we are not.

Brother Kenneth E. Hagin is the founder of Rhema Bible College in Tulsa, OK where I studied. I consider him my "spiritual grandfather." He used to say, "God will judge spiritual sins a lot quicker than He will physical sins."

Submitting to inappropriate control is actually a form of idolatry because you are allowing someone into a position in your life where only God belongs. Exerting inappropriate control is a form of the sin of witchcraft. It is dangerously dark and cunningly carnal. *Stop it.* Why? Because eventually it will destroy you.

The fourth cause of domination is fear. Simply stated, it happens when people feel out of control. The worse dominators are people who have had pain in their past. Someone took control from them.

Some studies reveal a higher level of childhood abuse among the serial killer prison population than in the general population. (Article Cited: Crime Traveller (crimetraveller.org) by Fiona Guy (2023, June 28) Serial Killers and Childhood Abuse: Is There a Link?)

They have lived in chaotic, violent, addictive homes. Within the perceived need to be in control, some people get violent because they think it to be the most effective way to get what they seek. This is another great deception of the enemy of our soul.

Too many make an inner vow, *"Nobody will ever be allowed to treat me like that again."* Or, *"No man is ever going to dominate me."* And this: *"No woman is ever gonna…"*

When you make an inner vow, you stop maturing in that area of your personality and become what you despise. If you were abused as a child and think, *"I'll never be an abuser,"* remember the illustration of the drunk man trying to get on a horse—it just doesn't work out. You become what you hate. Who traditionally becomes a child abuser? Children who were abused. Why? Because they made an inner vow. When you make an inner vow, you are declaring yourself as God in that area of your life. So, what do you do if you've been abused? Yes, get out of the abusive situation. And then forgive the abuser by saying something like, "God, please heal me of this. I trust You to take care of me. I don't have to take care of myself because You are my Provider and Lord."

You are a precious Christian person. God wants to set you free of that pain that has its roots in fear today.

SECRET OF A HAPPY MARRIAGE

You cannot become intimate with a dominator. That's why God doesn't dominate: instead, He loves you. Love may initiate, but it never intimidates or dominates. Love is patient and kind.

The University of Washington released an article, on February 20, 1998 entitled, "Husbands' willingness to be influenced by wife, share power, are key predictors of newlywed happiness and stability." The UW study revealed *shared control* as the secret to a happy marriage. (washington.edu)

Dominance misrepresents God to society. Dominance represents a distorted image of Who He really is.

When we have dominance in our marriages, we are misrepresenting God to our kids. This is seriously wrong because our first jobs as parents are to be the image-bearers of God to our children. And I know: unlike God, you are not perfect. But, according to I Peter 4:8 (NKJV), "love covers a multitude of sins." So just love them.

Let's look at four causes as to why some people dominate others. The first three are listed here – the fourth will come later. Then we'll talk about the cure.

1. **Pride** – this could be an I'm-better-than-you manifestation.
2. **Deception** – spiritual deception. Remember Jim Jones? Or David Koresh from Waco, Texas? Or Reverend Moon?
3. **Personality** – an unsubmitted, unsanctified personality could be dominant or controlling.

Racism is both pride and deception. No matter if it's black -vs- white; white -vs- black; Hutus -vs- Tutsis; Nepalis -vs- Bengalis or any other form of tribalism. Our first consideration in understanding racism is that it is an evil spirit. It did not originate in heaven, and it is a form of deception. God created all people in His image and in Christ we are equal.

Sexual deception. Girls being trained to use sex to control men is a form of deception. By the way, God gave the ladies sexuality to glorify God through childbearing, to please their husbands, and to enjoy physical intimacy with their husbands. It's not just one or the other. It is not just, as some people teach, "You should glorify God by having kids." No. Ladies, your role is to please your man, and for you to enjoy it also. If you're not enjoying overall, try something different because somebody is doing something wrong. Allow me to suggest a good book such as, *Intended for Pleasure*, written by Ed Wheat, MD.

THE CURE

We must admit that we are not God and submit ourselves to God and to our spouses. That's the cure for domination and control.

I can hear some of you saying, "What do you mean? I'm the man and I don't have to submit myself to my wife."

Actually—you do. The Bible says Ephesians 5:21 (KJV),

> *"...submitting yourselves one to another."*

We have established a house rule in our home: When I'm acting like an idiot, will you tell me? You won't be punished. I'm not going to retaliate. As a result of our developed confidence, my wife will tell me. Then, I have to remember I made a commitment that she won't pay a price for calling me out on my misbehavior. Because let's be honest: all men have a natural ability to be jerks, but we are aiming higher than that aren't we? We are shooting for supernatural results. I remember one time when we got into an argument. Oh, gosh, I was frustrated about something! She got highly emotional, which I don't like. Let me share something with my female readers, when women cry, it just freaks us out. But it's okay. Go ahead and cry because we need to be freaked out. It helps us… sometimes.

BEHAVE LIKE YOUR GENDER

Don't act like a man towards us because we'll bow-up at you. If you bow-up at us, we will most likely bow-up at you, but if you cry, we will have more of a tendency to be tender. Tears throw us off balance. Just don't use it as a manipulative tactic. (Only God knows your heart and motive.)

My wife went to the Ladies Room, and while she was there, she prayed, "Lord, will you please tell him he is being a jerk?"

I kid you not – I was out in the living room being frustrated and it was like someone in the room spoke. I knew it was the Holy Spirit, "Kevin, you are being a jerk! You need to apologize to your wife."

Quickly I said, "Okay, Lord. I repent."

When she came out, I said, "Babe, do you know what the Holy Spirit told me?"

She said, "I might."

I answered, "He said, 'You're being a jerk and you need to apologize.' So, I'm sorry."

Then she cried and hugged my neck. She didn't say, "See, I'm right!"

No, she said, "I'm so happy and thankful that I'm married to a man who hears God's voice. I just prayed in the bathroom, 'God, please tell him he's being a jerk.'"

Those are the exact words God spoke to me! "You're being a jerk and you need to apologize to your wife."

Ask the Holy Spirit to anoint your personality. Galatians 5:22–23 (NKJV) tells us what an anointed personality looks like.

> *"But the fruit of the spirit is love, joy, peace, long-suffering, kindness, goodness, faithfulness, [23]gentleness, self-control. Against such there is no law."*

That's a God-anointed personality. And that requires yielding to a completely different Spirit.

How to Activate the Cure

As we close out this chapter, I want to give you some practical steps that will activate the cure for being controlled, or for being a Control Freak.

- **Submit Yourself to the Lord Jesus Christ.**
  In other words, if you've never made Jesus the Lord of your life, then you're never going to have success relationally, of any kind, long-term.

- **Humble Yourself.**
  Have a humble servant's attitude toward people that you disagree with, and with people that you lead. The only way to have a right relationship with other people is to humble yourself. And the greatest in Christ's Kingdom are the Servants of All.

- **Communicate Your Needs, and Let God Be God.**
  Remember when we played the Love card, instead of the Change card? If you're going to force a result, then you're playing God. Don't you really believe God can change somebody better than you can?

- **Train People How to Treat You.**
  Righteously Stand Up. Don't allow control. Don't be mean, but stand up, righteously. You have a choice in how you are treated.

Here's an example of that: My wife and I have learned to say, "Hey, please don't talk to me like that." Or, "I don't want you to treat me that way." Or, "I don't like it when you _____."

You might think, "*If I said that to my spouse, they would go off on me! After all, if Mama ain't happy, ain't nobody happy!*" Well, Mama needs to get sanctified, because in a relationship, you've got to have the ability to communicate about your likes and your dislikes. This type of back-and- forth talk has lots of benefits. From the living room to the bedroom—you need to vocalize what you like and what you do not like. When it comes to the meal preparation—if you don't want to eat something for the rest of your life, you had better learn to say so.

My wife will tell me, "Hey! I don't like it when you call me out in public in front of people." We've fought about it. I'd like to tell you we had one argument and it was done, but we fought about that for years. I don't do that anymore (much). I decided to change. And the Lord helps me.

Likewise, when we were younger, she'd bark at me and I'd say, "Hey! I don't want you talking to me like that, please." Now, because we can tell each other things, we can change. When you like being around somebody, you can end up being with them for fifty or eighty years. You will enjoy the benefits of long-term love. That's the good stuff: Abundant Life! It's kind of fun.

You're Not Obligated to Stay with an Abuser

Let me be clear: do not stay in a relationship with an abuser. Get out.

You may ask in return, "Are you telling me I should divorce my spouse?"

No, I'm saying get out of the abusive situation. Let God change that person, and if He doesn't or can't, (that's right, even God can't help some people, so why would you think you can?) then you have no obligation to remain in an abusive situation.

Why? You're too important, too special, and too precious to God to be attached to an abusive individual. Abuse is not God's plan for your life; abundance is. You are not suffering for Jesus when you stay in relationship with an abuser. Satan is the chief abuser, and Jesus came to liberate us from him.

Think about it this way. If it was your daughter, would you allow her to stay with a man who was beating her up? No? Okay. Then why are you staying with one? Get out of there. Today.

Every controller or abuser must have an enabler. Stop being that enabler. Separate for the purpose of reconciliation. If redemption and reconciliation happen, then you are free and have a beautiful love-story of redemption; if it does not occur, then you have a beautiful story of liberation and deliverance.

Either way, you are free and blessed.

QUESTIONS FOR SMALL GROUPS AND PERSONAL REFLECTION:

1. Are you in a relationship that feels like "a fight with no winner"?

2. Were you raised in a home where one parent was clearly dominate or controlling? What affect do you feel that had on you and your personality?

3. In what areas of life are you being a master when you are called to be a servant?

4. Is there someone in authority in your life that you need to pray more for? What do you hope God will do in their life?

5. How can you show honor or create an atmosphere of honor in your most important relationships?

6. Have you dabbled in any of the three levels of ungodly control? (Manipulation, Intimidation and Domination) Which ones?

7. Activating The Cure: Have you submitted your whole life to the Lordship of Jesus? Do you have a humble heart in all your relationships? How do you communicate your needs and then trust God? How could you train people to treat you? Share examples of how to righteously stand up for yourself in a relationship.

-5-
THE F-BOMB: FORGIVENESS

5

THE F-BOMB: FORGIVENESS

We All Want It. We all need it. We sometimes struggle to give it. When we don't, it binds us and blinds us. When we do, it liberates us. The big "it" … forgiveness. Forgiveness is "God's F-Bomb." When you don't forgive, it allows the devil to create all kinds of havoc in your life.

If you want to blow up what the devil is doing in your life, learn how to deploy God's F-Bomb. Learn to forgive. Especially learn to forgive *you*. Sometimes you've got to forgive yourself, as well as your neighbor. You may need to forgive a friend, or a former friend, someone we might call a "frenemy."

It's important to know that the act of forgiveness is a daily thing, by the way. It isn't just a one-time shot.

You can't just say, "I forgive everybody and we're all happy now."

Making the choice to practice daily forgiveness will help to change your personality. It will help you become a nicer person to be around.

"Where two or three are gathered in my name I Am there in the midst of them." Then Peter came to him and said,

> *"Lord, how often shall my brother sin against me and I*
> *forgive him?" Matthew 18:20–21 (NKJV)*

I can imagine Peter thinking, "*I've been hanging around Jesus long enough to know that seven is His favorite number. Watch how I impress Him by saying not one time, not two, but seven!"* Perhaps Peter thought, *"After all, if you can forgive somebody one time, you're a good person and you can feel good about yourself. If you forgive somebody two times, then you're a candidate for sainthood."*

No Magic Number

So Peter decided on seven times! His hopes and plans were to really impress Jesus with his benevolent bent towards compassion.

Notice what Jesus, in turn, says to Peter,

> *"I do not say to you up to seven times, but up to seventy times seven." Matt. 18:22 (NKJV)*

This number, 490 (70 X 7), is not a magic number, rather Jesus was teaching that we should forgive that many times in one day if need be. May I confess that this challenges me? There have been some people I've struggled to forgive once! But if I'm being honest with you, and myself, that has both hurt and hindered me.

> *"Therefore, the kingdom of heaven is like a certain king who wanted to settle accounts with his servant."*
> *Matt. 18:24 (NKJV)*

Jesus further responded to Peter's genuine question. He begins to describe what the culture of the kingdom of heaven is like so we can imitate it.

Jesus continues with the story of a master who wanted to settle accounts with his constituency, but in reality, we are the ones He wanted to "settle accounts" with. And therefore, this is an even more fascinating story!

Forgiveness Benefits the Forgiver

Perhaps you are thinking, *"This is easy for you. You are a pastor. You've never had to forgive anybody for anything. Everyone is nice to you."*

Firstly, wouldn't that be nice if it were true? I sometimes feel as though I get rejected for a living. (But don't worry—I'll work it out in therapy.) Secondly, I want to say that I also realize that many of you have been through things that are much worse than anything I have ever endured. Whatever the case may be, forgiveness **still** benefits **you**. It does not justify or make what another person did to you right, but it frees **you** from the toxicity those situations have injected into your life. It enables you to go ahead and live the abundant life that God has destined for you.

My wife uses a great illustration.

She says, "If you know someone who is a shin kicker, you can forgive them, and also choose not to walk near them anymore."

So, if somebody kicks you in the shins and says, "Oh, I'm sorry for kicking you in the shin; my fault."

You reply, "No problem." It's forgiven.

Then they kick you again, but quickly apologize. You accept their apology, forgive them, and move on.

When they kick you a third time you should realize the time has come to quit walking past the shin kicker. You can forgive them, and we are commanded to do so, but you don't have to hang out with them. You are not commanded to continue in a toxic or abusive relationship with someone who does not value you as the child of God that you are. You are free from that obligation. Some people disqualify themselves from becoming an intricate part of your life. Drop God's F-bomb on them and move nicely onward.

I don't like stating this, but there are some people you can't get along with. Nevertheless, you can and should try. Yet, the Bible says,

> *"If possible, so far as it depends on you, be at peace with all men." Romans 12:18 (NKJV)*

Sadly, with some folks, peace just isn't possible. That's not necessarily your fault; that's just life.

Like my pastor told me once, "Some bricks would do more damage to the structure of the wall by trying to get next to each other, so they should just stay in their place."

Keep in mind that forgiving is not for others. It is for you. Forgiving is not forgetting. It is remembering without anger. It frees up your power, heals your body, mind, and spirit.

"Forgiveness opens up a pathway to a new place of peace where you can persist despite what has happened to you."
—Les Brown (Motivational Speaker)

Something Unseen Revealed

Jesus told an amazing story about understanding the unseen program that runs the world, also known as The Kingdom of Heaven. He reveals a picture in Matthew 18:23 (NKJV) with these words,

"The Kingdom of Heaven is like a certain king who wanted to settle accounts with his servants. And when he had begun to settle accounts, one was brought to him who owed him 10,000 talents."

This amount is the equivalent of 10,000 years of wages. An impossible debt to repay. And just so we can get our mind around this illustration, let's use a billion dollars. I don't know how much ten thousand years of salary would be, but I'm sure it is a significant sum.

And the story continues in verse 25. The master commanded that he be sold along with his wife and children and all their possessions so a payment could be made. Not full payment, just a partial payment.

"The servant, therefore, fell down before him, saying, Master, have patience with me and I will pay you all. (I'm begging you, for my sake, in other words.) And the master of that servant was moved with compassion; released him and forgave him the debt."

"But the servant went out and found one of his fellow servants who owed him a hundred denarii (about $262 bucks).

He grabbed the man by the throat saying, "Pay me my $262

bucks, dude!" (Paraphrased)

His fellow servant fell down at his feet and begged him for mercy, saying, "Have patience with me and I will pay you all!" And he would not." Please note that the Bible does not say he *could* not, but that he *would* not. Instead, he went and threw the man into prison until he could pay his debt.

FORGIVENESS IS NOT AN OPTION

I've always been confused by the idea of being jailed for debt. How do you pay your debt if you're in jail and you can't create an income? I guess that's a ponderance for another time. Let's finish this story with verses 31–35.

> *"So, when his fellow servants saw what had been done, they were grieved and came and told their master all that had been done. Then his master, after he had called him to him, said, 'You wicked [twisted] servant. I forgave you all that debt because you begged me to. Should you not have had compassion on your fellow servant just as I had pity on you?' "*

The master was angry and delivered him to the torturers until he should pay all that was due him. This next verse is really heavy.

> *"So my Heavenly Father will also do to you if each of you, from your heart, does not forgive his brother his trespasses."*

Jesus is telling us, "If you don't forgive your brother his trespasses God will not forgive you." And we can't just give it lip-service: we have to really mean it from our hearts! And God can tell the difference too.

Do you remember this portion of The Lord's Prayer found in Matthew 6:8–13 (NKJV):

> *"Our Father, who is in heaven, hallowed be thy name. Thy*

kingdom come, Thy will be done on earth as it is in heaven.
Give us today our daily bread. Forgive us our trespasses
as we forgive those who trespass against us."

"Forgive us as we forgive those who trespass against us." This prayer represents Jesus teaching his disciples to pray, and in the process, boldly telling us that if we don't forgive those who trespass against us, God is not going to forgive us of our trespasses.

In truth, we all *deserve* hell. We all deserve eternal separation from God. In comparison to what you and I have done to God, nobody really owes us very much do they? When we think in terms of the debt that we owe God, how much does somebody else owe us? It really doesn't amount to a whole lot, comparatively speaking. Or have you possibly underestimated your sinfulness without Christ?

Because of what God has forgiven us of, it is petty in His sight if we will not forgive someone else. This parable is clearly telling us, "If you don't want to live a tormented life, then drop the F-Bomb and forgive." Unforgiveness releases you from torment. Forgiveness is not an option; it is a commandment.

POSSIBLE SIDE-EFFECTS OF NOT FORGIVING:

What kind of torment is released by unforgiveness? Let's explore three avenues.

Physical Ailments. Unforgiveness causes high blood pressure. It causes nervous issues. Have you ever had someone get on your nerves? Who hasn't? Unforgiveness can cause headaches. It is a headache. Let me read a quote from Dr. Don Colbert. He's the doctor to the "Christian Celebrities" or the name-brand preachers. "More important than vitamins to our health is a merry heart. It's important to rid yourself of deadly, toxic emotions like hatred, bitterness, resentment and unforgiveness. Almost every cancer patient I've ever served has had some sort of resentment, unforgiveness or even self-hatred. Once they combined forgiveness with healthy eating habits, their cancer went into remission." That's powerful! Unforgiveness releases physical torment. It is like a bomb exploding in our own life. Do you want to improve your health? Forgive. The F-Bomb blows up our health issues.

Emotional Torment. Unforgiveness releases emotional torment. Outbursts of anger and cynical behavior are damaging. Ever encountered another individual who was cynical about most anything and everything? Did you find it difficult to have a simple conversation with them? Everything had the possibility of turning into an argument. What's more draining than that? There is a better way to live, and it involves you dropping God's F-Bomb of forgiveness into the midst of situations like these.

Unforgiveness often leads to depression. Imagine this scenario with me. Suppose we wanted to see who could run the furthest. Speed is not a factor. We would judge by distance alone regardless of time.

Some folks could go three steps and say, "I'm out."

Others could run 100 yards. A fair few could run a mile. Many might run up to five miles. I'd probably be pushing my limit at five miles, but maybe I could squeak out six if I paced myself properly. And I don't mean power walking; you've got to at least jog.

Some of you, who feel really good about yourself, could probably run ten miles. We have a marathoner in our church, twenty-six miles and 385 yards. She might could squeak out thirty miles. My point is that we all have a certain amount of physical energy and endurance. At some point we will "tucker out." The same is true emotionally. We all have a certain amount of emotional energy and endurance. People can only take negativity for so long until they want to escape. And they usually do. Too many times in companies, churches, or any kind of relationship, people take the bait of being offended—either legitimately or not, and brokenness is the result.

Perhaps the only thing more toxic than being offended is second-hand offense: when you get offended on behalf of somebody else. That's super dangerous.

What if we assumed the best and kept moving along our own path of destiny? Otherwise, we may only succeed in getting ourselves off-track, wrongly thinking we are doing someone a favor.

"Well, what if I'm right? I know I'm right!"

It seems to me, as Christ-followers, we can either make a point or we can make a difference. I don't recall seeing anyone do both effectively.

The biggest consumer of emotional energy is, (take a guess), unforgiveness. Again, this is critically important because we all have a limited amount of emotional energy. By dropping God's F-Bomb of forgiveness, we remove the largest drain of emotional energy in our lives.

Better With Time

A clinical definition of depression is anger turned inward. The only reason I can think of how anger would turn inward is perhaps because the individual has waited too long to deal with it, or they just have never been taught how to use the tools available for processing this very real but powerful emotion.

Depression is aged anger. Some things do get better as they age, like cheese, wine, and marriage. Nevertheless, anger is not one of those things that gets better over time. You might cool off, but unless you resolve your anger, it will become toxic to your relationship, especially any relationship where there is unforgiveness. Then *you* become toxic and start sabotaging all of your relationships. God's F-Bomb of forgiveness destroys depression and guards you from the deadly effects of offense.

Get It Out Before Dark

All these negative things can happen because we have unresolved issues in our lives. Ephesians 4:26 (NKJV) says,

"Do not let the sun go down on your wrath."

What, then, do we do with our wrath? We get it out every day. Deal with it. And deal with it before dark. Don't let the blazing hot sun of your wrath go down before you go to sleep, else it will burn you up. Work it *out*. Paul said, in Philippians 2:12 (NKJV),

"Work out your own salvation with fear and trembling."

When you go to approach someone for restoration, there may be some fear and trembling, but it's worth it to work it out. And yes, sometimes it feels like a workout too. But when you work out regularly you get fit, stronger and in shape.

You can only run so long on the emotional treadmill until you get depressed. You've got to get off the emotional treadmill so you can make some real progress.

"But if you do not forgive men their trespasses neither will your Father forgive your trespasses."
Matthew 6:15 (NKJV)

Do you believe Jesus actually meant what He said in this verse? Or did He say one thing and mean another? Was He speaking in hyperbole? Metaphor? If you were to study the original Greek words this passage was written in, what do you think you would discover?

Right! Jesus meant... *forgive*!

Unburden yourself of the guilt, shame and anger attached to your issue. One of the heaviest things to carry in life is a grudge. Let it go. Before dark. You are God's sheep, and sheep are not beasts of burden. Load them down too much and they die.

Dropping The F-Bomb

You've got to drop the F-bomb of godly forgiveness in your life. When you forgive, this decision blows up all the mess the devil is trying to do in your life. This is not fun, but if we do not forgive men their trespasses, neither will our Father forgive our trespasses. And believe me, we all have some.

Many Christians don't forgive because they don't feel forgiven themselves. They still struggle with a sense of guilt. Perhaps the reason for this is because they haven't forgiven someone else, and therefore they, in fact, are not forgiven…

What Does The Bible Say?

God's Word says,

> "If we confess our sins, God is faithful and just to forgive
> us and cleanse us from all unrighteousness."
> 1 John 1:9 (NKJV)

Unforgiveness is a sin.
"But you don't know what they've done to me."
Okay. How many times are you going to go around that same mountain on your emotional treadmill? The only one it's killing is you.

> "Forgive us our debts __as__ we forgive them our debtors."
> Matt. 6:12 (NJKV)

By the way, this is a *daily* prayer. "Give us this day our daily bread" is also a part of the prayer. This is not monthly bread, or annual bread. We need "Daily Bread!" Your loving Lord has provided what you need for each day. So, that means we have to forgive when? Today. How often? Daily. Every day? Yes. Each and every single day! That includes those tiny little grievances, but also the big ones. (Let me give you a hint. If you practice forgiveness on the little ones, it gets easier with the big ones.)

Developing a Good Habit

Walking in forgiveness will become second nature to you. More accurately, it will become first nature: you have been made a new creature in Christ and God's Love has been poured out inside of your heart by the Holy Spirit. Love is your nature now.

When someone grieves you, your response can become, "Ok, I

forgive you for that. I'm gonna cut you some slack here."

The "old creature" may have just said, "I'm gonna cut you."

The new creature says, with an Italian accent perhaps, "Don't worry 'bout it."

Why? It becomes your habit to forgive and not hold things against people. It is your way. This daily discipline sweeps out negative emotions every day. You end the day with a clean slate, a clean floor, emotionally speaking. Then you have nice dreams at night. Now life better for you.

Many people have jacked up dreams and don't know why. It's because their souls are cluttered; they are emotionally exhausted. They have piles of junk in their emotional closet and their mind is trying to work it out at night. They are trying to detox their brain within a sleep cycle. But they are missing the vital ingredient of detergent called forgiveness.

Just sweep that stuff out. "Don't let the sun go down on your wrath," then you will have sweet dreams (Ephesians 4:26 NKJV). Maybe you will have dreams about butterflies and being able to breathe underwater. That's one of my favorite recurring dreams. I'm under there like Aqua Man. I don't know what's that all about, but I like it. Have you ever had a dream about flying? I think we'll be able to fly when we get our glorified bodies. It will be awesome! But Joel 2:28 says you may have prophetic dreams. That's when the really funs stuff starts.

LOOKING FOR A WAY IN: ACCESS DENIED

The devil is looking for a way into your life. The number one point of entry is through anger, or cynicism, or offense. Forgiveness is a buttress against enemy tactics. It denies satan access to your soul. John Bevere wrote a fabulous book on offense called, "*The Bait of Satan.*" I encouraged the whole church to read it when I first started pastoring in Mobile, AL back in 2003. All sixty-seven of us read this book.

Don't take the bait! What is the bait? The bait is offense.

"That just offends me!"

Ace Ventura, a movie character played by Jim Carey, got offended because a lady was wearing an animal fur. Whether wearing the fur was right or wrong didn't even matter because he took the bait and got offended. It created big problems for him.

Offense, cynicism, and anger all work together to create the language and personality of satan. That's how he talks. He's always looking for someone of like personality, a person who is always angry like him. He constantly searches for someone who is easily offended like him. Somebody who is cynical. He thinks, *"I can work with them; they are just like me."*

Pharisees, one group of religious leaders during the time of Jesus-on-earth, looked good on the outside, but on the inside they were mean. We can learn from their negative example.

MEAN PEOPLE GO TO HELL

Did you know that? Mean people go to hell. You will not find any nice people down there. Everybody is bitter about something. I believe one reason I'm on earth to keep people from going to hell. I cannot imagine there being any nice people in hell; nor can I imagine any mean folks up in Heaven.

I've never been to hell personally; and I don't plan on going. Not my tribe. There will be no nice people there! I know this sounds awful, but there are some mean people who attend church. Don't become offended. Don't let them offend you. Don't take satan's bait: do not *take* offense! Leave it. Offense is a seedling of Satan sown into the souls of men to produce the bitter fruit of disconnection and death. Death is absence. II Corinthians 5:8 (NKJV) assures us that,

> *"to be absent from the body and to be present with the Lord."*

Love is greater than offense.

Only spiritual babies get offended. Let us decide to grow up. Offense may feel justified in the moment, but in the end, it hurts like hell and disconnects you from the body you desperately need. As a pastor, shepherd, and overseer of people's souls, being offended has been the number one thing I've seen stunt both church and individual spiritual growth. Offense robs relational riches, retards the body of Christ, and sabotages the perfect plan of God for His precious saints. Offense is like spraying Round-Up on your strawberries and taking a whiz in your cheerios. If you know what's good for you—you won't do it.

But if you have is it too late? Absolutely not. Turn to God and trust Him with your pain. His plan is not that fragile. He knows how to lead you back to the "paths of righteousness for His Name's sake." Psalm 23:3 (NKJV)

DUDE, YOU HAD ONE JOB!

The Bible says,

> *"Grapes are not gathered from thorns."*
> *Matthew 7:16 (NKJV)*

Grapes and thorns are two different things. Grapes are sweet; thorns will prick you and make you bleed. This fact reminds me of a group of people who came to Jesus and said, "Hey! We did powerful things in your Name. We cast out devils. We healed the sick. We worked miracles."

Jesus responded by saying, "Depart from me: I never knew you—you who works iniquity" (Matt. 7:23 KJV). The New Living Translation reads, "get away from Me you lawless ones, I never knew you." The PKT (Pastor Kevin Translation) says, "Dude! You only had one job: To Love! You were so busy 'casting out devils' you forgot to love God and love people."

Knowing Jesus intimately must be the key to operating by Love in all we do. For you see, God does not have any love; it's what He is. Love is not a thing. He is a person… He is Love. These people, possibly ministers, were casting out devils and working miracles. It sounds so spiritual. Yet, they were not willing to overcome offense and operate by "The Royal Law of Love." Instead Jesus labeled them "lawless" or not governed by Christ's Kingdom. You can cast out devils and heal the sick, but if you're not a person of love you're disqualified. If you're not walking in love and by love, motivated and animated with Love, then you are not abiding by God's one and only law for His people in the New Covenant: Love. We got one job bro.

> *"One step out of love is a step back into darkness."*
> —Rev. Kenneth E. (Dad) Hagin

THE GREATEST COMMANDMENT

His disciples asked Jesus,

> *"Lord, what is the greatest commandment?"*

In Matthew 22:37 and 39 (NKJV) Jesus gave them two.

> *"You shall love the Lord your God with all your heart, mind, and strength. And the second is like it; Love your neighbor as yourself."*

The most self-loving thing you can do is forgive those who have offended and hurt you. Forgiveness makes you sweet; offense makes you bitter. And it's better to get better than to get bitter. I like what one of my sons says. "Offense builds fences." Love welcomes and tears them down.

In the passage found in Matt. 7:23 (NJKV), and paraphrased by me, Jesus had just established the new law: The Law of Love. Jesus said, "Depart from me you mean people. I never got to know you. Depart from me those who do not keep 'The Royal Law of Love.' Get out of here. We're not on the same team. You have a different Spirit than I have."

THE SPIRIT OF LOVE

Jesus is the Spirit of Love. He also plainly stated in John 13:35

(NKJV),

"By this all will know that you are my disciples…"

By what? What evidence will people use to determine that we are disciples of Christ? By how we love one another. How we love one another is also how we are to love ourselves. Did Jesus say, "They'll know you're my disciples because you're always right about everything?" Some people think that's what it says. I've acted that way before. I like being right. But I'm learning to like Love more because, as I stated earlier, you can make a point or a difference. Not usually both.

Jesus also did not say, "They'll know you're my disciples because of your Christian bumper sticker, or because you have a fish on your business card." Nothing wrong with those things, but no. Is His light shining through you? That's His love. That light shines because we love Him, love ourselves, and love one another. I often wonder how many people realize we live in a dark world and the light people are drawn to is Love. People know we're His disciples because of how we love ourselves, each other, and God. Why? Because love like that is out of this world!

How does a married couple go from madly in love to just mad? How do they go from being totally head-over-heels in love with each other to hatred in a divorce court? It all starts with one, single, small drop of toxic offense. A single drop. That's all it takes.

Jesus told us the same way you measure it out, it's being measured back to us. As you sow it you will reap it. If you give drops of mercy, you will get a little drop when you need it. But if you give oceans of mercy, you will get an ocean when you need it. I would rather have the ocean on tap when needed.

WHEN YOU SAY "FORGIVE," WHAT DOES THAT LOOK LIKE?

What does it mean to forgive? Let's walk through it.

Permanently forgiving all debt. The offender owes you nothing, zero, not even an apology. You're all good. We are even. Square.

Permanently forfeiting disapproval. That means when I see you on the street, I will deliberately be nice to you. I'm not going to avoid you. I don't have to hang out with you if you are a "shin kicker," but I will be kind, not because you deserve it, but because that's who I am in Christ.

Permanently forgoing all expressions of judgment. No throwing shade in private or public. This one is a little harder, at least speaking from my own experience. I cannot afford to adopt the posture, "When it's just you and me behind closed doors, this is really what I think about them." If you've forgiven, you even forego those types of self-conversation in your own inner mind. You forfeit any reasonable approach and favor the spiritual approach. You say nothing but nice things about them. Again, you don't have to invest any time with them, if they are a repeat offender, but you must lay down your rights to malign them verbally or inwardly. Let it go. (Insert Disney song here.)

REMEMBERING BROTHER HAGIN

This reminds me of a story told by Reverend Kenneth E. Hagin. Brother Hagin was my spiritual grandfather. I attended his Rhema Bible College in Broken Arrow, Oklahoma. It changed my life. He used to tell us about a man, in a town where he pastored, who was not in his right mind. In fact, the whole population feared him because he was prone to violence. People kept their distance and let him do his thing.

One day, the deranged man had a knife. The sheriff had to get involved.

He refused the sheriff's requests to, "Put the knife down."

He not only refused but attempted to attack the sheriff. The sheriff, in self-defense, had to shoot him. The man died. Some of the local people, if I recall the story correctly, including a group of preachers, were standing around talking about it. It seemed as if a sigh of relief had filled the town. They were both sad, but glad he was gone, because he was such a menace. His threatening behavior had put such fear in people's hearts. Some were glad they would not have to deal with him anymore.

As they stood around one said, "I'm so glad he's gone. He was mean."

Then they asked, "What do you think about it Brother Hagin?"

Brother Hagin said, "Well, he sure had pretty eyes."

"Excuse me. What?"

"Yeah, he had pretty eyes. They were kind of a blueish green."

"Yeah, but what about how mean he was?"

"I just remember those pretty eyes."

He wouldn't say anything negative about the man. He refused to malign him.

A KEY TO LONGEVITY

Brother Hagin was also known to tell a story of a man in his nineties. The man he spoke of was the picture of health.

One day the man was standing with his wife when Brother Hagin asked, "What's the key to your health and longevity?"

"Well, Brother Hagin, I am the picture of health. My wife and I have been married for a long, long time and we're still *actively* married."

Then he kind of winked at Brother Hagin. The wife blushed.

He continued, "I've asked the Lord to let me keep all my hair, and I've kept my hair. I've asked the Lord to help me keep my teeth, and I've kept my teeth.

"Above all that, I asked the Lord to help me keep this" and he pointed to his mouth. "I've asked the Lord to help me keep my tongue."

If you keep your tongue, I believe you get to keep the rest. If you're willing to control that, then God is willing to forgive any sin you've committed. If you're willing to permanently forgive the debt, permanently forfeit reproach, and forego all expressions of disapproval, private or public, then there is no sin or trespass that the Blood of Jesus cannot cleanse.

There is a condition. You might not have known that. You may be thinking, *"But I thought God loves me unconditionally?"* Sure, He does. However, we have studied His Word, "I will forgive you, so I require you to forgive others." Matt. 6:12–14 (my paraphrase) Love and forgiveness is what makes the Kingdom work and what makes it attractive to those outside of it. This is the inner workings, the gears that cause the wheels of the Kingdom of Heaven to turn. At our church we have a core value: "Love is our language and kindness our accent."

Many still ask, "Why can't we all get along?"

We can. If you're in the Kingdom of Love, we can "work out our salvation." And we should. It is work, but it is worth it. In God's kingdom, Love is King!

Others have exclaimed, "This is not realistic. Normal people do not live this way."

My reply, "You are right: normal people do not live this way. But we are not normal. We are a supernatural people. Called to live a supernatural life. Normal people don't live to be 120 years old either, but the Way of Love is our new-normal." The proof lies in Psalm 91:16 (NKJV)

> *"...with long life I will satisfy you and show you My salvation."*

FACES OF UNFORGIVENESS

What are some forms of unforgiveness? Murder is a form of unforgiveness. Hate, slander, revenge, withholding good, and sarcasm are other faces of unforgiveness.

Sarcasm is an interesting word in the Greek translation. *Sarc* means flesh. It often refers to a wolf because the wolf comes to prey on the sheep's flesh. Sarcasm, therefore, could be interpreted to mean "flesh eater."

Labeling is a form of unforgiveness. If you call somebody a name, that can be an expression of unforgiveness. Racial slurs are a form of unforgiveness. I'm sure we don't have that in the church but walk outside the church doors and it's everywhere. Name-calling. We learn early, on the playground, how to call people names. We still do it to this day. And it's the spirit of the world at best.

Divorce is a form of unforgiveness. It is unresolved conflict.

Bigotry. Prejudice. A general wish _for_ bad things to happen to people is a type of unforgiveness.

Praying against people is a form of witchcraft often based upon unforgiveness or an extreme desire to control. By the way, when you pray for bad things to happen to somebody, God isn't listening to that prayer. Praying that someone will do what you want them to do instead of what God wants them to do is also a form of yielding to the wrong spirit.

Criticism is a form of unforgiveness. (As opposed to critique that wants someone to improve and get better.)

Rejection in the form of avoiding people to punish them counts too.

Unforgiveness often brings about a transfer of affection. In marriage it may mean something so awful as, *"I'll go love somebody else."* In friendship, it may lead to, *"I'll show somebody else the kindness I was demonstrating to you."*

Unforgiveness too often leads to judgmentalism. This leads to a lack of mercy and compassion. Not very Christ-like attributes, right? We are called to be conformed to the image of Christ. Jesus never held anything against anyone. He never took satan's bait of offense. He forgave Judas, one of his closest friends, who betrayed Him. He even forgave those who crucified Him. How do we get so offended over petty grievances?

REMEMBERING RELEASES THE BOMB

Let's get into some practical steps of releasing the F-Bomb of For-giveness in your life so you stop the enemy in his tracks.

Remember how much you've been forgiven. Your sin and mine put Jesus on the cross. When we forget this, we become very critical of other people and their shortcomings. We were on our way to hell and Jesus saved us. By the Grace of God, we've been saved. This truth ought to turn us into people who are walking around trying to give away what we have received—which is kindness and goodness. If you want mercy, then give mercy. You still reap what you sow. In Matthew 7:1 (KJV), Jesus says,

> *"Judge not that you be not judged."*

He goes on to say,

> *"In the same measure you mete it out it will be measured back to you."*

This truth is reinforced in Luke 6:38 (NJKV),

> *"Give and it will be given unto you; pressed down, shaken together and running over."*

This verse is most often heard during the offering when the plate is passed. We teach it correctly. This is a universal truth. But it was first spoken in regard to forgiveness, mercy, judgment and criticism. Whenever you give judgment and criticism, you're going to receive it back. You will receive back the full amount, "Good measure, pressed down, shaken together and running over." If you give mercy, that's what you're going to receive back. The good news is you'll receive it in abundance too.

I once read a book called, *How to Stop the Pain*, by Dr. James B. Richards. *Pain is Inevitable, Suffering is Optional*, is the sub-title. Pain happens to all of us. If you've never read the book, it's a good one to go through every few years to clean out the cobwebs of your soul.

How much grace do you want? A little or a lot? The more you give away, the more you're gonna get. That's a very good deal, especially when it comes to mercy and forgiveness.

Remember the death of Christ, on our behalf, was in vain if we will not forgive others. One of His final acts, while hanging on the cross of suffering, was to forgive those who placed him there to afflict him.

Remember the detrimental consequences of unforgiveness. Also remember the potential torment. Think of the spiritual bondages unleashed. Consider the broken relationships, fellowship and havoc that unforgiveness releases into your life.

LOVE AND HATE DON'T MIX

I've never seen a believer consistently walk in the power of the Holy Spirit who also chose simultaneously to walk in unforgiveness. The power of the Holy Spirit and unforgiveness will not flow together, no more than oil and water can mix. In Acts 8:19–24 (NKJV), Simon the magician said, "Give me this power of the Holy Spirit."

Peter told him. "You are full of all gall of bitterness."

Simon, the magician, it seems, was only asking for the power of the Holy Spirit so he could use it to hurt people he didn't like. Peter, discerning the motive of Simon's heart, rebuked him. (Love does that sometimes.)

Remember the phrase Acts 8:22 (NKJV). Peter told Simon,

> *"Repent therefore of this your wickedness, and pray God if perhaps the thought of your heart may be forgiven you."*

Most reading this will think, *"Well of course God will forgive. Our Lord will forgive anybody who asks for forgiveness."* Why would Peter say such a thing? Peter recognized that Simon, the sorcerer, was walking in a heavy level of unforgiveness and he needed to forgive somebody. Once Simon forgave, then he could be forgiven.

THE F-BOMB: FORGIVENESS

Remember God loves your offender as much as he loves you. When you find or manufacture a reason to devalue someone, you discount the power, the process, and the Person of Calvary. You are cheapening the death, burial, and resurrection of Jesus.

When you call someone an idiot, or find some reason to devalue them, you've just disqualified yourself from ever reaching that person with the Gospel. You will never reach a person that you have judged. No, not ever. We have been given the Ministry of Reconciliation and not of condemnation.

A LESSON REINFORCED

A few years ago, I was with one of my dear friends, Pastor Joel, in an airport in Northeast India. We were trying to get tickets on a helicopter to go up the mountain where our friend Mike lived. He leads a wonderful ministry. Both Mike and Joel are two of my favorite people on Earth.

A guy cut in front of us and bought one of the four seats out from under us. I became irritated and I told the guy about my irritation. I let him know I didn't appreciate his actions very much. It was not only irritating but, now most inconvenient. The Indian guy resorted to calling me a very bad name, which made me even angrier. I recall thinking, *"I'm here to reach and help your people and you're calling me an imperialist pig and...worse?"* As I sat quietly near my highly spiritual, friend, Pastor Joel, I remained quiet, but still thinking, *"I'd like to go lay hands on that guy! Suddenly and repeatedly!"*

The Holy Spirit suddenly spoke to me, *"Go apologize to him."*

I thought, *"I don't want to apologize to him. He stole our seat and called me a bad name!"*

"Go apologize to him. That is your next step in following Me."

I finally said inwardly, *"Alright. Yes, Sir."*

But that was not enough for the Holy Spirit. He wanted an act of contrition, which felt especially irritating.

The Holy Spirit, The Great Counselor added, *"Offer to pay for his seat."*

I thought, *"Now You're making me mad."*

Within a couple of moments, I yielded and went to the man. "Sir, I lost my temper. I apologize. I shouldn't have spoken to you like that. Please forgive me."

Then an amazing thing happened.

He said, "I shouldn't have gotten so upset so quickly."

We forgave each other. Total strangers had a meaningful conversation.

Remembering the direction of the Holy Spirit, I said, "Let me pay for your ticket."

He said, "No, no, no. I've got it. Please, please."

We had a great talk, and it's a good thing because we had a helicopter ride together up the mountain, and there was no "social distancing".

CLEAN HANDS AND A CLEAN HEART

After a few minutes, I came back to Pastor Joel and sat beside him. I was so relieved. I thought, *"This feels so much better than being mad at somebody."*

Pastor Joel smiled at me and said, "Clean hands and a clean heart."

We all have to deal with this issue. This was my reminder that God loves our offenders as much as He loves us. And if we don't forgive them, we can never reach them.

Remember to create a permanent release of debt. Decide and speak this aloud, "The same thing my Master did for me is what I'm going to do for you." We must bless them and pray for them. I believe Matthew 5:44 (NKJV) is one of the greatest scriptures in the Bible in regards to restoring relationships and getting out of satan's trap of offense. The Strong's Exhaustive Concordance of the Bible gives us some insight into the practical application of this verse. Look how it defines the words *love* and *bless*:

"Love (Agape – love unconditionally) your enemies.

Bless (<u>Eulogize</u> – speak well of and invoke a benediction to prosper upon) those who curse you; do good to those who hate you and pray for those who spitefully use you and persecute you."

That means pray, bless, eulogize, and only say nice things about those who spitefully use you. For example, as a minister, when I officiate a funeral, I always bring up the good stuff on the deceased. I speak of their good attributes and contributions. I never get up and talk about what a jerk they were or spotlight their struggle with addiction. I "eulogize" them. I focus on the good. I recall the positive.

I remember one time I had a situation where I had to work through some forgiveness with a guy. This was before the Lord brought alive Matthew 5:44 to me. I was upset and said, "Lord, do you remember in your Word about Ananias and Sapphira and how you killed two people in church? Lord, do you know how much the city of Mobile would come to fear you if a couple of people in our church dropped dead? I'd humbly like to offer you a short list of names, sir that I feel, strictly from a pastoral perspective, qualify."

Now that's not exactly what I said, but that was my way of thinking. I wasn't praying nice things for them if I'm being completely honest. But the Lord helped me. He's The Great Counselor; The Helper!

The Lord spoke to me saying, *"Okay, continue on with your request for them."*

"Alright," I said. "Your Word says, 'Vengeance is mine, saith the Lord'"

Then it was almost like the Lord leaned down with a notepad and asked, *"Can you just speak slowly here before you go on with the details of what you want me to do to them? I want to get everything down that you say, because I will do twice as much for you, son."*

Quickly I said, "What I meant to pray Lord was, that you would bless them really good. Do some nice stuff for them. Pay off their house. Bless and help their kids. Bless their marriage. Give them more money. Help their ministry to grow. Lord, just bless 'em, bless em', bless 'em, bless 'em. Let all their dreams come true. Give them favor! Do more for them than they could ask or think or dare dream or imagine!"

This is actually a true story. I'm exaggerating only a very little bit. I didn't really pray that God would kill them, but I was not happy with them, and I was not praying nice things for them because I was hurt and angry. But the Lord truly did respond with words I will never forget, *"Now I want to get exactly what you're saying, Son, because I want to do twice as much for you."* By the time I finished, I got caught up in praying such a blessing on these people that I couldn't be angry or hurt any longer. Can you guess the result? I was healed. I dropped the F-Bomb, it healed me, and blew up all the enemies plans.

You can't stay mad at somebody and consistently pray good things for them at the same time. I got somewhat caught up in blessing them and was healed. Then I sent them an offering. Yep, I sent them some money. Then I felt even better. God's medicine was working in my sour soul, making it sweet like Jesus. Then I thought, *"Lord, now I really do want you to do good things for them. Now I'm sincere about it."* That took a little while; I'm not gonna lie, but I got to the point where I really did want to see these people do well.

Let God drain the bitterness out of your heart today because, if you apply this, God's Word is medicine. Forgiving others will change your personality. You don't like your personality? Start loving, forgiving, and having mercy on others. And "eulogize" them. Bless them. Pray for them. It will heal your heart. It will soothe your soul. It will set you free. It will change your personality. It will make you more like Jesus.

The most self-loving thing you can do is forgive. Do you want to show yourself some love? Stop drinking the bitter poison of resentment. It's only hurting you. Forgive those who have harmed you. Go ahead. Drop the F-Bomb: forgiveness.

QUESTIONS FOR SMALL GROUPS AND PERSONAL REFLECTION:

1. What are some of the faces of unforgiveness that have shown up in your life?

2. What are some things we must remember to release the power of forgiveness for in our lives?

3. In the story of the man in his 90's, what was the key to his health and longevity? What are 2 or 3 specific ways you can improve in this?

4. Do you have "clean hands and a clean heart" today? Is there someone you need to forgive? Who? How would you "eulogize" him/her?

5. The most self-loving thing you can do is forgive. Show yourself some love. Stop drinking the bitter poison of resentment. It's only hurting you. Discuss or journal about these concepts.

-6-
SHAME ON JESUS

6

SHAME ON JESUS

Has anyone ever said, "Shame on you?" I remember when I was kid hearing, "Shame! Shame! Shame! Everybody knows your name!" Most folks, at one time and in some form or another, have been told such. The last thing humans need is more shame, most of us have more than enough.

Yet, there is a clear remedy for shame and that is the redemptive work of Jesus. He paid the price for our sin, so the truth for the Christ-Follower is not, "shame on you" but rather, "shame on Jesus!" He bore our sin AND He bore our shame. (See Isaiah 53:1–12.)

PUT IT OUT OF YOUR MIND

> *"Therefore, since we are surrounded by such a great cloud of witnesses, let us also lay aside every weight, and sin which clings so closely, and let us run with endurance the race that is set before us, looking to Jesus, the founder and perfecter of our faith, who for the joy that was set before him endured the cross, despising the shame, and is seated at the right hand of the throne of God."*
> *Hebrews 12:1–2 (ESV)*

Jesus is our example of faith. He lived and died as a human. Perfect. Sinless. On the worst day of His life, He *endured* AND *despised* shame. Despise – is the Greek word, *kataphroneo*, pronounced, "karat-fern-A-o." It means: to put out or keep out of your mind.

JESUS FOUGHT SATAN, TOO

Satan does nothing new. He is still doing what he's always done. The way he attacked Jesus is how he attacks us, as well. Not only was Jesus hanging naked at the crossroads of the world on a cross for all to see, but satan was also there jeering at Him in the midst of His horrific suffering. When Jesus was exposed Satan mocked, scorned, and showered our Suffering Savior with shame. As shame relentlessly battered Christ's soul with accusation, insult and inferiority, somehow Jesus put it out and kept it out of His mind. He "endured the cross; despised the shame."

BEWARE DURING WEAK MOMENTS

Satan attacks during our weaknesses when we feel exposed and helpless. Luke records a particularly revealing attack on Jesus. Satan came to tempt Jesus after He had been fasting for forty days. He had been led into the wilderness by The Spirit, whom we have come to know as The Counselor. Satan is always waiting for when we are weak. He is not a gentleman, but a vicious and cruel adversary. Amazingly, satan attacked Jesus with a spirit of shame! Jesus won His victory by despising the shame satan attacked with. Success leaves clues so now let's learn from Jesus' success.

A SNAKE IN THE GRASS

> *"And they were both naked, the man and his wife, and they were not ashamed." Genesis 2:25 (NKJV)*

There is no shame in the Presence of God. Because of this, we know heaven is a place without shame. The manifest Presence of God is shame-free. God only operates in an atmosphere of faith, grace, and acceptance. Encouragement and gratitude make the entry and mark the exit to His domain. In His presence there is tangible, strength-building joy! He refuses to operate in the toxic atmosphere of shame.

Shame was the first emotion felt and expressed by fallen man. It caused mankind to hide from the One who loved us the most. Shame is the most insidious thing that satan uses to destroy God's will for our lives!

Genesis 3:6–11 (NKJV) describes the scene,

> *When the woman saw that the fruit of the tree was good for food and pleasing to the eye and also desirable for gaining wisdom, she took some and ate it. She also gave some to her husband, who was with her, and he ate it. Then the eyes of both of them were opened, and they realized they were naked; so, they sewed fig leaves together and made coverings for themselves. Then the man and his wife heard the sound of the Lord God as he was walking in the garden in the cool of the day, and they hid from the Lord God among the trees of the garden. But the Lord God called to the man, "Where are you?" He answered, "I heard you in the garden, and I was afraid because I was naked; so, I hid." And he said, "Who told you that you were naked? Have you eaten from the tree that I commanded you not to eat from?"*

THE TEMPTER AND THE TORTURER

There is a reason satan is described as a serpent. Serpents are dangerous because they are camouflaged creatures and can be difficult to see. We've already discussed that satan never truthfully identifies himself. You will never hear him reveal his true motives to steal, kill and destroy you. No, he's subtle. Sneaky. Tricky. Stealthy. And poisonous.

Remember, Adam and Eve were gloriously naked (not pornographically naked). However, shame came and robbed them of their original, stunning glory and covered it with cheap, fig leaves! If you struggle with shame, it is also covering your true glory with some- thing dull, common, and most likely, uncomfortable. (Fig leaves are scratchy!)

There is an uncommon conqueror in you! But satan is a master manipulator, a sensational seducer, and a dispenser of deception.

"This is everything you want. It will make you happy! Come on in! Eat the fruit! It will make you smart. It will make you like God!"

But the instant you yield to the temptation, you find satan stand- ing on the other side of your sin saying, "I can't believe you did that! You are so dirty! How could God ever love YOU? You can't talk to Him anymore. He knows you're a weak, dirty, naked liar, and those are two qualities that God especially hates. So, He probably hates you too now."

Shame, defined, is the constant feeling you are flawed; knowing you have to measure up while also knowing you cannot. On the one hand satan is The Tempter, and then on the other, he is the Torturer. He is your enemy. And his intentions are cruel indeed.

THREE PURPOSES OF SHAME

- **To change the way you see yourself.** If satan can get you to think about yourself inaccurately, looking at your distorted reflection in the mirror of shame, then he can limit your suc- cess and effectiveness in this life. If he can't kill you he will settle for crippling you.

- **To change the way you interact with others.** If he can get you coated in shame, then you will sabotage relationships and destroy your relational potential. You will commit relational suicide and make his job easier.

- **To change the way you think about and relate to God.** This is, I believe, the devil's ultimate weapon of deception. If he can get you all shamed-up, then you will see God as your op- pressor, and suspect Him of malintent. You will draw away and hide from the One Who constantly thinks of and plans your eternal good.

Now, to be forewarned is to be forearmed. Exposing satan's tactics gives you a competitive advantage over your adversary. Give him no reprieve! Whatever he tells you, declare and do the opposite. His native tongue is deceit; his accent is shame.

CONVICTION -VS- CONDEMNATION

God uses conviction. Conviction is very sweet and specific. It is God's way of simply convincing us of our need for life-giving change. Jesus will never bring a negative emotion without a solution.

You may be sad about the fact Jesus died, but that is not the whole story. The reason He died was to pay the penalty for our sin. Furthermore, He did not stay dead: He defeated death, hell, and the grave, and arose The Victor! His death seemed negative, but it brought the solution. It purchased our salvation. And when The Counselor convicts us, He is leading us into a deeper reality and experience of that salvation.

COME OUT OF THE CAVE

Satan will try to cause you to withdraw. He always employs this strategy not if, but when we fail or make a mistake. He would like nothing better than for you to live in seclusion. Joy is released when you learn that Jesus doesn't want you to hide in shame after failure. He wants us to exit isolation and confess our sin openly to Him. His promise is constant, *"I will forgive you and remove both the sin and shame."*

The devil uses condemnation to tell you that you are defective, or just plain hopeless. You hear that inner accusing voice, *"There is something wrong with you. You are completely unacceptable. I know that nobody is perfect but geesh! You are exceptionally broken and dysfunctional. No wonder no one can be around you long-term."* (**Q:** Pastor Kevin, how do you know so well the kinds of things the devil is saying to people? **A:** I've conducted hundreds of counseling appointments and the same devil attacks preachers too.)

This is how you can tell the difference between Conviction and Condemnation—

Conviction says, "You *made* a mistake."

Condemnation says, "You *are* a mistake."

God never condemns you. NEVER. But because He loves you, He will *convict* you. He wants you to stand strong and walk confidently through life. And for that, you need clear and strong convictions; a life built not just around *values*, but upon strong, biblical *virtues*. So, when this conviction arises in your life, and if you are following Christ, it often will arise, take heed to what it is saying and where it is guiding.

THE WAY SHAME COMES

- Abuse.
- Failure.
- Poverty.
- Physical appearance.
- Parental authority figures.
- Faulty beliefs.
- Etc. (Fill in the blank.)

As awful as shame can feel, it is a preference for some people over other emotions that shame might be covering up such as loneliness, grief, sadness, or heartbrokenness. In the same way as anger, shame could also be a cover-up for difficult feelings.

We can originate feelings of shame within ourselves by our own faulty beliefs, but loneliness, grief, or sadness are feelings that are a by-product of life. Our hearts are broken and we may grieve over losing someone we cared about. We may feel loneliness when we want to connect with someone and there is no one available for connection. Many people would rather feel the dreadful feeling of shame, than feel the actual, authentic pain caused by real life, because they don't have the tools to address them. But this is one reason that Jesus sent us "another comforter" so that The Counselor can guide us to freedom, no matter what life throws at us.

CALAMITOUS CHOICES

Life is about choices. Poor choices can produce catastrophe. Unrest continues today in the Middle East because of a poor decision made in Biblical times. Abraham, the father of our faith, got into the wrong tent, with the wrong woman, at the wrong time, and had the wrong baby. Through Ishmael the Arab nations were born. Conflict remains between them and the Jewish people to this day.

STILL IMPACTED BY ABRAHAM

Gentile salvation was on the line. You may not realize how important that was. However, your salvation and mine was literally hanging in the balance. Why? It was through Isaac that The Promise came. Abraham had to overcome the shame of wronging Hagar (and the ensuing birth of Ishmael) in order to get into the right tent, with the right woman, and have the right baby to produce the right result: The Messiah.

CONSIDER MOSES

"Thou shall not kill." Exodus 20:13 (KJV)

Those words must have mocked Moses. As he walked down from Mt. Sinai, he had the opportunity to be overwhelmed. You will never convince me his past was not screaming back at him as Moses read the words freshly inscribed by the Finger of God upon those stone tablets, "Thou shalt not kill." He must have remembered killing the Egyptian forty years earlier, having buried him in the sand.

THE IRONY OF GOD

God seems to deal in irony. His message is one of peace and love. Yet, He used a murderer to carry the stone tablets carrying the commandment, "Thou shalt not kill." King David broke the barrier of shame created by his own sin with Bathsheba in order to marry her so she could bear Solomon, the future king and lineage of the Messiah. The apostle, Peter, denied knowing Jesus and had to break the shame barrier of rejecting Christ in order to preach the first Pentecostal sermon where 3,000 people accepted Christ and were saved. And finally, Jesus was accused of being illegitimate.

"He came unto His own and His own received Him not."
John 1:11 (KJV)

All of His disciples, except John, forsook Him. The Romans stripped away His clothes and beat Him with a metal studded whip, and if that were not enough, Jesus was publicly hanged on that old, rugged cross while naked! Shame was lurking. But Jesus despised it. He dealt with our shame. He suffered it for us and as us so we would not have to. Shame off me; shame on Jesus. This is part of our inheritance as God's Children.

I Have Fought Shame

I remember when the message came into my spirit: *"You are a freak—a defective weirdo. You deserve to experience this kind of suffering and depression for the rest of your life."* Satan may be a liar, but he is a convincing one. **Shame causes us to fear exposure and fear intimacy.** We never feel we are doing well enough, so we become self-haters. This causes us to become performance motivated. We fall into the trap of judging ourselves by what others think of us vs. what GOD thinks of us. As a result, we become easily devastated by criticism and overly dependent on praise that may or may not even be genuine.

The Tale of Two Goats

Once upon a time there were two goats…. Leviticus 16 shares the story. One was to be a sin offering by the priest. The other was called "the scapegoat." It took the blame for sin and was released to wander alone and unprotected in the wilderness. Far too many believers are wandering alone in the wilderness today. They may know they are forgiven, but shame still separates them from the family.

Let me say this another way. Two goats were offered. One to satisfy sin, while the other was offered for shame! Provision has been made. You can come out of hiding and go free. Shame has been dealt with. You don't have to carry it anymore.

God's Solution

One of the goats had to go to an uninhabited land because God didn't want shame socializing in His camp of people! Like a virus, shame can sweep through a community. The scape-goat would be walked from the temple, through the camp in the sight of all, and sent out into the dangerous wilderness. This animal went out of the camp, a visual announcement to the people, "It's over! Not only is your sin forgiven, but God does not even offer a reminder of your mistakes and sins!" By doing this, God not only solved the sin problem, but He also handled the shame problem. Of course, this was a symbol of what Christ would complete for us at Calvary. He is our Scape-Goat!

Receive Freedom From Torment

A young lady had an abortion. A voice came accusing, *"Murderer!"*

So, she began to rescue animals. She believed, *"If I can save enough lives, I can heal the shame in mine."*

She was born-again later and believed God forgave her, but she still could not deal with her own sense of defectiveness and shame. This is true of a lot of Christians: they continue to carry something that Jesus has already carried for us.

The Woman With The Issue of Blood

We were ministering with one of our dearest friends on one of the islands of Samoa in the South Pacific a few years ago. After I finished preaching a sermon entitled, *Shame on Jesus*, a lovely young Samoan lady approached me and my wife. She explained, through her embarrassment, how that she had been bleeding, non-stop for months. But her pain and suffering had finally become greater than the embarrassment. She desperately needed help. She had received both prayer for healing and medical attention. Neither had helped. She was a woman with an issue of blood. (See the Biblical version in Mark 5:25–34)

Of course, my wife and I were willing to pray for her. But would our prayers be more powerful than the last minister who offered prayer for her healing? We were *not* more anointed than they! As we reached out our hands to place them on her shoulder, that's when it happened. Suddenly and silently, this question drifted up from my spirit, *"When did this condition start?"* So, I paused and asked her that question.

"About eight months ago."

Then the next question floated up from my spirit, "What happened eight months ago?"

She blushed and responded tearfully, "I slept with my boyfriend…".

My wife and I hugged her as she softly wept in our arms. We did not condone her sin, but we did set a captive free. We reminded her of The Father's great love for her, and the great price Jesus paid for her sin *and* shame. We did *not* pray for her healing. It wasn't necessary. She prayed for forgiveness. It was then that she was released from the talons of shame. She was instantly "healed." She went away happy, smiling, grateful and free. Shame is a slow bleed from the inside. But thankfully salvation is an inside job too. So if the Son sets you free, you really will indeed be free (John 8:36 NASB).

The Sacrificial Lamb

The price for sin and shame has been paid. No "if's, and's or but's," the work has been done. The account settled. God's Sacrificial Lamb, Jesus, paid the price for all humanity.

"The next day John the Baptist saw Jesus coming toward

him, and said, 'Behold! The Lamb of God who takes away
the sin of the world.'" John 1:29 (NKJV)

Well, He took away the shame of the world too. It's a really good deal.

THINK WITH ME

Sin is the cause of shame. Yet, our sin has been removed. Should we then be ashamed? No, not at all.

"He is despised and rejected by men, a man of sorrows and
acquainted with grief. And we hid, as it were, our faces from
Him; He was despised, and we did not esteem Him. Surely
He has borne our griefs and carried our sorrows; Yet we es-
teemed Him stricken, Smitten by God, and afflicted. But He
was wounded for our transgressions, He was bruised for
our iniquities, the chastisement for our peace was upon
Him, and by His stripes we are healed. All we like sheep
have gone astray; We have turned, every one, to his own
way; and the Lord has laid on Him the iniquity of us all."
Isaiah 53:3–6 (NKJV)

Through a tree and a naked man's sin, shame came into the world. Through another tree, a naked man dealt a blow to death and carried away the sin and shame of the world. As a result, we have been restored to God and His destiny for our lives.

"Therefore, if anyone is in Christ, he is a new creation; old
things have passed away; behold, all things have become
new. Now all things are of God, who has reconciled us to
Himself through Jesus Christ, and has given us the ministry
of reconciliation, that is that God was in Christ reconciling
the world to Himself, not imputing their trespasses to them,
and has committed to us the word of reconciliation. Now
then, we are ambassadors for Christ, as though God were

pleading through us: we implore you on Christ's behalf, be reconciled to God. For He made Him who knew no sin to be sin for us, that we might become the righteousness of God in Him." 2 Corinthians 5:17–21 (NKJV)

FOUR WAYS TO EFFECTIVELY DEAL WITH SHAME

1. **Get Naked.** Be honestly transparent or naked before God. Adam and Eve hid from God and covered themselves with fig leaves. FYI, God can see through fig leaves. If everyone knew everything about you, it would reduce your number of followers on social media. But God knows everything about you, and He loves you anyway. You will NEVER SHOCK Him! He IS our safe place! Because of Christ's finished work of redemption, you can be "naked and not ashamed" in the presence of God once again, like Adam and Eve originally were in the Garden of Eden.

2. **Own it.** Take responsibility for your behavior and don't blame other people. Adam and Eve began to point fingers at one another. Adam pronounced his sin on his wife, Eve! God pronounced the sin of the world, your sin and mine, on JESUS. God accepts no scapegoat but Christ alone. Someone may have done something to me, but I must take responsibility (Response-Ability) for my life. Your perspective, and your response, is YOUR choice! You may not be able to control how someone treats you, but you can control your response to that treatment. Unless you stop blaming the government, your wife, the church, and your parents, you will never be an overcomer. We have the ability, through the Blood of Jesus, to overcome! One symptom of dealing with shame is always blaming someone else for all our woes. James gives a clear breakthrough formula,

   "Submit to God; resist the devil; he will flee!"
   (In that order.) *James 4:7 (NKJV)*

   Too many Christ-Followers try to resist the devil before they have submitted themselves to God. That never goes well. Ask the Seven Sons of Sceva (Acts 19:11–20 NKJV).

3. **Believe it.** Believe you are forgiven, and that the sin and shame have been removed by Jesus Christ. It is a faith issue.

> *"If we confess our sins He is faithful and just to forgive us*
> *our sins and to cleanse us from all unrighteousness."*
> *1 John 1:9 (NKJV)*

God not only has removed the sin, but the record of sin, too! Our lives are hidden with Christ in God, so when God sees you, He doesn't view you as defective, but as whole and perfect. When He sees you, He sees Jesus! Believe you are His favorite kid—because you are.

4. **Zero Tolerance Policy.** Refuse the vile spirit of shame when it comes and choose to fight it with the Blood of Jesus. Jesus did His part on the Cross, but WE have a part to play in this too.

> *"For the weapons of our warfare are not carnal* [natural],
> *but mighty* [supernatural] *through God for pulling down*
> *strongholds, casting down arguments and every high thing*
> *that exalts itself against the knowledge of God, bringing*
> *every thought into captivity to the obedience of Christ."*
> *2 Corinthians 10:4–5 (NKJV)*

There is a war going on **in** our minds and **for** our minds. Shame is a high place; it is a stronghold that exalts itself above Christ. In other words, the devil wants to get a strong hold on your thought-life through shame, unforgiveness, addiction, regret, or any number of other devices he employs. Exercise your free-will and simply decide not to allow it.

In some of the most vulnerable moments of your lifetime, during some of your greatest tragedies, the devil has whispered lies into your soul about who you are to keep you from living life as who you *really* are! Satan knows he is no match for you if you are walking in your true, God-given identity, so he schemes and maneuvers to trick you into believing you are actually someone else or something else other than a precious, redeemed child of the Most High God. But it's too late! We have discovered that we are More than Conquerors in Christ Jesus! And nothing can separate us from His Love. Nothing.

SOME HAVE BEEN VICTIMIZED BY EVIL WORDS

A young couple in their early 20's could not have children. One day while making a hospital visit, their obstetrician stepped into the elevator with their pastor. Small talk led to the young couple coming up in conversation. "There is no physical reason why they can't have kids," the doctor explained to the preacher.

Later, the pastor told the young couple, "Your doc says there's nothing wrong with you physically. Is there something that you know of that would keep you from having children?"

The young lady said, "I think I may know. When I was about ten, my mom caught me with some boys doing some inappropriate things. As a result, Mom said God would never allow me to have babies."

A curse had been spoken over her. I'm sure that was not the mother's intention, but her words released shame and bound the conception of her posterity. The young lady thought she was defective! The shame-monster was so powerful it kept her from conceiving. But once that curse was broken off her, and she was washed in the Water of God's Word, she went free. She did not need physical healing. She needed a lie exposed and deposed by The Light of God's Love and Truth. And after some time, they conceived a child.

What lie is keeping you from the desire of your heart? The Counselor is present with you right now to reveal Jesus and guide you into all truth. And truth makes you free! Shame Off You; Shame On Jesus. Choose to stop believing the lie today. You can go free.

LOVING MOM AND GETTING FREE

If something like this has happened to you, yes, love your mom. If necessary, forgive her. I'm sure that momma was trying to inspire her daughter to chastity, albeit through twisted methods. But, if momma's words (or anybody else's) don't line up with what GOD'S Word says, we are going to break those words off of your life and release Abundant Life over you, in Jesus Name! Are you ready?

DECLARE THIS PRAYER OUT LOUD:

"Father, I break the power of negative words spoken over me in Jesus 'Name! I break the power of curses, intentional or unintentional, that were put on me. Jesus became a curse for me that I might inherit the Blessing of Abraham. I renounce and revoke words of poverty, failure, barrenness, sinfulness and death. I release abundance, success, joy, holiness and abundant-life over me and my family—In Jesus 'Name!"

Jesus hung naked at the crossroads of the world, with a sign over His head mocking Him, and satan is still trying to defeat Him, not just physically, but emotionally and spiritually with the weapon of mass destruction, called shame. But Jesus didn't receive it! He rejected shame. He despised it: He pushed it out and wouldn't let it in. That's what you just did too. Well done. Good job. For some this issue has defined your entire life! Are you tired of dealing with shame? It is exhausting, isn't it? No more serpent of shame: refuse those lies! The Lamb has born your shame. Jesus, our Scapegoat, carried it out of your life.

BOLDLY DECLARE

"My sin has been removed as far as the east is from the west! I am sufficient by the Blood of Jesus! I am whole and set free from any and all deficiencies! In the Name of Jesus, I bind the spirit of shame! Through bondages, addictions, sexual problems, devastations & tragedies... I bind satan and declare that I am FREE by the power of the pure, sinless Blood of Jesus. I tear down this stronghold. I reject shame! Shame, I put you out of every area of my life! The concept I now have of myself and of God is changed today. I take off the fig leaves of shame I've been using to cover my inadequacies and I say aloud, 'Yes, I have issues, but Jesus loves me anyway and He has forgiven me and given me the ability to live as an overcomer by His grace.' I receive the Lamb as being my total sacrifice for my sin AND shame. I reject shame off my person. And from this day forward, I walk in Your glory and in the warm light of Your love and acceptance. And I love and accept myself. I choose to walk in the glorious destiny God has for me! Amen! So be it! In Jesus' Name I am free."

QUESTIONS FOR SMALL GROUPS AND PERSONAL REFLECTION:

1. Some people use shame as a cover-up emotion for a deeper feeling they don't have the tools to address. What other feeling are you using shame to cover up? What feelings, memories or habits do you need/want the tools to deal with?

2. The author mentioned 4 ways to effectively deal with shame: Get naked, Own it, Believe it, and Zero Tolerance. Which of these are you doing well? Why? Which of these is still "eating your lunch?" How can you advance in the area(s) where you have previously been suffering at the hands of shame?

3. Have words or curses been spoken over you that could be having ill-effects on your life in any way? Explain, discuss, and journal. Describe how the prayer and declaration at the end of the chapter affected you?

-7-
THE SEVEN WOUNDS OF THE SUFFERING SAVIOR

7

THE SEVEN WOUNDS OF THE SUFFERING SAVIOR

Seven. It's been called The Number of God. The number of Perfection. The number of Completion. It is more than symbolic, it is vital.

Remission is a powerful word. It means payment for sin that enables. Enables what? Our ability to receive something we all need: forgiveness.

> *"For this is My blood of the new covenant, which is shed*
> *for many for the remission of sins."*
> *Matthew 26:28 (NKJV)*

JESUS BLED SEVEN WAYS

Seven is the number of perfect completion. Jesus bled seven ways to provide a perfect and complete redemption for you and me. We've been redeemed…bought back from sin and satan; redeemed from sickness and selfishness; delivered from the power and penalty of sin. The Redemption Jesus procured for us is total and perfect. The Salvation He created for us is complete! Jesus bled seven ways because He would only provide a salvation that was complete and perfect. So, when Jesus said from the cross, "It is finished," He was not speaking metaphorically. He was speaking absolute and complete truth.

Can you think of the seven ways Jesus bled for you?

Let's look:

1. **From His Pores**: He sweat as if it was great drops of blood. Luke 22:44 (NKJV)

2. **From His Back**: By His stripes we are healed. I Peter 2:24 (NKJV)

3. **From His Brow**: "And the soldiers twisted a **crown of thorns** and put *it* on His head, and they put on Him a purple robe. Then they said, 'Hail, King of the Jews!' And they struck Him with their hands." John 19:2–3 (NKJV)

4. **From His Hands**: "Reach your finger here, and look at My hands; and reach your hand *here,* and put *it* into My side. Do not be unbelieving, but believing." John 20:27 (NKJV)

5. **From His Feet**: "And they crucified him…" Matthew 27:35 (NKJV)

6. **His Side**: "But when they came to Jesus, and saw that he was dead already, they brake not his legs: but one of the soldiers with a spear pierced his side, and forthwith came there out blood and water." John 19:33–34 (KJV)

7. **He Was Bruised for Our Iniquity**: Internal Bleeding. Isaiah 53:5 (NKJV)

Let us further explore these seven ways our Savior suffered for our total freedom:

#1

SWEATING BLOOD: REDEEMED FROM PSYCHOSIS

"And being in agony, He prayed more earnestly. Then His sweat became like great drops of blood falling down to the ground." Luke 22:44 (NJKV)

Has mental illness ever negatively impacted someone in your life or family? More and more these days, I hear of people suffering from mental illnesses. But Jesus suffered the excruciating agony of mental illness, not only for us, but AS us! He was our substitute. What does this mean for us practically? You don't have to be "crazy" or bipolar. You don't have to accept it. In our humanity, we may all visit "crazy" every now and again, but you don't have to get stuck living there!

Can you imagine such enormous levels of emotional stress that physical pain radiates through your body? Have you ever worried so much that there was an actual bursting of tiny blood vessels that released blood to ooze out of the pores of your skin? This happened to Jesus. The World Health Organization has declared the combination of depression, anxiety, stress, and worry as the Number One health risk in the world today. (Pre-COVID.) Of course, the pandemic of 2020 took everyone's stress to a whole new level!

But Jesus is the Prince of PEACE. His suffering in this way paid the price for us to be redeemed from mental illness of all varieties. The most repeated commandment in the Bible is **"Fear Not!"** God didn't create us to be afraid, but to rule and reign on earth. We are not wired to worry. We are built to lead and govern and create. We are to live in dominion, be at peace and walk in peace — to establish His peace everywhere we go. We could not do this if God had not made provision for us to do so. But in the Atonement He provided peace and wholeness.

Hematidrosis is an actual rare condition in which capillary blood vessels that feed the sweat glands rupture, causing them to exude blood. This is known to occur under conditions of extreme physical or emotional stress. According to the Indian Journal of Dermatology, hysterical mechanisms and psychosomatic disorders are also believed to induce bleeding. Stress is a dangerous little monster. It seems to be lurking everywhere these days, coiling to strike. But Jesus took the bite for us. Many of the physical conditions people suffer have their root in the mind:

> *"As a man thinks in his heart so is he."*
> *Proverbs 23:7 (NKJV)*

JESUS IS OUR PEACE

"For He Himself [Jesus] *is our peace..."*
Ephesians 2:14a (NKJV)

This is a critically important truth to know and wholeheartedly embrace. Why would Jesus allow Himself to undergo this level of excruciating mental anguish and torment? He looked ahead in time and saw what was coming. And Anxiety came and began to pressure Jesus in such a way that enormous tension pressed upon him until the blood-vessels under the surface of His skin burst and trickled out onto the surface of His skin.

Physicians believe the top reason for sickness and disease is anxiety. Jesus never wants you to have to endure such levels of mental torment. As our Substitute, Jesus suffered this kind of anxiety so that we would not have to. **Yet we have to enforce it**. Because He suffered this for us, we can now cast all our care upon the Lord and not cast away our confidence in the Lord.

"Casting all your care upon Him for He cares for you."
I Peter 5:7 (NKJV)

Just knowing He cares for us so passionately is comforting. I've heard it said that depression is living wrongly in the past. Anxiety is living wrongly in the future. Peace is living appropriately in the present.

Jesus perfectly redeemed us from both depression and anxiety. His Blood both cleanses our past and empowers our future, while enriching our present. It's intense! :-)

Philippians 4:6–7 (NKJV) exhorts us,

"Be anxious for nothing, but in everything by prayer and supplication, with thanksgiving, let your requests be made known to God; and the peace of God, which surpasses all understanding, will guard your hearts and minds through Christ Jesus."

When we turn our worry-list into our prayer-list a Divine Peace is released into our souls that protects us from the damaging effects of anxiety.

A Peaceful Prayer for You

Before we go deeper in this chapter, I feel the urge to pray. I invite you to read this prayer aloud:

> "Thank You, Jesus, for suffering severe stress for me and as me. Therefore, I refuse to worry or have any anxiety about anything. But, in everything, with prayer and thanksgiving, I make my needs known to You! You are my faithful provider. You meet all my needs abundantly and generously. By faith, I believe and declare that God is my Loving Dad Who cares for me watchfully and passionately. Finally, I determine whatever things are true, whatever things are noble, just, pure, lovely, and are of good report, if there is any virtue and if there is anything praiseworthy—I will think on these things. Thank you for redeeming me from mental illness of any and every kind. In Jesus' Name!"

#2

By His Stripes: Redeemed from Physical Sickness

"Then Pilate therefore took Jesus, and scourged him."
John 19:1 (NKJV)

Sickness is death in slow motion. Sickness breaks people. It damages your body and it can drain your finances. It is a scourge upon anyone's life. Jesus provided a solution for our brokenness. Jesus purchased our wholeness. Sickness and disease are no exception to this whole-life policy that legally belongs to you. It is part of your birthright. Your physical symptoms do not and cannot nullify the provision of healing made available to us by the Atonement of Christ. It was given by God's grace and can be appropriated by faith. Once again, the suffering Savior became our Substitute when He bore stripes upon His own back for us and also AS us—He is our Substitute!

The scourging He endured was at the hands of a prolific torture-master. The Roman soldier who delivered the beating was skilled in his sadistic trade of inflicting pain. But our God, who wastes nothing, counted Jesus' affliction as payment for our comfort. His face and form were marred beyond human recognition! The Roman soldiers mutilated Jesus, yet they kept Him alive to suffer every ounce of agony and leave absolute none for you and me. None.

Why would such suffering be necessary? Because your health is this valuable to our loving, heavenly Father. In fact, scripture teaches us that all disease was laid upon Jesus. In the medical community it has been said there are thirty-nine major types or categories of disease. Jesus took a blow upon His back for each ancient seed of sickness. The root cause of each kind of sickness was placed upon Him: He became our disease just as He became our sin. Therefore, there is now no category of disease that can come upon you that you cannot rightfully, effectively and legally resist and deny access to your body! Just as He became sin with our sin, He became sickness with our sickness.

Jesus was the "serpent on a pole" that is now the medical community's symbol for heath and healing. Yes, our sinless Savior was likened unto a snake! Not a lamb. What is the meaning of this prophetic photograph we find in scripture? (Numbers 21:3–7; John 3:14–16). It means that everything vile and venomous, everything dangerously deadly... everything that we were... sinful and sick... Jesus became. He said,

> *"If I be lifted up I will draw all men unto Me."*
> *John 12:32 (KJV)*

Jesus drew the venom of sin and sickness of all mankind into Himself when He was lifted up on that cross. And if anyone will look to Him, they will live!

And now we can legally become everything He was.

> *"Thy will be done on Earth as it is in Heaven..."*
> *Matt. 6:10 (KJV)*

And when people look to Jesus, like the Israelites fixed their gaze upon the serpent on the pole, they too are healed.

> *Then they journeyed from Mount Hor by the Way of the Red Sea, to go around the land of Edom; and the soul of the people became very discouraged on the way. [5]And the people spoke against God and against Moses: "Why have you brought us up out of Egypt to die in the wilderness? For there is no food and no water, and our soul loathes this worthless bread." [6]So the Lord sent fiery serpents among the people, and they bit the people; and many of the people of Israel died. [7]Therefore the people came to Moses, and said, "We have sinned, for we have spoken against the Lord and against you; pray to the Lord that He take away the serpents from us." So Moses prayed for the people. [8]Then the Lord said to Moses, "Make a fiery serpent, and set it on a pole; and it shall be that everyone who is bitten, when he looks at it, shall live." [9]So Moses made a bronze serpent, and put it on a pole; and so it was, if a serpent had bitten anyone, when he looked at the bronze serpent, he lived.*
> *Numbers 21:4–9 (NKJV)*

> *For He made Him who knew no sin to be sin for us, that we might become the righteousness of God in Him.*
> *II Corinthians 5:21 (NKJV)*

ANOTHER GREAT EXCHANGE

The commonly known Great Exchange was created at salvation. Yet, it was just one of several. In each case, Jesus became what we were, so we can become what He is. Jesus became sick that we might be healed. Isaiah prophesied this. We are told in Isaiah 53:3–4 (NKJV) that

> "He was despised and rejected of men, a man of sorrows and acquainted with grief... surely he has borne our griefs [pains] and carried our sorrows [sickness & diseases]."

So beloved, Jesus suffered indescribable pain in His body and on His back so that your body and back could be made whole and healed. As you're reading this, I believe back pain is leaving some in this very moment. Kidneys are being restored. Bones are being adjusted. Crohn's disease and Fibromyalgia are being expelled from bodies. 1 Peter 2:23–24 (NKV) further explains,

> "who, when He was reviled, did not revile in return; when He suffered, He did not threaten, but committed Himself to Him who judges righteously; who Himself bore our sins in His own body on the tree, that we, having died to sins, might live for righteousness—by whose stripes you were healed."

Your healing has already been paid for. Jesus carried sickness away to another place and left it there. In fact, all maladies and diseases were carried away. He became them in our stead. He bore them for us. He does not want you sick any more than He wants you to sin.

Healing is not something God wants to do; it is something He has already done.

> "I AM The Lord that Heals you." Exodus 15:26 (NKJV)

He is *not* the Lord Who *ills* you. He is the Lord that *heals* you. If God put sickness on His children to teach them a lesson, does He also now place us in sin to teach us things too? Of course not. That's just bad logic and even worse theology.

Your Bill is Already Paid

Would it be right for someone to pay a bill that's already been paid? Of course not. Allowing such a thing would be dishonest at best. In the same way, why would you continue to bear sickness and disease in your body when Jesus bore it for you in His own body? Remember the cost that has been afforded. The price has been paid. God's Word tells us in 1 Corinthians 11:24 (NKJV),

"and when He had given thanks, He broke it and said, 'Take, eat; this is My body which is broken for you; do this in remembrance of Me.'"

We should regularly recount the expense of our healing and salvation. Remember the stripes that were laid upon His back. Recall the price that was paid for healing is not wishful thinking, but a spiritual fact. It is a product that has been purchased by the tangible commodity of the broken body of Jesus. Power released from Christ's wounds for healing still surges from the Eucharist. Partake. "…do this in remembrance of Me." In other words, enjoy the benefits of what He has done for you.

If you struggle with wondering about the willingness of God to manifest His healing power in your body, consider this passage from Mark 1. A disfigured leper approached Jesus one day. He said,

"If You are willing, You can make me clean."
Mark 1:40 (NKJV)

One of God's Names

Jesus' answer within the passage noted above is one for the ages.

"I Am Willing." And Jesus touched the sick man and announced, "Be cleansed!"

And he was.
Our Lord has several compound Hebrew names. "I Am Willing"

is obviously one of them. And how reassuring it is. We all know He is able. But once and for all He settles the issue of His willingness. Is it God's will to heal? If you could ask that leper he would say an emphatic, "Yes!" To whom did Jesus ever deny when requesting healing mercies? Jesus is the Yes-Man. And He never changes.

Still not convinced? I feel God would rather you doubt His *ability* to heal than His *willingness. "My Child, I want to heal you but alas I cannot,"* as opposed to, *"My Child, I could heal you but alas I will not."* Doubting His willingness and intention is to doubt His very character and nature. He is a good Father, and we are His children.

Some may argue, "But what if I deserve my ailments? I have been a poor steward of my health and body. I have self-abused and used up my vigor." Allow me to voice three thoughts. First, we serve a merciful God. Throw yourself over onto His mercy. Secondly, take responsibility (Response-Ability) for any actions that may have put your health at risk. And third, repent of your poor stewardship and make the appropriate adjustments. The Law of Sowing and Reaping is still in effect. Take advantage of this reality. Eat cleaner, exercise, and quit any destructive habits. Let your body do what it was designed to do: Heal. If you need medical attention, then get it. But, most of all, trust God's grace.

Walk through the process of eliminating bents of iniquity in your life: Recognize. Repent. Renounce. Replace. Return. (See chapter one.) Finally, we receive healing the same way we receive salvation: by grace through faith. Healing and health are by God's grace, not our works. True Christianity begins not with what you have done, but with what Christ has done for you, and as you. Receive it.

"For by grace you have been saved through faith, and that not of yourselves; it is the gift of God, not works, lest anyone should boast." Ephesians 2:8–9 (NKJV)

#3
REDEEMED FROM MENTAL ILLNESS, CHEMICAL IMBALANCES AND HEAD TRAUMA

"And the soldiers twisted a crown of thorns and put it on His head, and they put on Him a purple robe."
John 19:2 (NKJV)

God the Father is omniscient. Omniscient means all science or all-knowing. The Father knew all the various ways that our archenemy would attack and seek to destroy us. He knew the number one way of attack would be with piercing thoughts to the mind. This is evidenced by the fact that the stealthy serpent of old has whispered to all of us, "Hath God said?" Satan would love to keep you from ever hearing God's Word or convince you to doubt what God has spoken. Why?

"He sent His Word and healed them, and delivered them from their destructions." Psalm 107:20 (NKJV)

HE PAID A DEBT HE DIDN'T OWE

Jesus has redeemed us from head and brain trauma. Jesus has bought us back from the tormentors that cause mental suffering of all kinds. God pre-ordained that our Savior, the Christ, would suffer with the piercing of both His mental soul and His physical brain. This is a key point to understand as all the suffering of our Savior is on our behalf and for our benefit. His suffering was the purchase price that procured our salvation, preservation, deliverance, and ongoing maintenance.

VICTORIOUS OVER THE WORST OF ATTACKS

The thorns from crucifixion's crown pierced through Christ's skull and entered Jesus' physical brain. Physicians call this traumatic brain injury. This diagnosis can produce wide ranging symptoms from mild to acute disorientation, partial or full paralysis and beyond. Nausea, dizziness, and vertigo are also common after such a violation. These symptoms can last from a few moments, to years, or in severe cases even be permanent.

"The chastisement of our peace was upon him."
Isaiah 53:5 (NKJV)

Jesus was harassed and aggravated that we may have peace. Jesus suffered brain-trauma so that you could avoid it or fully recover from it.

Jesus has redeemed us… *bought us back…*from mental torment, mental illness, and physical head-trauma. Therefore, we may boldly say,

"For God has not been us a spirit of fear but of love,
power, and a sound [disciplined, self-controlled] *mind."*
2 Timothy 1:7 (NKJV)

DECLARE IT ALOUD RIGHT NOW

"My mind thinks the thoughts of God. My brain is blessed. The mind of the Master is the Master of my mind. I have a spirit of love. I have a spirit of power. I have a sound and disciplined mind. I operate in self-control. No habit, injury, thought, or person controls my mind. I am not my own. I belong to God. He keeps and preserves me. He surrounds me with His favor like a shield. The chastisement of my peace was upon Jesus. He suffered aggravation that I may live in peace. The peace of God that passes understanding belongs to me. I cast all my cares, worries and anxieties upon the Lord for He cares for me watchfully, and He cares about me fervently! I let this mind be in me that is also in Christ Jesus. Christ has been made unto to me righteousness, peace, and wisdom. I am not unwise, but I know the will of God. My steps are ordered of the Lord. He leads me beside still, pure, peaceful waters, and He restores my soul. He renovates and updates my mind, will and emotions. He leads me in the paths of righteousness for His Name' sake. The Name of the Lord is my strong tower. I run into it and I am safe."

#4
REDEEMED FROM PURPOSELESSNESS

"Unless I see in His hands the print of the nails, and put my finger into the print of the nails…" John 20:25 (NKJV)

Heavenly Hands. Nail-Pierced Hands. These hands are unique. They are the hands of God and of man. They reached down from eternity and formed the dust of the earth into the image of the first man, Adam. Now they suffered the painful piercings of disobedience and self-determination.

ETERNALLY EXISTENT

Mankind originated in God. In His heart and in His mind. When God used His imagination, He envisioned us! From the beginning the Divine fingerprint has been upon Humanity. Formed in the image of God; filled with the breath of the Spirit; made of the stuff of Earth; filled with the elements of Heaven. But when man committed high treason and disobeyed God's Word in the Garden of Eden, he fell from the glory that had been inherently his. From that time man labored with his hands, but the earth only produced thistles and thorns as man sweat profusely from his brow. Jesus ended fruitless labor and meaningless existence. Mankind's non-productive work ended when Jesus said, "It is finished."

When Jesus' hands were pierced with those nails on the cross, He was suffering to redeem us from fruitless and meaningless labor. No longer will man have to toil so much, for so little. Man's efforts could now be blessed again by God's hands. Now whatever we put our hand to will prosper. Jesus was suffering the wages of sin that is still death. But His Hands bled so that with our hands we may serve God, our

Creator, Who's Image we bear, with gladness. Through the redemptive work of Christ Jesus, Mankind has the opportunity to rediscover his Divine Destiny.

The Blood flowed from Christ's Hands that we may have a clean heart **and** clean hands. Therefore, we may serve the Lord with gladness, and also serve our fellow man with kindness. And fruit that remains is placed in our eternal account. It matters that you lived. We see this in 1 Timothy 2:3–8 (NKJV)

> *"For this is good and acceptable in the sight of God our Savior, who desires **all** men to be saved and to come to the knowledge of the truth. For there is one God and one Mediator between God and men, the Man Christ Jesus, who gave Himself a ransom for **all**, to be testified in due time, for which I was appointed a preacher and an apostle—I am speaking the truth in Christ and not lying—a teacher of the Gentiles in faith and truth. I desire therefore that the men pray everywhere, lifting up **holy hands**, without wrath and doubting..."*

GOD GOT HIS HANDS DIRTY

Mankind's hands are stained with blood. Our hands were filthy and dirtied by works of sin and the rotten fruit of self-reliance. Grit and grime were symbolic of the treachery beneath our fingernails. Cruelty and suffering were among forensic evidence of our brutal nature and evil heart. By Man's rejection of God's Plan and Purpose, he adopted a satanic version of history unfolding in famine, wars, slavery, abuse, manipulation, pain, sickness, death, and even religion. Polluted by leprosy on the skin, and motivated by darkness in the heart, Mankind's hands are a putrid abomination to a holy God. How could they ever be lifted to Him as holy in service, prayer and worship?

This could only happen if God's Hands were pierced so that holy blood might flow from them cleansing the rest. It was settled. God became a Man to serve as our Great Substitute. Operation Buy-Them-

161

Back had been launched. It was time for God to get His Hands dirty.

This God-Man, Christ Jesus, lived a sinless life and He operated as the Holy Spirit aided Him. And that sinless Man's Hands bled for sinful Mankind, so that their hands may be redeemed and cleaned. God got His Hands dirty that ours may be clean! What kind of Love is this, that a King would die for His subjects?

THE ULTIMATE RANSOM

Jesus was our ransom. He was the price that was paid: Eternity's Jewel of Heaven given that you and I may go free! He exchanged Himself for us. It's what Love does. He gave Himself to darkness that we might come back into the light, and that The Light may abide in us, forever. Because the Hands of Jesus bled, we can lift our hands in holy worship to a holy God.

Your hands represent your creativity. They are a reminder of our Divine Pathway. God has a destiny for each human born on earth… a purpose and plan. Our God is the Creator-God, and we are made in His stunning likeness and image.

REDEEMED CREATIVITY

Our creativity has been redeemed. That is why your purpose can now be realized and fulfilled. Your life does not have to be idle or meaningless. Your purpose is restored. The destiny hums beneath the surface of your soul, like the finely tuned engine of a muscle-car ready to devour the road. Because His Hands were pierced, your hands now have purpose. Because His Hands resigned to punishment, yours now have power.

Put your hands to the plow and do not look back! Do the good works foreordained for you to do and in so doing you will find satisfaction beyond your wildest dreams. We do good works, not to BE saved, but because we ARE saved. There is joy in the call and satisfaction in fulfilling it! What is your calling? Be about it. Destiny delayed is the devil's delight. Consider yourself, from here on, living on purpose and for a purpose. You don't decide your destiny—you discover it on the journey of faith with your Guide, the Holy Spirit.

Lift your holy hands in worship. Use your clean, holy hands in service to your blessed Savior! And with them point to the Lamb of God that takes away the sin of the world.

DECLARE THIS BOLDLY

"My hands are holy hands. They will touch no unclean thing. I lift them in worship of my Holy God. I refuse to raise them in anger against another human or in defiance against authority or my Healer-King. I will serve the Lord with gladness; I serve my fellowman with kindness. I will use my hands for good and not evil. For fruitful, productive labor and not idle laziness, for creation not destruction. My children and grandchildren will remember my hands as loving conduits of kindness and blessing. Everything I put my hands to prospers. For I know the One who made me and I know why I was made: to be the recipient of God's kind benevolence and a conduit of His Love and Truth. I was born to worship Him. When I lay hands on the sick, they shall recover. Jesus' hands were pierced that mine may be blessed and a conduit of His blessings. I am not unwise, but I know the will of God."

#5
REDEEMED FROM ISOLATION

"Then they crucified Him, and divided His garments..."
Matthew 27:35 (NJKV)

God values preaching. It is one of the tools He uses to bring forth the Gospel. Feet, in scripture, always represent the ministry of preaching the Gospel and declaring the Good News.

It says so in Isaiah 52:7 (NLV),

*"How lovely on the mountains are the feet of them that
brings good news, who tells of peace and brings good news
of happiness."*

Did you know that you have beautiful feet? That's what scripture
says. If you bring good news, then you have lovely feet! Why then
were the Savior's feet pierced, marred and battered? So that ours
could be made into something completely lovely. Why were giant
nails thrust through the Messiah's feet? What did this act purchase
for us?

A God of Restoration

God always intended and desired relationship with Man. But when
he sinned, it separated and isolated him from the Presence of God.
Adam and his wife actually hid from God. Earlier in this book, we
discussed their attempt to cover their own mistake by taking fig
leaves and making coverings for themselves. But religion is Man's
effort to cover his own sin. The Gospel declares God's efforts to remove that same sin and restore us to His wonderful Presence where
His very glory covers our life. God has got you covered! Jesus called
it "Abundant Life."

Nails through Jesus' feet restored our companionship with God,
like God slaughtering animals to take their coats to cover Adam and
Eve after their fall. Jesus is our Sacrificial Lamb, but He doesn't
cover our sin; He removes it. He is the Lamb of God Who *takes away*
the sins of the world.

In the beginning, in the garden, Adam *walked* with God in the
cool of the day... in the spirit realm! You see, before man sinned and
was separated from God, he could walk both in the natural and in the
supernatural realm simultaneously. Man was a multi-dimensional being! He could traverse in the earth, as well as in the spirit. But once
he chose to be separated from God, he could no longer walk in the
Pathways of the Almighty.

RESTORING THE HIGHWAY

*"And it shall be called the Highway of Holiness. The un-
clean shall not pass over it..." Isaiah 35:8 (NKJV)*

Sin caused the highway of holiness to be closed to Mankind. So, Jesus came and paid the toll. He suffered separation from God on our
behalf, so that we might be united with Him. Jesus was isolated in the
belly of the earth for three days... the Eternal suffering for the finite!
(That's why it only took three days.) Because of His work we can
once again traverse the Highway of Holiness and walk with God. Our
access to the King's Highway has been restored. Your violation (if
you will) has been paid, and your license restored.

This redemptive reality keeps getting even better. Enemy forces
cannot walk there. No evil can come near where you walk when you
walk with The Almighty. Scripture tells us that the

*"But the path of the righteous is like the light of dawn That
shines brighter and brighter until the full day."
Proverbs 4:18 (NASB)*

It also says that our steps are

"ordered of the Lord." Psalm 37:23 (NJKV)

The piercing of the feet of Jesus feet caused our steps to be free from
the path of disorder and disorientation, isolation, and fearful confusion.

Prior to His piercing, our steps were not directed, but rather chaotic or random. The way of the transgressor is hard, but Jesus has
made a way for us to come into God's Presence as Sons.

*"I Am the Way, The Truth and the The Life. No man comes
to the Father except through Me." John 14:6 (NKJV)*

The Way has been made; fellowship has been restored. Because Jesus
suffered in His feet, we can once again walk with God "in the cool of

the day" or in the spirit. And consequently, if your Great Substitute suffered in His feet, then you are redeemed from foot injuries, disorders, and deformities as well. Our feet, legs, hips, bones, and joints are redeemed from the curse. Take some time to think on 1 Corinthians 1:9 (NKJV),

> *"For God is faithful through whom you were called into Fellowship with His Son Christ Jesus, our Lord."*

DECLARE THIS BOLDLY

"The way has been made for me to come boldly before God's throne of grace where I receive mercy and find grace to help in my time of need. I walk not in the counsel of the ungodly, but in the wisdom of The Counselor! He leads and guides me into all Truth and shows me things to come. My fellowship with my Heavenly Father is sweet. Thank You, Jesus, for redeeming my walk with God and showing me The Way and being my Way. Therefore, I walk in the Spirit and do not fulfill the lusts of the flesh. I no longer live in isolation from God, but in celebration with God. The joy of the Lord is my strength! So not only am I happy, but the Lord's joy is my strength: I am strong, focused in fellowship with God, and purposed! In Jesus' Name. Amen."

#6
HE BLED FROM HIS SIDE: REDEEMED FROM HEARTBREAK

> *"But one of the soldiers pierced His side with a spear, and immediately blood and water came out."*
> **John 19:34 (NKJV)**

Side by side. God wanted us there with Him. This is why He did not just die for us but died AS us. He didn't just suffer for us but AS us. He was not just raised from the dead victorious for us but he was raised victorious AS us! He is our Substitute in every way! He took our place.

Furthermore, we can see in Ephesians 2:6 (NKJV) that,

*"and raised us up **together**, and made us sit together in the heavenly places in Christ Jesus."* (Emphasis mine.)

We are seated **WITH** Jesus in Heavenly places **IN** Christ! That is where God hoped we would always be: With Him and In Him. We were created for community and connection. God has never liked the idea of man being by Himself.

"It's not good that man be alone…" Genesis 2:18 (NKJV)

Even the Godhead, Himself, dwells in *oikos*… This is a greek word meaning, "intimate community with at least three close associates." It means your family or like family. (It can also mean "yogurt" in most American grocery stores.) LOL

"LET US MAKE MAN IN OUR IMAGE, ACCORDING TO OUR LIKENESS…" GENESIS 1:26 (NKJV)

Self-image is important. God wants our image to be like His. What does that image look like? A triune image: The Father, The Son, The Spirit. Three-in-one. The trichotomy of man is like that of his Creator: Spirit, Soul, and Body. Three-in-one.

And God took action in Genesis 2:21–22 (NJKV), because a helper comparable to him was desired and needed (a bride, if you will),

"And the Lord God caused a deep sleep to fall on Adam, and he slept; and He took one of his ribs, and closed up the flesh in its place. Then the rib which the Lord God had taken from man He made [built] *into a woman, and He brought her to the man."*

A surgery of sorts occurred. The first bloodshed in human history was over marriage. God made an incision, removed the curved bone next to Adam's heart, and from the bone, built the first man his bride, Eve. Marriage and intimacy was God's idea. This is how we know it's good. And a bonus thought: God did His best work when man was asleep! Sometimes the most spiritual thing you can do is take a nap and let God do what only He can do for you.

The Bone Used Was Quite Important

The bone was not taken from Adam's head, that she may rule over him. The bone was not taken from Adam's foot, that he may walk all over her. God intentionally and purposefully took the bone from Adam's side, near his heart, that she may be dear to him and by his side as an equal. As in peers. She was taken from near his heart that she would remain close and dear to him, and that Adam may cover her with his arms of strength. She was designed to be always by his side, not behind him. That way man would always be able to put his arm of affection and protection around his wife. She was taken from his side that she might remain at his side. The Bride of Adam was taken from his side.

The Spearing of Jesus Was Not Random Barbarity

The barbarity of this scene defies description. Yet, everything that happened had prophetic importance and practical application as a benefit for us today. In this chapter, I have been describing, for you, the legal ramifications of Christ's Redemption. Every wound bought something back that God originally outfitted Adam with. When the soldiers came by to inspect their victims on the cross, they discovered that the two thieves on each side of the King of the Jews were still alive. Their legs were broken that death may come for them more quickly.

But upon discovering that Jesus had already given up the ghost and died, they took a spear and pierced his side! The spear was inserted between his ribs and went up and into his heart. Water and blood flowed out of the wound. It was a confirmation for these death-specialists that The Man had already expired when the water came out first. And what they did next is of great significance for you and me.

You see, it wasn't only Jesus' side that was pierced. God's very heart, incarnate in Christ, was pierced. God suffered a broken heart that ours might be mended. I mean this both quite literally and figuratively. This act redeemed us from heart disease, and also from heartbreak. Not that no one will ever hurt and disappoint us, but that healing and strength is available to help us mend in our times of need.

ANOTHER BRIDE

Just as from Adam's side came his bride, from the side of the Christ was carved His bride, The Church! She was not taken from his head that she would rule over Him. Nor was she taken from his foot that He may walk upon Her. But she was gloriously taken from His side that she may stand by Him for all time and eternity. Equals and peers! Of course, she submits to Him as the Head of the Church, but He is making her glorious! Without spot or wrinkle, in fact. And has empowered her with dominion and the usage of His Name through the power of attorney. We even have joint bank accounts. I know that sounds funny, but this is how healthy marriages work. They share resources! All of human history is about God's Son getting a bride and that we, the church, may rule and reign with Him.

No, we are not exalting ourselves to this lofty place. Jesus, Himself, stooped down for the purpose of lifting us up. Because of this we are seated with Jesus in heavenly places in Christ.

> "...and lifted us up from the grave into glory along with Christ, where we sit with him in the heavenly realms—all because of what Christ Jesus did." Ephesians 2:6 (TLB)

This is quite different than Adam's self-determination and self-reliance. This is God's determination. We are God-reliant. God's Spirit has quickened us and made us alive together with Christ and made us "joint heirs with Jesus Christ!" Romans 8:17 (NKJV)

169

DECLARE THIS BOLDLY

"The spear thrust into Jesus' side produced a miraculous flow of restoration into my life. I have been elevated back to my place of right standing with God in His Kingdom. My daily walk is not one of isolation, but I walk side-by-side, united with the King of the Universe. No evil thing can separate me from His Love. I am the apple of His eye. He has given me the power of attorney and the use of His Name! He has opened to me His treasure and shares His resources with me. He protects me with His strong arms and keeps me close to His heart. I am His and He is mine! All that I have is His; all that He has is mine. We are covenant partners. We are forever united. I am by His Side. And because His heart was broken, my is mended. And because He allowed His heart to be pierced, mine is healthy and whole, beating with the rhythm of life."

#7
INTERNAL BLEEDING: REDEEMED FROM DESTRUCTIVE PATTERNS

"...He was bruised for our iniquities..."
Isaiah 53:5 (NKJV)

I love the game of soccer. It held a big spot in my life for many years. I played soccer from middle school all the way up to college and even in our city's adult league. My kids played for school and club. I even coached some of their teams and those are some of our best father-son memories. We still like playing it and watching it. But once, in my early 20's, I received such a contusion on my ankle that I was sure it had to be broken.

As the doctor examined it, he said, "Kevin, it would probably hurt less if it were broken. It's just deeply bruised."

THE BODY-BLOWS OF LIFE

Have you ever had a bruise? Bruises can be invisible on the outside. Nonetheless the pain can be almost unbearable. The slightest graze or innocent touch can send excruciating pain shooting throughout your entire being.

Unintentionally, a passerby can become a perpetrator of more pain to an area that's already sensitive from past abuse. When these "bruises" are in our soul, we sometimes mistakenly conclude that "this person" or passerby is the cause of our pain, when in reality the internal damage has been beneath the surface all the while.

AN OVERLOOKED SUFFERING

This is a much-overlooked pain endured by Christ. The seventh Way our Savior suffered is often the most overlooked to the point of being virtually forgotten. And sometimes I wonder to myself if this could be one of the reasons for such extreme levels of disfunction in the Body of Christ today. Everyone remembers that Jesus bled from His Brow, Hands, Feet, and Side. Many remember His Back and some recall His bloody sweat. But to date, I have yet to meet someone who has passed my little pop quiz: List the seven ways Jesus bled. Yet, scripture tells us clearly and plainly,

> *"He was **bruised** for our iniquity." Isaiah 53:5 (NKJV)*

THREE KINDS OF SIN IN THE BIBLE

Definitions always tend to put everyone on the same page. Let's look at these:

1. **Sin** – to miss the mark.
2. **Transgression** – to go beyond a known boundary.
3. **Iniquity** – a sometimes unconscious pattern or inward bent toward a certain and often destructive behavior.

The Hebrew word for iniquity is "avon." (It has nothing to do with make-up.) It's where we get our word "wicker" from, as in wicker furniture. It means twisted. Bent. Wicked. Because of the condition of the fallen human race, there are people who do things and don't know why they do them. They just have a bent or twist in certain directions. But that's why Jesus came: to straighten us out. (Pun intended.)

Have you ever driven a vehicle that was severely out of alignment? So much so, that if you relaxed your grip on the wheel, you would be jerked into the wrong lane or even into a ditch! This is what iniquity is like. It pulls your life in a dangerous direction. You can try to manage and cope with it, but if you relax for even a moment, you are headed to a dangerous place. Some of you have prayed about this issue in your life dozens or even hundreds of times with no long-term relief. I want to reveal to you the power and healing Jesus has afforded you by His being "bruised for our iniquity." The apostle, Paul, said it this way in Romans 7:15,24–8:1 (NJKV),

> *"For what I am doing I do not understand. For what I will*
> *to do that I do not practice; but what I hate, that I do…*
> *Oh, wretched man that I am. Who will deliver me from this*
> *body of death? I Thank God through our Jesus Christ our*
> *Lord… There is therefore now no condemnation for those*
> *that are in Christ, who walk not according to the flesh but*
> *according to the spirit."*

Tell Me About Your Childhood

Many years ago, my youngest son was crying and complaining about something. He was still a little boy back them. I jokingly said, "Tell me about your childhood."

Shocked, he retorted, "But I'm still in it!"

How often, in our formative years, pain sneaks and creeps in through various experiences ranging from suffered abuse to stupid decisions, of our own making or someone else's. But often, iniquities and strongholds grab us during this impressionable time of life. It

172

happens to almost everyone, but provision has been made to overcome childhood traumas and disappointments. Allowing The Counselor to bring them to light is the first step for the healing to begin. Take a moment and tell The Counselor about your childhood. Seriously, He's waiting.

STRONGHOLDS

Everyone has "bents" from their family of origins. Many believers live with these bents. They have strongholds or things that have a strong hold on their soul or flesh. These ways of thinking and behavioral patterns produce forms of bondage that for some, become ways of life. A stronghold is a place in your soul where a particular cause or belief is strongly defended or upheld. It's believing a lie is actually the truth. This gives the kingdom of darkness a strong hold in your mind and produces a negative or destructive pattern in your life.

HOW STRONGHOLDS COME

Some strongholds come through sin perpetrated against us or performed by us. Other strongholds come through generational bloodlines or what the Scripture calls *iniquities*. Whatever the route hell took in attacking your life, Jesus has already paid for the healing of your emotions, bents, and patterns of struggle. For that matter, Luke tells us in Luke 4:18 (KJV) that part of the mission of Jesus was to

> *"...set at liberty them that are **bruised** [wounded internally]."*

PAIN IS A BONDAGE MAKER

Past wounds can hold you in bondage. Every one of us has had our hearts broken. Every person has experienced some kind of extreme pain. Almost everyone I know has experienced the tragedy of broken relationships. Too many have seen friendships collapse, and even marriages end in divorce. Rejection from some and abuse from others. Many adult children are suffering from the lingering pain of parental issues, especially unrealistic expectations and the harsh words that were attached to those disappointments. Not to mention actual abuse.

BUT THERE IS GOOD NEWS

Jesus came to heal the brokenhearted! It is one of the major reasons the Spirit of the Lord was upon Him. Not just to heal the physically sick, but to also heal the brokenhearted. Besides, many physical ailments stem from these internal, emotional bruises anyway. We don't need to learn to cope. We need to overcome and be healed!

But you can't just tell someone with a broken bone to "get over it!" NO, it must be set and put into alignment. The same is true with someone experiencing a broken heart. It's the same with a past hurt or wound. You have to go to an expert. And, most importantly, you have The Counselor on the inside to lead and guide you into all Truth. He will transform your reality if you let Him help and set your thinking into alignment with His Word. He will tell you the Truth, and that will make you free.

BETTER THAN A SHRINK

Jesus can do for you what the psychiatrist can't. Jesus is outcome-oriented and wants to bring your suffering to a permanent end. This is why He suffered in your place and then gave you a full-time, live-in Counselor, The Holy Spirit. Sometimes, we try to control people, so they won't reject us. Sadly, this behavior actually often causes people to reject us and thus causes our fear of rejection to come to pass. But again, why was the Spirit of the Lord upon Jesus? To set at liberty them that are **BRUISED**! If you're bleeding on the inside, He brings you freedom!

Then we have people-pleasers, manipulators, and controllers. (Tragically, most of them seem to get married to each other. Not impossible to fix, but in the meantime — "ouch!") By the way, most relationships and even marriages could be mended if people were emotionally healed... if somehow crushed people could receive their pardon from a Great Liberator! What hope do we have of this? *"He was crushed for our iniquities."* Because humanity is injured on the inside, Jesus suffered internal bruising. He has paid for your pain that others cannot even see.

DEFINING THE PAIN

The doctor pushes and asks, "Does this hurt?"

You scream, "YES! Did you not go to Medical School?!? Of course, that hurts! What is wrong with you? Stop pressing there…"

There could be emotional, internal bleeding if someone tries to point out an area of hurt or dysfunction in your life and your response is defensive or accusatory.

When someone offers constructive criticism, you lash out, "Well you are the same way!"

Or the old favorite, "So do you!"

This could be a sign of an internal issue as people either transfer their pain or transform it. Most transfer it to their own future and children. But though the redemptive work of Christ it can be transformed into a testimony of victory! ***Sin comes by internal desire aided by external enticement.*** Aligning yourself with Jesus is the only way to overcome.

> *"But in every nation whoever fears Him and works right-*
> *eousness is accepted by Him… how God anointed Jesus of*
> *Nazareth with the Holy Spirit and power who went about*
> *doing good and healing all that were oppressed by the*
> *devil, for God was with Him." Acts 10:35, 38 (NKJV)*

DISCOVER YOUR REAL ENEMY

People are not our problem. No matter what your mother-in-law says! Ephesians 6:12 reveals that we don't fight people or wrestle against flesh and blood. You can't "think" or "reason" the devil away. But you can appropriate your faith and **speak** him away.

ALIGNMENT IS PARAMOUNT

Who and what you are aligned to is of paramount importance. Submit to God. Align yourself with Christ through repentance. Acts 3:19 (NKJV) says to,

> *"Repent therefore and be converted, that your sins may be blotted out, so that times of refreshing may come from the presence of the Lord."*

A time of refreshing would do wonders for your souls! It's better than catching a second wind. It's more like catching your breath.

King Solomon, the wisest man to ever live, shares a powerful insight in Proverbs 28:13 (NKJV).

> *"He who covers his sins will not prosper, but whoever confesses and forsakes them will have mercy."*

SIN IS LIKE FUNGUS; IT GROWS IN THE DARK.

What remains hidden cannot heal. But if you expose it and bring it into the light (by accountability; confession; prayer) it will die! And like a fungus in sunlight, it will lose its grip on you. And that refreshing from Heaven will pour into your weary soul.

Jesus will always deal tenderly with His people.

> *"A bruised reed He will not break, and smoking flax He will not quench, till He sends forth justice to victory."*
> *Matthew 12:20 (NKJV)*

Are you bruised? The Counselor is gentle and kind. Your healing, wellbeing and supplying help are His goals. His role is to guide you to a greater understanding and intimate knowledge of Jesus. Let Him reveal to you the Healing Power of the Seven Wounds of the Suffering Savior! He did it all for you.

THE SEVEN WOUNDS OF THE SUFFERING SAVIOR

WHAT ABOUT THE SCARS?

After Jesus' death, his disciples went into hiding. But Jesus later appeared to them. To prove his identity, He showed them His scars. Pain is unavoidable. Not even the innocent escape, else Jesus would have. But I like the subtitle of James B. Richard's book, *How to Stop the Pain: Pain is Inevitable; Suffering is Optional.*

Secondly, When Jesus appeared to His followers it was as if He was saying, "I'm not bleeding or hurting anymore. The suffering is over." What if we offered our scars to the world, not only to prove our identity, but to demonstrate the healing power of Jesus in our life? Your suffering is over too. Don't hide your scars: they tell a story and show that God has healed you. If He did it for you, then He can do it for them too.

Time doesn't heal all wounds—love does. Scars are proof that you are still alive and that you are very loved.

USE THIS PRAYER TO REALIGN YOUR LIFE

"Father, in Jesus' Name, I come boldly before your Throne of Grace to accept Mercy and find Grace to help. I acknowledged that Jesus, my Savior, Lord, and King, bled seven ways to procure and complete total and perfect redemption for me in Spirit, Soul and Body. Remove from my life anything that was not planted by You. I now **Recognize** the sin, sickness, selfishness, and generational iniquity that has held me back from my Divine destiny. I **Repent** of _____ (call it by name: sin, injury, insecurity, confusion, prejudice, destructive habits, depression, anxiety, lingering sicknesses, bents, patterns, etc.). I change my mind about this and declare it is unacceptable to You and is now unacceptable to me. If Jesus suffered for me to be free from it, then I receive that freedom. I **Renounce** _____ (call it by name) and command it to get out of my life in Jesus' Name! I now use the power of attorney granted to me and invoke the Name above every name and state: I no longer have anything to do with _____. I kick you out of my life and I close the door behind you. LEAVE! NOW! In Jesus' Name. I purpose and will, from this moment forward, to **Replace** _____ (call it by name) with God's Word, God's Presence, God's Power, God's People, God's Spirit, and Godly Habits. I **Return** to my God-given position as a son or daughter of The Most High God. I am seated with Jesus in heavenly places in Christ. I **Return** to my First Love and to do the good works I was preordained by God to do. And I will return to a good, bible-teaching, Jesus-preaching, people-reaching local church. I am **Restored** to right standing with God and I am as bold as The Lion of the Tribe of Judah! In Jesus' Name, Amen."

Enjoy your new freedom. I hope you have enjoyed your time on The Couch.

QUESTIONS FOR SMALL GROUPS AND PERSONAL REFLECTION:

1. Had you ever considered the seven ways Jesus bled? List them. Why does it matter to us that He bled in seven different ways?

2. Are you currently in need of physical healing? Which of Jesus's redemptive wounds would apply to your situation?

3. Which of the seven wounds from which Jesus bled spoke to you the most where you're currently at, and why?

4. If "you have not because you ask not" then ASK God for your healing right now. Read Mark 11:22–25. Then claim your healing and health. Be sure to thank God for blessing you with this gift.

5. Is there a generational "bent" that you are ready to be free from?

-8-
A ROADMAP TO PERSONAL REVIVAL

8

A ROADMAP TO PERSONAL REVIVAL

"If My people who are called by My name will humble themselves, and pray and seek My face, and turn from their wicked ways, then I will hear from heaven, and will forgive their sin and heal their land."
2 Chronicles 7:14 (NKJV)

In this final chapter, I want to lay out a road map for you to personal, sustained revival. It's great that you have shaken off the chains of bondage from your past. Now take up the tools to stay free and sustain your fervor in Christ. In the famous passage above, there is a key to why revival gets short-circuited, instead of being sustained generationally. But it is also a recipe for experiencing personal, sustained, on-going revival as well. If iniquity and depression can run from generation to generation, then how much more can righteousness and revival? Let's take a look at each of the nine phrases contained is this eternal script penned in antiquity. Then we will hone in on the phrase-that-pays, and leave you with more practical handles to walk in **permanent** victory over any and all of your previously "twisted ways." This is the stuff that changes family trees for future generations! Let's dive in.

STEP ONE: DECIDE
"IF..."

"If My people..." God could have said "*When* My people..." But He didn't. He said "IF." The word "if" indicates the presence of alternatives. It means you may or you may not receive the invitation being offered. As it always is with The Sovereign Almighty—the decision is yours. Choice is the greatest gift God has given Mankind, other than The Man, Himself, Christ Jesus.

You have made some quality decisions. Now, what's next? More choices. And among them we must choose a vibrant relationship with God and we can also choose revival. And it only takes a handful of people to bring change and reform to an entire community and even a nation. But before God judges the affairs of Mankind, He looks first to see what His people are doing. For example, in Genesis 18:16–32, God went to investigate the wickedness of Sodom, but first He stopped by His friend, Abraham's home, to both inform him and get Abe's input on the situation. Like when God created all the animal in the garden but brought them to Adam to see what he would name them. In other words, The Lord doesn't hide His agenda and activities from His close, trusted friends. You are one of those now.

I once heard Brother Kenneth E. Hagin teach that The Lord will hold the church accountable for the way the nation goes. We have more power than we've realized! And, therefore, more responsibility. And like God's friend Abraham, we must intercede and pray. Satan tries to make our life seem futile, for the fate of nations rests in the hands of the righteous.

If. Let's decide here and now that we will play our role and do our part. No longer meandering in the maze of mediocrity or pondering at the pool of popularity. Like the prophet of old let us also declare, "Here I am. Send me!"

POUR INTO YOUR CORE

Now this I know:

183

"The Lord gives victory to his anointed. He answers him from his heavenly sanctuary with the victorious power of his right hand." Psalms 20:6 (NIV)

I'm going to assume that you are a leader. If not, you are now. Establish a Core. It's one of the things leaders do. Identify who is hungry for God and then invest into them. Pour into the core of believers who express a hunger for God. Whatever God has called you to do, you cannot do it alone. As my mentor, Jim Wideman, says, "Before Jesus ever worked a miracle, the first thing He did was recruit some help." If Jesus needed a team, so do we. God seeks a Core! In Samuel 14:6 (NKJV), we are told,

"Nothing restrains the Lord from saving by many or saving by few."

Establish a core that will set itself aside as a living sacrifice.

God seeks to find, in us, a spark that He can transform into a life that can change the course of history. A revival core exists to meet God and receive His power! It makes me think of the Book of Acts, in Chapter 2. Now that was a Core of Revival people hungry for all God had to offer! And they received the greatest outpouring that the world has ever seen heretofore. But I want to announce, there is a greater outpouring on the horizon. The Lord once spoke this to me, *"The Shadows of Time are Gathering upon the Horizon of History, and the final grains of time are slipping through the hourglass. The Son of Righteousness is Rising with Healing in His Wings. And the Days of Nominal Christianity are becoming extinct; only those Skilled at Knowing God and His Word and are Led by His Spirit will be those that Thrive in these Last-Days!"*

LOYALTY RHYMES WITH ROYALTY

2 Chronicles 16:9 (NKJV) reminds us,

"For the eyes of the Lord run to and fro throughout the

whole earth, to show Himself strong on behalf of those
whose heart is loyal to Him."

Loyalty is a greatly neglected virtue in our culture today. But it is on behalf of the loyal that God, the Royal, shows Himself strong. To be loyal means to be fully committed. Dedicated. Taking on someone else's agenda as your own.

Wade is a dear friend of mine. He's also a retired FBI Agent. I would tell you more about him, but then he'd have to kill you. (Not really. I think…)

He once told me that before they ever hired anyone they would ask, "Will this candidate be loyal to the Bureau?"

If loyalty to the agency is vital for employment, how much more is our loyalty to God's agenda and His people essential for our employ within God's Kingdom? He shares His power with the loyal.

THE FABRIC OF CIVILIZATION

Loyalty is the fabric of civilization. A marriage where the husband is not loyal to the wife will not endure. A staff that is not loyal to their leader will not advance. Dr. Mark Rutland says in his book entitled, *Character Matters*,

> "Loyalty is the willingness, because of relational commitment, to deflect praise, admiration, and success onto another. This loyalty may well be at great personal expense, but it will edify and bless its object…. Loyalty is the glue that holds relationships together, makes families functional and armies victorious."

Loyalty, like Love, is not a feeling but rather a decision. So here we see the power of choice again. Will we choose God's way over our own?

> *"And if you have not been faithful in what is another*
> *man's, who will give you what is your own?"*
> *Luke 16:12 (NKJV)*

What is God's agenda? I believe it is people. Souls. The Great Commission. His family and His church. That none should perish. The mission of the church is missions; the mission of missions is the church. Do our prayers reflect these priorities? Does our giving? How about our serving? What about our words? Or our loving? Our Witness? Our loyalty? Faithfulness is a fruit of the spirit. Grow it. Do justice. Love mercy. Walk humbly with your God. These are among your next steps.

We must ask ourselves, "If I'm being honest, in what ways is my heart disloyal to my God?" And then respectfully follow with, "I humbly put myself in agreement with Your agenda, dear God!"

QUESTIONS FOR SMALL GROUPS AND PERSONAL REFLECTION:

1. If loyalty is taking on someone else's agenda as your own, are you loyal to Christ's agenda? Explain how or how not.

2. In what ways is my heart disloyal to my God? What 3 changes can I make that would be most pleasing to God?

3. "IF." Will you decide to receive the invitation in God's grace being offered to you to be a part of what God is doing in these last days? What might that look like for you?

A ROADMAP TO PERSONAL REVIVAL

STEP TWO: KNOW THYSELF
"...MY PEOPLE CALLED BY MY NAME..."

As Christ-followers, God calls us by His own Name. Names identify, and The Almighty gave us His Name when we accepted His Son as our Lord. You are no longer called, by God, according to your family of earthly origin, or by the decisions of your past, but by His own Name. You've been transferred out of The Adam's Family into The Lord's Family! Now, begin to feed your soul a steady diet of who you really are. God the Father (not to be confused with "The Godfather") sent His Son, Jesus, to show us God's nature and character. But He also sent His Son, Jesus, to show us... US! ...who we now are in Christ. Who Jesus is reveals who we are and what we are capable of being as born-again, recreated, Spirit-filled, children of The Most High God. Love has fashioned us into the Image of Him that not only created us, but also re-created us! Are you willing to continuously renew your mind to know who you are in Christ and to know who Christ is in you? It will transform your entire life spiritually, emotionally, intellectually, physically, and financially. Like a worm that grows wings, renewing your mind with scripture will metamorphosize your entire being. It builds into your conscientiousness, not only who you are, but Whose you are. You will no longer crawl through life: you will soar!

"If My People, Who are Called by My Name..."

You are not what your past calls you or what your family calls you, but what the God of the universe calls you. This must become your dominate pattern of thinking. Your life will always move in the direction of your most dominate thought. He calls you by His own, family Name. He claims you! That's My child! He's your happy, proud Papa. In fact, until you know *Whose* you are, you will never know *who* you are. Children who lack the knowledge of knowing their father have to overcome an identity crisis at some level. Today's

187

culture and society demonstrates the damaging effects of fatherless-
ness.

> *"Behold what manner of love the Father has bestowed*
> *upon us that we should be called the children of God."*
> *1 John 3:1 (NKJV)*

Only when we know Whose we are can we gain confidence. Developing a relationship with God through scripture, prayer and godly
relationships enlightens us to know who He is in us, and who we are
in Him. We must discover our identity in Christ and see ourselves as
He sees us: Sons of The Most High God! The apostle, Paul, said it
this way,

> *"In Him we live, and move, and have our being."*
> *Acts 17:28 (NKJV)*

You can't move in the things of God if you don't live in the things
of God. In other words, the core of your being is now IN CHRIST. If
we live in Him, we will move in Him and have our identity and being
in Him. I read a book entitled, *Atomic Habits*, written by James Clear.
It describes a powerful concept called, "Identity habits." In brief, the
concept states that if you will take on the mindset of the kind of person you want to be, you will in fact, move toward living out of that
identity, as that kind of person. For example, one man lost a hundred
pounds by simply asking this questions before he made any decisions,
"What would a healthy man do?" A healthy man takes the stairs not
the elevator. A healthy man orders the grilled chicken salad, instead
of the fried catfish. A healthy man gets adequate sleep. So, when "life
happens," and we all know it does, simply ask, "What would a
healthy man do?" And then, do that! Because that is who you are.
That is your identity.

Let me put it to you another way and offer an even more powerful
question to use. What would a bold, Spirit-filled, tongue talking, revival walking, sin hating, devil chasing, Jesus preaching, people
reaching, God loving, true blue, red hot, Holy Ghost, Heaven sent

man or woman of God do in each situation you find yourself in? Then, just do that! And I bet you can imagine the kind of person you are metamorphosing into! You will begin to look a lot like Jesus, and that is what revival looks like. You will begin to soar through life, instead of crawling.

STICK WITH THE PROCESS

Robert struggled in his relationship with God. Memories kept reminding him of the awful person he was. His self-image was broken and poor. As a result, he often found himself self-medicating and on the wrong side of the law.

But one day, someone told him, "You know, that's not your real momma and your real daddy. Now that you are in Christ your family tree has changed."

So, Robert's inner image of himself began to change. He began to renew his mind with who he is in Christ, not who or what he was B.C. (before Christ). Because his inner picture changed, his outward picture has begun to change. Like all of us, Robert is not perfect, but he is sticking with the process of being a disciple of Christ and working out his salvation. Sometimes he acts like a jerk. Sometimes Robert still falls. But more importantly, Robert gets back up.

Stick with the process, God's process, and it will stick with you. If you do, like cream, you will rise to the top in life. And like most things, rising up is a choice.

WHO WILL RISE UP?

Psalm 94:16–19 (NJKV) submits an interesting question for our consideration:

> *"Who will rise up for Me against the wicked? Who will take a stand for Me against evildoers? Unless the Lord had given me help, I would soon have dwelt in the silence of death. When I said, 'My foot is slipping,' your unfailing love, Lord, supported me. When anxiety was great within*

me, your consolation brought me joy."

In other words, remember Whose you are and Whose Name you bear! Constantly keep in mind who you are and Whose you are. It is a key to sustaining both personal and generational revival. Because who wants to have revival without God's love or without joy?

Here's a practical exercise for you. Read through the New Testament epistles and underline every place it says, "in Him", "in Whom", "in Christ", etc. Meditate, think, and chew on these redemptive realities that belong to you in Christ Jesus our Lord. Memorize some of those passages. I can't think of anything else that will accelerate your spiritual growth and maturity as quickly as this exercise.

QUESTIONS FOR SMALL GROUPS AND PERSONAL REFLECTION:

1. If God sent Jesus to show us US then who are you now in Christ?

2. If your life will move in the direction of your most dominate thought, what direction is your life moving in? Do you need to totally change directions or just make minor adjustments?

3. Renewing your mind with scripture "gives you wings." What's your current go-to scripture?

STEP THREE: ATTITUDE ADJUSTMENT
"...WILL HUMBLE THEMSELVES..."

Your will is involved. Will you do it? Will you humble yourself? Will you choose to adjust your attitude before God and man? Will you wait patiently before God while recognizing a deep realization of your need for change? Will you confess your need for repentance, revival, renewal, restoration, and the rekindling of the flame of your First Love? Matthew 22:14 (NKJV) reminds us,

> *"For many are called* [invited], *but few are chosen* [selected]. *"*

Just because you are invited to a job interview doesn't guarantee you will get the position. Naturally speaking, you've got to have the resume and dress for success to impress. But then you have to have character, competence, and chemistry with the rest of the team. In other words, you have a part to play if you hope to get the job.

A level of humility includes simply agreeing with God. The Lord is looking for those clothed in humility, and their resume is Jesus. A humble person is a submitted person... someone who has a proper relationship with authority. God has designed it so that you will only walk in authority to the degree that you are submitted to authority. A rebellious person needs personal revival but will never have it. Only those who humble themselves can walk through the door of awakening. Submit to God. Resist the devil. In that order. Only then will Satan flee.

God sends this invitation to many but opens the door for few. This door is not salvation. Salvation comes through faith in the finished work of Christ alone, and whosoever believes will not perish. But I'm speaking of the door of revival. This door is not opened by talent, persistence, nor even intelligence. A very specific attitude is the key. Isaiah 57:15 (NKJV) says,

"For thus says the high and lofty One Who inhabits eter-nity, whose name is Holy: 'I dwell in the high and holy place, with him who has a contrite and humble spirit, to re-vive the spirit of the humble, and to revive the heart of the contrite ones.'"

Who gets revived? The humble and the contrite. Being quick to repent is a key to attaining personal revival and sustaining it.

Acknowledge your brokenness before God, and your deficiency without Him. And there is a proper time and place to acknowledge the same before appropriate people too. We are instructed to confess our faults, one to another, that we may be healed. (James 5:16)

We confess to God for forgiveness; we confess to one another for healing.

CLEAN HANDS AND A PURE HEART

Psalm 24:3–4 (NKJV) says,

"Who may ascend into the hill of the Lord? Or who may stand in His holy place? He who has clean hands and a pure heart, Who has not lifted up his soul to an idol, Nor sworn deceitfully."

Let's look at four very important definitions pertaining to this verse.

1. **Cleans hands:** doing what is right, living with honor and integrity.
2. **Pure heart:** not allowing the actions and attitudes of mean people to create toxicity, anger, resentment, and disappointment in your heart, walking in love, and never working ill toward any other person. Ever. (See Romans 13:10.)
3. **Not giving your soul to an idol:** An idol is anything that has taken the place that only God deserves. It can be a "good thing" that if we elevate it to become our "ultimate thing" causes it to become a "bad thing". It's a priorities-issue. It

can be the right things in the wrong order. If your priorities are out of, then pause, evaluate your priorities in the presence of God, and ask Him to reorder things for you. Order proceeds increase and outpouring.

4. **Nor swearing deceitfully:** Be a man or woman of your word. It is a key ingredient to living with the tangible Presence of God upon your life. God cannot lie. He keeps His Word. And as His kids, so should we. We don't trick or manipulate to get our way. We deal honestly.

THE GREAT RESET

Can we just pray to receive revival? Absolutely not! Can we receive revival without prayer? Absolutely not. *"If My people,"* God says, in effect, *"will wake up, hit the spiritual reset button, and realize what they have done, what they have left undone, and what they now must do...."* We can't instantly shake ourselves from a sedentary Christian life and stroll casually before God's throne of Grace and demand a revival from a holy, awesome God who happens to be an all-consuming fire. We must be as the prodigal son. "He came to himself..." Luke 15:17 (KJV) He humbly admitted to himself that he was in the wrong place at the wrong time with the wrong pigs. That is the kind of entrance that is recognized by God: humility. Because true humility is simply agreeing with the truth. God's Word is Truth. That is the great reset.

I think it's okay to experience the grief of what we have lost as we recognize those areas where we have not measured up to God's Word and we see what our true condition is before a holy God. But we cannot live there. Hit the reset button. After the COVID-19 global pandemic, many speak of our need for "the great reset." Perhaps this is that reset button: a deep realization of our need for a spiritual awakening and revival! Ephesians 5:14 (NKJV) tell us to,

"Wake up Sleeper! Rise from the dead, and Christ will shine on you."

God looks for people who have been sobered, and are no longer drunk on culture and the world, who have humbled themselves with a godly sorrow of conviction for which there is no relief except one... revival! A mighty outpouring of God's Spirit as promised would come in Joel 2:28!

Leonard Ravenhill wrote a powerful book entitled, *Why Revival Tarries.*

One story I heard says that years after that writing he was asked, "Brother Ravenhill, aren't you writing another book? If so, what is it titled?"

He answered yes. Then with tears in his eyes he stated the title would be, *Why Revival _Still_ Tarries.* Oh, my friends, hasn't it tarried for way too long? Do you think The Benevolent, Almighty will forget this generation? A nursing mother may forget her baby, but our Heavenly Father cannot forget His children that cry out to Him night and day. Let us cry out to Him once more and do it with great expectation of His kind response of refreshing (Acts 3:19).

And what is revival? It is quite simply and profoundly when God comes! And if we have ever needed Him to come it is now! Only His Presence will cure our sin sick world and rescue this generation from godlessness. Let us humble ourselves and cry out to Him to come among us in His goodness and His might.

Check out these confirming and affirming verses:

"Oh that You would rend the Heavens! That You would come down!" Isaiah 64:1 (NKJV)

"Repent therefore and be converted, that your sins may be blotted out, so that times of refreshing may come from the presence of the Lord, and that He may send Jesus Christ..." Acts 3:19–20a (NJKV)

"The generous will prosper; those who refresh others will themselves be refreshed." Proverbs 11:25 (NLV)

The Passion Translation says,

"Those who live to bless others will have blessings heaped upon them, and the one who pours out his life to pour out blessings will be saturated with favor."

The author and revivalist Leonard Ravenhill once said, "The man who can get believers to praying would, under God, usher in the greatest revival that the world has ever know."

PLANNING IS PART OF PRAYING

But to pray for a river of revival, you must think where that river would flow. Before you pray for revival, a city-shaking outpouring of God's Holy Presence and Power, you must consider what it would do. Endeavoring to calculate the total consequences of a spiritual awakening shows God you mean business and that you really expect it to happen. Faith gets ready. Of course, God does "exceedingly abundantly above all we could ask or think." Ephesians 3:20 (KJV) Faith plans for increase. Faith prepares as an expecting woman prepares for the arrival of her new baby. Envision the moving of God's Spirit throughout your home and church and city. Engage your godly imagination! Let it run wild with the impossibilities becoming realities. Visualize notorious sinners coming to Christ. Picture entire school campuses falling under the convicting power of the Holy Spirit.

"For without faith it is impossible to please God. For those that come to Him must believe that He is and is a rewarder of them that diligently seek Him." Hebrews 11:6 (NKJV)

Oh friend, God rewards those who diligently seek Him. It is a promise! Planning for, is part of praying for. If you pray for something, you must expect it from The Rewarder. Expecting it means we train ourselves to handle and receive the thing we have requested. In this case, a sudden influx of new believers. It means pastors study accounts of past revivals to see the potential dangers and prepare a congregation to absorb and sustain revival-life without it destroying our life. Leaders must *complete* one another not *compete* with one another. We not only cooperate, but even repent for competition if needs be!

> *Psalm 66:18 (KJV) says, "If I regard iniquity in my heart the Lord will not hear me."*

Harbor a secret sin and you will not be heard by God? That is what this book has been all about: rooting out sin, twisted thinking, and initiating the healing and renewing of our minds. Have your past redeemed, so that we can step into your future to discover your destiny in God. For destiny delayed is the devil's delight! Jealously, lust, pride, gossip, prejudice, offense, etc…we no longer give them place in our hearts and lives. We humble ourselves, make it right, before entering God's Presence for revival. If we can't make it right then we enter into His Presence crying out for deliverance as we fall upon His mercy.

Let us keep reading. Psalm 66:19 (NKJV) says,

> *"But certainly God has heard me; He has attended to the voice of my prayer."*

Why? Because we have not approved filth and naughtiness in our lives. We are not perfect, but we are perfectly His! We walk humbly clean and honestly before our Lord and our God.

STRONG IN THE BROKEN PLACES

God is attracted to brokenness. Can we humble ourselves completely today? On behalf of our church? On behalf of our city? Our nation? God is attracted to spiritual hunger too. Can we have as much sense as a newborn baby that's hungry and cry out today for what we need?

I encourage you to express your humility to God right now. Change your mind once and for all about unholy things you have tolerated in the past. God will embrace and uplift you, and times of refreshing will come from His Presence! Let us assume the attitude that delights our Heavenly Father: honesty and humility! And He will make you strong where you were once broken.

QUESTIONS FOR SMALL GROUPS AND PERSONAL REFLECTION:

1. Describe how you personally plan to wait patiently before God to help you recognize a deep need for change? What would "expressing your humility to God" look or sound like?

2. Engage your godly imagination! Discuss some of the mighty things that God may do in an outpouring of His Spirit upon your community. Describe what you would love to see Him do.

3. What are some practical preparations you can make to receive God's outpouring? Make a list.

4. If revival is simply "when God comes," then in what area of your life do you need revival? If you're reading and discussing this with a group, stop now and lift those things up to God in prayer. May a time of refreshing come to you now.

Step Four: Give Birth
"AND PRAY..."

Revival is not the church's response to God pouring out His Spirit; it is God's response to His church pouring out their spirit! When we cry out in humility, repenting and praying, God cannot resist.

> *"Call unto Me and I will answer you and show you great*
> *and mighty things that you do not know."*
> *Jeremiah 33:3 (NKJV)*

Jesus did not say He was coming for a culturally relevant church. He is, however, coming for a glorious church! Not a poor, bedraggled church, but a bride without spot or wrinkle. And I think that must mean a praying church too.

> *"If My People who are called by My Name, will humble*
> *themselves AND PRAY..."*

Pray for what? Pray for God to pour out of His Spirit. Pray specifically for the fulfillment of Joel 2:28–30 (NASB),

> *"It will come about after this that I will pour out My Spirit*
> *on all mankind; And your sons and your daughters will*
> *prophesy, Your old men will have dreams, Your young men*
> *will see visions. And even on the male and female servants*
> *I will pour out My Spirit in those days. I will display won-*
> *ders in the sky and on the earth, blood, fire, and columns*
> *of smoke."*

I'm talking about a birthing-kind-of-prayer that releases eternal things into this temporal earth for the glory of God and the advancement of Christ's holy and soon coming Kingdom. God's pre-condition for revival-prayer and intercession is to be willing to die, albeit to your flesh, to see and experience renewal and revival. My best friend, Reverend Jeff Taylor, has a saying, "As long as you can live without a move of God, you will." I don't think I can anymore.

I'm ready to be a part of a church that's ignited by a holy fire. That will bow in worship to seek God's face with or without a "paid, professional worship band" and care less if the fancy lights and screens are on or not. They can bring the life-changing power and Presence of Almighty God with a simple box-guitar or by passionately lifting their voice in one accord, or falling humbly silent in a holy hush before their Maker. Where is the apostolic church of a by-gone era where sinful men could simply walk in and their bondages of addiction and affliction would be melted off in the heat of a holy God's love as His people PRAY?

IF YOU AIM AT NOTHING YOU WILL HIT IT

The children's pastor that led me to Jesus, when I was 5 years old, is still my mentor in leadership and my friend today. He conducted my wedding in 1993. I have heard Brother Jim Wideman say my whole life, "If you aim at nothing you will hit it every time." Our prayer needs a target. What exactly are we praying for?

There is a book in the New Testament called, *The Acts of the Apostles*. But accurately it could be called, "The Acts of the Holy Spirit Through the Church." In revival-prayer, a person presents himself before God to give birth to an *act of God* in his city, but first in his own heart and life. But your prayer must have a clear target and be focused. Nothing is more important in experiencing this forceful praying than to focus your concern. Do not ask amiss. Tied to our lack of power in prayer is our lack of a target for our faith and compassion. It's fine to ask God for your wants and needs, but do we also ask Him for souls? If not, then let our repentance start there. If we move in faith, God will move in power. And if we will travail in prayer, another chapter will be written in the Heavenly copy of The Book of Acts!

In the words of the revivalist and preacher, Charles G. Finney, "If the church does not have a burden for souls it is backslidden." And as the Holy Spirit spoke to my soul once in prayer before I mounted the pulpit to preach in a partner-church, "A church that is not concerned with souls—I Am is not concerned with that church!" Let us be concerned for what concerns God.

the pulpit to preach in a partner-church, "A church that is not concerned with souls—I Am is not concerned with that church!" Let us be concerned for what concerns God.

In the kind of prayer that I am endeavoring to describe, we have to come to worship and pour out our deep grief over specific evils in specific places at specific times. The ancient prophet, Daniel, gives us an example. (I've inserted my city and made some emphasis.)

> **Daniel 9:15–19 (NKJV)** "And now, O Lord our God, who brought Your people out of the land of Egypt with a mighty hand, and made Yourself a Name, as it is this day—**we** have sinned, **we** have done wickedly! O Lord, according to all Your righteousness, I pray, let Your anger and Your fury be turned away from Your city **MOBILE**, **Alabama** because for **our** sins, and for the iniquities of our fathers, and Your people are a reproach to all those around us. Now therefore, our God, hear the prayer of Your servant, and his supplications, and for the Lord's sake cause **Your face to shine on** Your sanctuary (The Church: Revival!), which is desolate. O my God, incline Your ear and hear; open Your eyes and see our desolations, and the city which is called by Your name; for we do not present our supplications before You because of our righteous deeds, **but because of Your great mercies.** O Lord, hear! O Lord, forgive! O Lord, listen and act! **Do not delay** for Your own sake, my God, for Your city (insert the name of your city here) and Your people (the church) are called by Your name."

We must also know when to pause in prayer and wait for a release of the Holy Spirit. Then follow His instruction. As one man of God, who was the pastor of the largest church in the world at the time said, "I pray, and I obey." We must stay in prayer until God is satisfied that this particular season of prayer has fulfilled its purpose. *How would you know such a thing?* Well, how do you know when you're satisfied at the dinner table? You're full. Stay in His Presence until you are filled. Your heart will be satisfied.

A Matter of Life and Death

Keep in mind that what you're doing is of eternal life-and-death importance. Nothing you're doing is more important than expending your soul on this kind of prayer and praying.

I like how one of my preaching heroes, Mario Murrello, defines revival: "Defeating the local demonic authorities by prayer." Or we could also say that revival is *enforcing* our dominion and authority in Christ because demons have been defeated through the cross and resurrection of Jesus the Christ. Matthew 12:28–29 (NKJV) states,

> *"But if I cast out demons by the Spirit of God, surely the*
> *kingdom of God has come upon you. Or how can one enter*
> *a strong man's house and plunder his goods, unless he first*
> *binds the strong man? Then he **will** plunder his house."*

Jesus was drawing us a picture of what he did to satan through His death, burial and resurrection. He completely plundered him. And to the Victor goes the spoil! And one way we apprehend the spoil is in prayer.

The Last Days

God longs to reveal end-time events to those of us who are His friends. When you set your heart toward the Lord, to seek Him and His will, prophetic things are set in motion that have been hidden in the mind of God from eternity past. Like certain vitamins and medications, these plans are time-released, and I believe the Holy Spirit is searching for people to network with and who will cooperate with Him in these last days. The prophet Daniel is an example of this kind of cooperation with God. Let's look at Daniel 10:11–14 (NKJV) *(emphasis mine)*.

> "And he said to me, "O Daniel, man greatly beloved, **understand** the words that I speak to you, and stand upright,

for I have now been sent to you." While he was speaking this word to me, I stood trembling. Then he said to me, "Do not fear, Daniel, for from the first day that you **set your heart** (You can set your heart today) to understand, and to **humble yourself** before your God, **your words were heard**; and I **have come because of your words**. But the prince of the kingdom of Persia withstood me twenty-one days; and behold, Michael, one of the chief princes, came to help me, for I had been left alone there with the kings of Persia. Now I have come to make you understand **what will happen** to your people in **the last days**, for the vision refers to many days yet to come..." (Perhaps those days have arrived.)

Jesus promised, in John 16:13, that the Holy Spirit would guide us into truth and show us things to come. But this doesn't happen by chance, it happens by intentionally humbling oneself and setting one's heart to understand The Architect of the universe and His holy plans. How can we fathom the Unfathomable? How can the finite comprehend the Infinite? Intentionally turn your heart towards God. He is no longer the "Unknown God" that cannot be discovered. "He has put Eternity in their hearts" (Ecclesiastes 3:11 NKJV). Our Heavenly Father longs to reveal Himself to His family! And Jesus made the way. In fact, He is The Way, The Truth, and The Life. He made us His joint heirs! Because we share His *position,* we also share His *possession*.

THE CITY SHAKING POWER OF PRAYER

A suffering city is the result of a weakened church. Rochester, NY was a den of debauchery and spiritual lethargy. But in September of 1830, revivalist, Charles G. Finney, saw somewhere around 100,000 souls swept into the Kingdom inside of a six-month period. When he came to preach in a pastor-less church, the Fire of God fell, and people were pierced in their souls by the conviction of the mighty Holy

Ghost. Bars became Bible studies. Influential, so-called powerful, people humbled themselves and publicly repented of their sins. They invited and brought their friends to church. (Oh, that the Saints would bring the lost to church today, and they could hear a pure Gospel sermon!) The crime-rate dropped so dramatically that the local police formed singing quartets, as there was little-to-no crime to be stopped. These church members labored for souls in prayer and wrestled for salvations! It bothered them that people they knew did not know Jesus. And God visited their city in such dramatic fashion that the very cultural fiber of it was transfigured by Heaven's Glory.

Could it happen again today? Could notorious sinners be slain by Love and resurrected as saints made in the likeness of Christ? Would the Fire of God fall on Earth in the likes that haven't been seen since Pentecost and the Book of Acts? Set your heart to praying and you shall know! How Heaven longs to invade Earth once again with the goodness of the Savior and the Power of The Spirit! We need prayer that births revival and releases the Kingdom of God into the Earth like the apostolic men of old. Not weak, wimpy prayers that are not convinced that God is Good, Heaven is real, and Hell is hot. We have to P.U.S.H.—Pray Until Something Happens. Where are the Elijah's that know how to call down fire from heaven upon altars of sacrifice? Where are the people who fear an eternal God more than the temporary pain of offering those sacrifices? Where is the Moses of today that will ascend the mountain to seek God's Glory and carry His Holy Commandments to the people? Where are the David's who will dance before Him and be a man after God's own heart and slay the giants of the epoch? Who will pray like the Prophet Isaiah, "Rend the heavens and come down?" Who can say like Jeremiah, the weeping prophet, "Your Word is like fire shut up in my bones!" Where are the sons and daughters of God, who, like Jesus will pray, "Not My will but Thine be done." You show me those praying people, and The Great Commission shall be accomplished and we will see the return of King Jesus in our lifetime! Let us be those people.

To Pray God's Word is to Pray God's Will

"To pray effectively you must pray in submission to the will of God."
—Charles G. Finney (Revivalist)

But to know the Will of God you must know the Word of God. And we have a generation that prefers social media over spiritual meditation. Many spend more time questioning the veracity of scripture than receiving it with meekness as the engrafted, living, eternal Word of Truth which is able to save one's soul. God forgive us! Honor God's Word as your chief priority and highest standard for living and He will honor your word when you speak. *Well, how can reading an ancient book have any application to my modern life?* It is not an "ancient book." It is an Eternal Book from outside of the bounds of time. And you do not read the Bible my friend; the Bible reads you! Make it first place in your life and it will transform every area of your life where you submit to it!

Believe It to Receive It

You must believe that an outpouring of God's Spirit is His will for your life. You must come to know that He wants to revive your soul, and your city. To know God's Word is to know God's Will. God expects us to play our part in this process. Do your part and God will do His. Go out weeping, bearing precious seed, and you will doubtless come home rejoicing, bring harvest with you. Pray in faith expecting God to answer. Why wouldn't He? We are praying out His Word and His Will into the Earth, not our own after all. He wants to pour out His Spirit upon Mankind more than we want Him to do so. We must live inside James 5:16 (NKJV) continually,

"Confess your trespasses to one another, and pray for one another, that you may be healed. The effective, fervent prayer of a righteous man avails much."

Here we see powerful praying and godly community working together. It reminds me of a quote by Rev. John Wesley,

> "I continue to dream and pray about a revival of holiness in our day that moves forth in mission and creates authentic community in which each person can be unleashed through the empowerment of the Spirit to fulfill God's creational intentions."

Esther 4:1 (NKJV) speaks of a man of passionate prayer,

> *"When Mordecai learned all that had happened, he tore his clothes and put on sackcloth and ashes, and went out into the midst of the city. He cried out with a loud and bitter cry."*

Mordecai prayed an agonizing prayer to His God. He wasn't afraid to fill His prayers with faith... expectancy... and to couch them with his passion. Travailing praying has passed out of vogue in the modern church, but it will return to fashion in these final hours of the Age of Grace. Let's look at Joel 2:12–14 (NKJV),

> *"Now, therefore," says the Lord, "Turn to Me with all your heart, with fasting, with weeping, and with mourning. So rend your heart, and not your garments; Return to the Lord your God, For He is gracious and merciful, Slow to anger, and of great kindness; and He relents from doing harm. Who knows if He will turn and relent, and leave a blessing behind Him."*

What do you think the "blessing" is that God leaves behind Him? It is His Glorious Presence that changes everything and everyone it touches. It must be what we call revival! Let's rend out hearts I prayer and find out! I am not willing to live without it anymore.

The Holy Spirit still falls on hungry humanity; let Him fall on us today! Rend the heavens and come down, Lord! Don't stay up there;

come down here! Some religious people argue, "But the Holy Spirit has already fallen on the Day of Pentecost. Now He lives inside of us." Be that as it may, some say this to justify their own lack of ardor, zeal, and spiritual hunger. In Acts 8:16, a multitude had received The Word of God and been born again, but speaking of the Holy Spirit it says,

"For as yet He had fallen upon none of them."

But He soon did. And they were all filled with the Spirit when hands were laid upon them. And the mighty Holy Ghost of God will fall on us too, if we will receive Him. He still answers those who call unto Him.

When God Comes

What is revival? One of my favorite definitions is simply, "when God comes." Do you need Him to come into your life? If you've wrecked it, He can fix it. Do you need Him to come to your family? If it's broken, He can mend it. Do you need Him to come to your parched soul, withered marriage or ineffective ministry? When He comes, He brings dead things back to life. What is revival? It is when the Fire Falls! It is when God comes, not in His Omnipresence, but in His Manifest Presence!

Cancel Culture

Would you believe that part of our job as Christ-followers, our mandate even, as the church, is to counterbalance the culture that's been trying to kick Christ out? It's a part of the "cancel culture" agenda: kick churches and ministers of the Good News off social media platforms and close down their ministries. So how do we counteract cancel culture? By lifting our united voice and crying out for Him to come. By crying out, "God, pour out Your Spirit on our sons and daughters! We repent for the sins of our nation. We repent of our own sin! And we fall on our face asking for mercy… for revival and awakening!" You Can't Cancel Christ. And you can't cancel a church that prays.

So, will we agonize in prayer for the lostness of our city, and the darkness in the core of our modern culture? The old-timers used to groan in the spirit for the lost souls of their day. It bothered them that people were entering into a Christ-less eternity. May it bother us too! Make a list of people you know are without Christ and set your soul to praying for their encounter with The King. And may it be on Earth as it is in Heaven: a Christ-Culture instead of this Cancel-Culture. I realize not everyone is going to call on the Name of the Lord and be saved. But on our watch, let us lift our hearts and voices to God in intercession for the lost souls of our day. And may God grant us clemency and show His glory to this generation, that as many as will come to Him would do just that. Let us plunder hell and populate heaven with molten hot prayers that penetrate the darkness of our day. And let's make it hard to go to hell from our town.

THE GOLDEN TRIANGLE

How are you doing with the internal formation of your spiritual discipline? Are you investing time to pray, reading the scriptures, fellowshipping in a small group with other believers, giving generously into the work of God, enjoying a weekly sabbath, and investing into your marriage? The late Theologian, Dallas Willard, in his book, *The Great Omission*, describes what he calls the "Golden Triangle" of Christianity. One side is the fruit of the spirit, the other is the gifts of the spirit, but the foundation is spiritual disciplines. God forbid that our giftings take us where our character cannot keep and sustain us.

HOW'S YOUR FOUNDATION?

Recently the Lord spoke to my heart, "*The more you grow in the fruit of the spirit, the more you will flow in the gifts of the spirit.*" How can one grow in these spiritual fruits? By tending to your foundation. By getting back to the basics of feeding daily on God's Word, practicing prayer and fasting, choosing godly friends, taking time off to rest, and being a generous giver.

Check your foundation. We all need regular maintenance and checkups. Get before God and examine your heart... better yet, let Him examine it. If He wants any adjustments, He has many, kind and loving ways of letting us know just that. And this helps to us avoid the trap of self-condemnation and self-criticism. It's easy to find our dirt. Let our loving heavenly Father help us find our gold. That happens when we keep the right company: Him and the right "them".

SPECIAL FORCES UNIT

Take up the mandate of prayer. Prayer is not for sissies or just for women. Pray-ers are God's Special Forces. Our Commander and Chief is recruiting you to join the unit. I am here to **bestow this mandate** upon you as you read these pages. Take up the mandate. You won't be disappointed. Lift your voice today and cry out to God for an out-pouring of His Spirit. No longer are you a person who prays from time to time. You are now a pray-er!

Welcome to the frontline.

*"If My people...will humble themselves and **pray**..."*

QUESTIONS FOR SMALL GROUPS AND PERSONAL REFLECTION:

1. If revival is not the Church responding to God pouring out His Spirit but God responding to His Church pouring out her spirit, has your church poured its spirit out to God in prayer? Have you?

2. "If you aim at nothing you will hit it every time." Our prayer needs a target. What exactly are we praying for? Why? What do we expect it to look like when it comes?

3. Is dominion praying a part of your revival-praying? Are you exercising your authority in Christ over the defeated foes of darkness? Describe your experiences in this area or what questions you may have about this kind of praying?

4. Like God revealed to Daniel things to come, what "things to come" has the Holy Spirit been showing you? Discuss.

5. Could it happen again today? Could notorious sinners be slain by Love and resurrected as saints made in the likeness of Christ? Would the Fire of God fall on Earth again like the Day of Pentecost and the Book of Acts? Are we really expecting it?

6. Does it bother you that people were entering into a Christ-less eternity? Make a list of people you know are without Christ and set your soul to praying for their encounter with The King. Make a "holy hit list" of people. Write down their names. Pray now.

7. Evaluate your foundation. The author mentioned prayer, scripture reading, fellowshipping with other believers, giving generously into the work of God, a weekly sabbath, and investing into your marriage and family. How is your "foundation"? Take a moment in the presence of the Lord to evaluate these vital areas of your life.

STEP FIVE: FOCUS
...AND SEEK MY FACE...

The scene is an upper-room above the streets of Jerusalem. The day was Pentecost: fifty days after Passover. The gathering was kosher: perhaps ten representatives from each of the twelve tribes. They were together for a specific purpose, and they would not be denied. Their Savior-King and Lord, after plundering the dark caverns of Hell, was lifted back to life by His Father, God, and now issued the decree to

"tarry in Jerusalem until you are endued with power from on high." Luke 24:49 (NKJV)

And when it happened it was sudden! The wind blew; The Fire fell. They were all filled with the Spirit and spoke in tongues as the Spirit gave them the heavenly words they were to utter. Then, like a torrent of white, hot lava from a volcanic eruption, these brand-new believers poured out of that same upper room and stunned the diverse crowd of thousands who were milling around below in the dusty streets of that holy city. The message of repentance and salvation through Jesus was preached by Peter, and it was almost too good to be true! Every person heard it in his own language, spoken by those who could not possibly know it. Ethnic diversity is a hallmark of a genuine outpouring of God's Spirit. And we shall see it again in the Body of Christ before the catching away of His church, composed of "every tribe, tongue, people and nation" (Revelation 5:9 NKJV).

It's a small wonder that 3000 men (perhaps well over 10,000 new believers) were added to their number within minutes of the miracle. They had spiritually reached the boiling point. The infant church of the Lord Jesus Christ had been seeking the Face of their King, and something akin to a nuclear chain reaction was set off in the spirit realm. Now it was spilling out into the streets! Whenever we seek His Face in our upper room, His power and Presence will be flowing in our streets too.

America needs to spiritually see this again. The nations of the earth must experience it too. The question isn't God's power; the question is: will anyone seek His face? He is the same yesterday, today and forever (Hebrews 13:8 NKJV). We are the variable in this equation. Can we, the church, renounce pride and face the fact that we have built, in many cases, Christian corporations we call mega-churches that lack the power of Pentecost that has failed to heal our land? If it lacks New Testament, soul-winning, miracle-working power, it may be "mega," but it is not "church." I am not against good business practices or "mega-churches," (I want the churches I lead to grow) but I am longing for the "glorious church" that Jesus said He was returning for.

FACE VALUE

> *"...the mystery which has been hidden from ages and from generations, but now has been revealed to His saints. [27] To them God willed to make known what are the riches of the glory of this mystery among the Nations: which is Christ in you, the hope of glory." Colossians 1:26–27 (NKJV)*

There's something in you that your city needs. Your community needs it. It's the burden removing, yoke destroying, power of God: Christ, in you, is the hope of glory. It is why God coaches us to seek His face, perhaps. Faces tell us a lot. If the eyes are the window of the soul, then the face is like an LED screen.

Seek means to search out by any method, but in this case, specifically in worship and prayer. It means to ask, beg, desire, make request: require! Moses did, as we can witness in Exodus 33:10–20 (NKJV).

> *"All the people saw the pillar of cloud standing at the tabernacle door, and all the people rose and worshiped, each man in his tent door. So the Lord spoke to Moses face to face, as a man speaks to his friend. And he would return to the camp, but his servant Joshua the son of Nun, a young*

man, did not depart from the tabernacle. Then Moses said to the Lord, "You say to me, 'Bring up this people.' But You have not let me know whom You will send with me. Yet You have said, 'I know you by name, and you have also found grace in My sight.' Now therefore, I pray, if I have found grace in Your sight, show me now Your ways, that I may know You and that I may find grace in Your sight. And consider that this nation is Your people." And He said, "My Presence will go with you, and I will give you rest." Then he said to Him, "If Your Presence does not go with us, do not bring us up from here. For how then will it be known that Your people and I have found grace in Your sight, except You go with us? So we shall be separate, Your people and I, from all the people who are upon the face of the earth." So the Lord said to Moses, "I will also do this thing that you have spoken; for you have found grace in My sight, and I know you by name." And he said, "Please, show me Your glory." Then He said, "I will make all My goodness pass before you, and I will proclaim the name of the Lord before you. I will be gracious to whom I will be gracious, and I will have compassion on whom I will have compassion." But He said, "You cannot see My face; for no man shall see Me, and live."

I heard a story once about a scarred, little child who crawled into bed with his dad and groped his dad's face: "It's dark and I'm scarred. I just wanted to make sure your face was looking at me."

There's something about having the face of the one you love turned toward you. When God sent Jesus, He turned His face towards us.

His Presence is the Reward

"By faith Enoch was taken away so that he did not see death, 'and was not found, because God had taken him';

*for before he was taken he had this testimony, that he
pleased God. But without faith it is impossible to please
Him, for he who comes to God must believe that He is, and
that He is a rewarder of those who diligently seek Him."*
Hebrews 11:5–6 (NKJV)

Enoch was the seventh from Adam. In other words, Adam was
Enoch's great grandfather to the seventh power. Can you imagine the
stories little Enoch would beg his great granddaddy to disclose to
him! Enoch was especially fond of the garden variety stories, when
God walked with his great grandparents "in the cool of the day."

Perhaps young Enoch would inquire, "Where is God now? I want
to walk with Him and talk with Him like you did. Where did He go?
What happened?"

To which Grandpa Adam would explain, "Well, your grand-
mother… ate us out of house and home! Now we have to wear these
fur coats and God never comes to visit anymore."

But a hunger for God and His Presence grew inside of young
Enoch. And there came a day, when he was sixty-five years old, that
Enoch began to reach out to God with his spirit. Enoch tapped into
the powers of an age yet to come! He began to walk with God for 300
years, and he did it by faith. This pleased the Lord.

In fact, God liked it so much that, one day, He said something
like this (perhaps), "Enoch, we are a lot closer to My house than
yours. Why don't you just come on home with Me?"

And so, he did. Check out Genesis 5:24. And one day very soon,
all those who walk with God, like Enoch did, will also "be taken."

PRESENTS OR PRESENCE?

I used to travel a lot, earlier in my ministry. And the Lord has revealed
to me that I will travel again later in my ministry. But anyway, as a
young father, I would bring gifts home to my two precious sons that
are two of my best friends. They are grown men now. And I still think
they are amazing.

But when they were little, I'd get a hug, then, before my bags hit the ground, "What did you bring me, Papa?"

But the older they got, the less my *presents* mattered and the more my *presence* mattered. In fact, the reason I slowed my traveling ministry down was because my family needed my presence. What was in my hand became less important than the touch of my hand. The giver has become more valuable than the gift as our relationship has developed over the years. Like any normal parent, I still love to bless my boys with *presents*, but nothing replaces *presence*.

SHOW US YOUR GLORY

There are some things within us that must be released. God's Presence. His Love. His Power. Our prayers must break through the greatest obstacles to revival. We must seek His Face. From God's perspective, seeking His face is the same as seeking His glory. Moses asked to see the Face of God in Exodus 33:18–23 (NKJV).

> *"And he said, 'Please, show me Your glory.' Then He said, 'I will make all My goodness pass before you, and I will proclaim the name of the Lord before you. I will be gracious to whom I will be gracious, and I will have compassion on whom I will have compassion.' But He said, 'You cannot see My Face; for no man shall see Me, and live.'*
> [That's why Jesus died so we can see His face again!]
> *And the Lord said, 'Here is a place by Me, and you shall stand on The Rock. So it shall be, while My glory passes by, I will put you in the cleft of The Rock and will cover you with My hand while I pass by. Then I will take away My hand, and you shall see My back; but My face shall not be seen.'"*

In Step 4—we are *praying*; but in Step 5—we are asking to be inundated with the rays of God's glory that radiate from His Face and break hard hearts and mend broken ones. Heaven starts to look our way, so to speak. The nature of the revival-praying-core that you gathered in the beginning changes. It is has come to the boiling point. This is why the number "212" is my favorite number. At 211 degrees, water is just really hot. But one more degree, and it's boiling! Too many people stop one degree shy of erupting into a holy boil! Only the glory of God will bring our revival-core to the desired temperature. Settle it in your heart. God warned Moses, that if he saw His Face, it would mean certain death, so our exposure to God's glory will mean the death of our pride, lust, anger, prejudices, selfishness and fear. It will shatter the barrier. It will bring revival!

VACCINATED OR UNVACCINATED

Much of the church in America has been inoculated with a small dose of Christianity perhaps to ensure they won't catch a full-blown case. But an unprecedented outpouring of God's Spirit is coming that will shake our sleeping land. An awakening of genuine, infectious faith will soon ignite in the heart of Christ's Bride and erupt in holy fear and the fires of evangelism and personal devotion to Christ. The only immunity we will have will then be towards religion and our own agenda. **Before He comes in His Glory, His Glory is coming!** And all of humanity will be without excuse on judgment day, for

> *"the glory of the Lord shall be revealed and all flesh will*
> *see it together, for the mouth of the Lord has spoken."*
> *Isaiah 40:5 (NKJV)*

A NEW BREED

My spiritual grandfather is Dr. Kenneth E. Hagin (aka: Dad Hagin). He prophesied of a "new breed" coming on the scene in the last days. And a new breed of believer is arising that will set fire to the dry grass of religion and command life into the dead bones of small thinking believers. It isn't sufficient to simply be polite or nice. This is a call to become the army that God needs to convict the conscience of nations, become the dread of demons, and a supernatural river of life for the total gamut of humanity's need. Only the manifest goodness of God will do that. Revival includes a sudden bursting forth of God's tangible power that is undeniable. The power that is already in us overwhelms the gates of hell. Satanic hordes flee in terror before the tsunami of God in Christ's earthly body, the church. Nothing travels as fast as The Light and nothing penetrates the conscience like righteousness. To seek His Face and live in His Presence is worth everything. Whatever the cost, revival is worth it, because His Presence is our present. We must be willing to die for it; not only physically, if need be, but die to our carnal desires and man-made agendas. The price for Moses to see God's face? "No man can see My Face and live." The price of your revival? Your life! Will you "Pray the Price" and seek His Face?

QUESTIONS FOR SMALL GROUPS AND PERSONAL REFLECTION:

1. Do you prefer God's presence over His presents? Explain. Describe your time of devotion set aside for seeking His face.

2. How did it make you feel when reading about seeing God's face means certain death? What are the top 3 things that need to die in your life?

3. Before Jesus comes in His glory, His glory is coming! How do you think this will impact unbelievers in our society? How will it affect the church? How will it affect you?

4. Will you "pray the price" for revival? Why or why not?

STEP SIX: UNTWISTED
"AND TURN FROM THEIR WICKED WAYS..."

"Her Mind is Definitely Twisted..." Can you hear the old Eagles band singing those lyrics in your mind? The story-song is an accurate depiction of life without Christ for many: bondage. And many well-meaning, Christians have "checked in" to what they thought would be a life of luxury and pleasure to find that they had checked into a prison of their own making. But I'd like to show you The Way out.

I want to turn now to the concept that this book has really focused on: being set free from wicked, twisted ways, whether inherited, adopted or perpetrated upon you. It is no coincidence that the phrase *"and turn from their wicked ways..."* is embedded into the scripture that reveals Heaven's recipe for an outpouring on Earth. It is our outline for personal, as well as corporate, revival.

LOST AND FOUND

Some argue, "Mankind is so depraved he would never seek God."

And that is true. We were all lost, and without hope. But God so loved the whole world, that He sent Jesus to "seek and save the lost." Luke 19:10 (NKJV) Well, that's everyone. He is seeking all of us. And He has done everything in His power to make a way of escape for all people so that the lost can be found. The apostle, Paul, chose his words carefully in relation to our opportunity to seek God, saying, "...therefore I persuade men..." (2 Corinthians 5:11 NKJV) and "...we implore you, be reconciled to God..." (2 Corinthians 5:20 NKJV). In this Age of Grace, God is at work, to influence the will of men to choose His Son, Jesus. In like manner, by God's grace, you can choose freedom from your twisted ways. Whosoever *will* let him come!

OUT WITH THE OLD; IN WITH THE NEW

Let's move on with our phrase by phrase study of 2 Chronicles 7:14. We have covered six out of nine phases prescribed in the text for an awakening, but let's refresh ourselves with the entire verse once again:

> *"If My people who are called by My name will humble themselves, and pray and seek My face, and turn from their wicked ways, then I will hear from heaven, and will forgive their sin and heal their land."*

In many cases people are too full of themselves to be filled with anything else. We have no shortage of churches, but we do have a shortage of the outpouring of the Spirit of God in and through our churches. We do have a shortage of Christ-followers that are practicing the spiritual disciplines that builds a strong foundation on the Rock of Jesus.

> *"We have consolable and inconsolable longings."*
> — **C.S. Lewis**

We cry over our sin, but not the place we've given it in our lives. How many come to Jesus because of guilt, but not because it helps us love and honor Him more? Do we come for healing because we don't like to hurt or because it honors God and makes Him look good? Do we come for safety, wanting to be secure, or because we want to demonstrate the preeminence of Christ? Do we come for prosperity, because we love money and comfort, or because we want to build Christ's Kingdom and be a blessing? Do we come to Jesus because we don't want to go to hell (it's a good start). Or because our hearts know He, alone, deserves our worship and obedience? Let us cry for eternity because we cannot be nourished any longer by temporary things. May we stop seeking *them* and instead seek *Him*. Perhaps now is the perfect time to pray aloud, "Jesus, I repent for seeking first anything other than You!"

DISTANCE FROM GOD CREATES PAIN

Many of us have constructed our faith around the benefits we get from it. Thank God for those benefits and it's better than being ignorant of all Christ has procured for us. However, too often "us" is at the center, instead of Christ. We "use God" to make life better for us. Please know that He came to make life abundant for us but stopping there is stopping far short of His ultimate intention. Let us not allow the *benefits* to become *entitlements*. Same blessings; different mentality. Press into Him. Remember that "i" is always at the center of pride. Hosea 7:13–14 (NKJV) remind us,

> *"Woe to them, for they have fled from Me. Destruction to them, because they have transgressed against Me! Though I redeemed them, yet they have spoken lies against Me. They did not cry out to Me with their heart when they wailed upon their beds. They assemble together for grain and new wine, but they rebel against Me..."*

DARK NIGHT OF THE SOUL

This section, "Dark Night of the Soul", is inspired by one of my preaching heroes, Reverend Mario Murrillo and his 1985 book entitled, *Critical Mass*. I read the small book as a senior in high school in 1988. I sat in the public library in Jackson, Mississippi and created preaching outlines from the content. I not only recommend you read the book, but shamelessly plagiarize his brilliant writings in this section as an invitation and contribution to personal, generational, sustained revival. Brother Mario writes,

> "Right before an atom splits and the nuclear chain-reaction is set in unstoppable motion, the nucleus actually depresses. Scientists observe that the neutron bombardment, which seemed to be changing the nucleus, now shows no sign of reaching critical mass; nothing seems to be happening. That is what seems to be happening right before a manifestation of God's glory too. The revival core we mentioned earlier will be praying and sensing a rising tide of power and expectancy. All of the sudden, you hit a brick wall. The

power is gone. God's presence seems to have lifted. Your prayers feel trapped in your mouth. A deep despair settles in. You feel physically drained. **The Dark Night of the Soul has begun.** Every revival pioneer has been here before and now it's you! It will take everything within you to keep moving. Do Not Retreat! Why does this happen? The person God uses to bring revival receives praise from man and attacks from Satan. A person lacking humility won't survive the praise of man; and without perseverance won't overcome Satan. Stand the Test. How? Turn up the prayer. If you don't go by what you see or feel, God will know He can trust you with revival. In the heat of battle, you will not rely on circumstances or feelings to keep you on a straight course. By this step, you would think God would know we have abandoned sin. The issue, however, is something deeper; it deals with our *ways*. Our repentance has dealt with what we have done, now the purification focuses on what we are."

Psalm 103:7 says,

"He made known His ways to Moses, His acts to the children of Israel."

"We must understand the essence, heartbeat, and direction of God: His ways. To turn from our wicked ways doesn't only mean we need to repent of our sins. Hitherto, we have repented of our acts; now we need deliverance from our ways. The dark night of the soul is a very baffling test, for it comes at the least expected time and with special conditions. The inner man must be surprised, caught off guard, in order to be exposed and conquered. For Example: (1) So, on the mountain top Elijah calls down fire, but then he battles depression in the cave. (2) Joseph had glorious dreams – then he's in a pit and sold as a slave to Potiphar. (3) David hears, 'Saul has slain his thousands and David his ten-thou-sands!' Then he wakes up in a cave being hunted like an animal. (4) Jesus, Hosannas still ringing in his ears, then alone, cold, sweating drops of blood, praying around eleven, sleeping disciples. The battlements of heaven are waiting for that unmistakable ring of genuine obedience where the dragon of human nature has been met and beheaded. *'Not my will but Thy will be done!'* The cup cannot pass. In re-penting of sin, we rid ourselves of evil, but when we turn from our wicked ways, we surrender the things we dearly love... things we can't readily identify as being in conflict with God. The issue is not right and wrong, but high and low purpose of living. **Spiritual awakening is not simply get-ting rid of sin; it is giving God what He wants.** We must pour ourselves out to God as a living sacrifice."

And to finish up,

> *"Spiritual awakening means that the faithful become fiery, the decent become dynamic, and the acceptable become excellent. But, most of all, we become disgusted with our evil, and totally dissatisfied with our good."*
> —Reverend Mario Murrillo

Do you see why this guy is one of my preaching heroes? Wow! The old saying rings true here, "If that doesn't light your fire, then your wood is wet!"

FRIENDS IN HIGH PLACES

Let's look at Exodus 34:1–35 (NKJV).

And the Lord said to Moses, "Cut two tablets of stone like the first ones, and I will write on these tablets the words that were on the first tablets which you broke. So be ready in the morning, and come up in the morning to Mount Sinai, and present yourself to Me there on the top of the mountain. And

221

*no man shall come up with you, and let no man be seen throughout all the mountain; let neither flocks nor herds feed before that mountain." So he cut two tablets of stone like the first. Then Moses rose early in the morning and went up Mount Sinai, as the Lord had commanded him; and he took in his hand the two tablets of stone. Now the Lord descended in the cloud and stood with him there, and proclaimed the name of the Lord. And the Lord passed before him and proclaimed, "The Lord, the Lord God, merciful and gracious, long-suffering, and abounding in goodness and truth, keeping mercy for thousands, forgiving **iniquity** and **transgression** and **sin**, by no means clearing the guilty, visiting the iniquity of the fathers upon the children and the children's children to the third and the fourth generation." So Moses made haste and bowed his head toward the earth, and worshiped. Then he said, "If now I have found grace in Your sight, O Lord, let my Lord, I pray, go among us, even though we are a stiff-necked people; and pardon our iniquity and our sin, and take us as Your inheritance." And He said: "Behold, I make a covenant. Before all your people I will do marvels such as have not been done in all the earth, nor in any nation; and all the people among whom you are shall see the work of the Lord. For it is an awesome thing that I will do with you. Observe what I command you this day. Behold, I am driving out from before you the Amorite and the Canaanite and the Hittite and the Perizzite and the Hivite and the Jebusite.* [No mention of the cellulite or termites: Sorry.] *Take heed to yourself, lest you make a covenant with the inhabitants of the land where you are going, lest it be a snare in your midst. But you shall destroy their altars, break their sacred pillars, and cut down their wooden images (for you shall worship no other god, for the Lord, whose name is Jealous, is a jealous God), lest you make a covenant with the inhabitants of the land, and they*

222

play the harlot with their gods and make sacrifice to their gods, and one of them invites you and you eat of his sacrifice, and you take of his daughters for your sons, and his daughters play the harlot with their gods and make your sons play the harlot with their gods. You shall make no molded gods for yourselves. **The Feast of Unleavened Bread** *you shall keep.* [This feast represents Freedom from Sin and Sickness: Get Free!] *Seven days you shall eat unleavened bread, as I commanded you, in the appointed time of the month of Abib; for in the month of Abib you came out from Egypt All that open the womb are Mine, and every male firstborn among your livestock, whether ox or sheep. But the firstborn of a* **donkey** *you shall redeem with a* **lamb**. [Jesus is The Lamb that redeemed a donkey like me.] *And if you will not redeem him, then you shall break his neck. All the firstborn of your sons you shall redeem. And none shall appear before Me empty-handed. Six days you shall work, but on the seventh day you shall rest; in plowing time and in harvest you shall rest. And you shall observe* **the Feast of Weeks** *of the firstfruits of wheat harvest* [This feast represents the Baptism of the Holy Spirit: Get Filled with the Holy Ghost!], *and the Feast of Ingathering or Tabernacles at the year's end* [This feast represents The Catching Away of the Church and GOD Tabernacling with His People]. *Three times in the year all your men shall appear before the Lord, the Lord God of Israel. For I will cast out the nations before you and enlarge your borders; neither will any man covet your land when you go up to appear before the Lord your God three times in the year. You shall not offer the blood of My sacrifice with leaven, nor shall the sacrifice of* **the Feast of the Passover** *be left until morning.* [This feast represents Redemption: Get Saved!] *The first of the firstfruits of your land you shall bring to the house of the Lord your God. You shall not boil a young goat in its mother's* *milk." Then the Lord said to Moses, "Write these words, for according to the tenor of these words I have made a covenant with you and with Israel." So he was there with the Lord forty days and forty nights; he neither ate bread nor drank water. And He wrote on the tablets the words of the covenant, the Ten Commandments. Now it was so, when Moses came down from Mount Sinai (and the two tablets of the Testimony were in Moses' hand when he came down from the mountain), that Moses did not know that the skin of his face shone while he talked with Him. So when Aaron and all the children of Israel saw Moses, behold, the skin of his face shone, and they were afraid to come near him. Then Moses called to them, and Aaron and all the rulers of the congregation returned to him; and Moses talked with them. Afterward all the children of Israel came near, and he gave them as commandments all that the Lord had spoken with him on Mount Sinai. And when Moses had finished speaking with them, he put a veil on his face. But whenever Moses went in before the Lord to speak with Him, he would take the veil off until he came out; and he would come out and speak to the children of Israel whatever he had been commanded. And whenever the children of Israel saw the face of Moses, that the skin of Moses' face shone, then Moses would put the veil on his face again, until he went in to speak with Him.*

Moses had spent so much quality time in the Presence of God that his face radiated with the glory of God! I desire to pastor a church, not where my faces glows, but where everyone's face shines! After all, Jesus is coming for a glorious church! So let us "turn from our wicked ways" and be healed of our generational "bents" by looking into the Face of Jesus in prayer and in the mirror of His Word. We become what we behold!

GO ON UP THE MOUNTAIN

It is necessary to take a look at 2 Corinthians 3:18 (NKJV).

> *"But even to this day, when Moses is read, a veil lies on their heart. Nevertheless, when one turns to the Lord, the veil is taken away. Now the Lord is the Spirit; and where the Spirit of the Lord is, there is liberty. But we all, with unveiled face, beholding as in a mirror the glory of the Lord, are being transformed into the same image from glory to glory, just as by the Spirit of the Lord."*

Has your veil been removed? Whatever "veil" you struggle with is taken away when you turn to Jesus! Let us consider our ways. Not just merely repenting of our misdeeds, but even surrendering to God the things we cherish. Is there someone or something in your life that brings you more satisfaction than Jesus? Fire falls on sacrifice. Not tokens. Offer it up to Him.

Like Moses was, are you ready to exchange low level living for living with God on a higher plain? After all, that is what Jesus came to make available to us, and this is what pleases God. So go on up the mountain of God's Presence. Let Him write His commands upon the tablets of your heart, and you too will shine! You have "Friends in high places."

QUESTIONS FOR SMALL GROUPS AND PERSONAL REFLECTION:

1. Jesus came to "seek and save the lost." Has He found you? Is Jesus your Lord? Describe your salvation experience. Is your mind still twisted in some way where you want the Lord to help you? If so explain. Will you allow Him to free you?

2. Is there anyone or anything that has become more important to you than Jesus? If so who or what? Discuss then take a moment to pray, "Jesus, I repent for seeking first anything other than You."

3. Spiritual awakening is not simply getting rid of sin; it is giving God what He wants. What do you think God wants from you, right now?

4. Is there someone or something in your life that brings you more satisfaction than Jesus? Fire falls on sacrifice. Not tokens. What would offering that up to God look like?

5. You have "Friends in high places." What one adjustment could you make that would enable you to have more time "on the mountain of God's presence?"

Step Seven: Heaven Responds
"...Then I Will Hear From Heaven..."

His "then" is predicated on your "if." God will never do for you what you can do for yourself. Conversely, never try to do for yourself what only God can do. When we do our part, THEN happens. Then God does His part. And that is the part only He can do.

With revival manifestation there comes a radius of the glory of God that reverses the works of darkness for all who enter into it. I've been praying for years that, within a fifty-mile radius, our local church, would be a "darkness-free zone." No disease, death, darkness, divorce, depression, addiction, or any such demonic thing that satan commonly uses to oppress humanity. But it has dawned on me that if we won't take responsibility for the one-mile radius around our church, and take action in that same realm, how can God do anything good there since He only works through people? We have to work with His Word in Acts 10:38 (NKJV),

"How God anointed Jesus of Nazareth, with the Holy Spirit and power, who went about doing good and healing all that were oppressed by the devil, for God was with Him."

"God's Sovereignty is when He does more than He promised He would."
—*Reverend Christopher Alam (Missionary/Evangelist)*

Prayers Build Monuments Before God

"There was a certain man in Caesarea called Cornelius, a centurion of what was called the Italian Regiment, a devout man and one who feared God with all his household, who gave alms generously to the people, and prayed to God always. About the ninth hour of the day he saw clearly in a vision an angel of God coming in and saying to him, 'Cornelius!' And when he observed him, he was afraid,

and said, 'What is it, lord?' So he said to him, 'Your pray-
ers and your alms have come up for a memorial before
God. Now send men to Joppa, and send for Simon whose
surname is Peter. He is lodging with Simon, a tanner,
whose house is by the sea. He will tell you what you must
do.' And when the angel who spoke to him had departed,
Cornelius called two of his household servants and a de-
vout soldier from among those who waited on him continu-
ally. So when he had explained all these things to them, he
sent them to Joppa." Acts 10:1–9 (NKJV)

Because this man honored God with his offerings of prayers and finances, it built a monument before God. And the Lord sent His angels
to make sure His ministers got the message to go and bring the life-
changing Gospel to Cornelius. God's ear is tuned to prayer. He is the
God who hears.

Never doubt that God is listening. Here are three verses that cor-
relate this truth.

"Call to Me, and I will answer you, and show you great
and mighty things, which you do not know."
Jeremiah 33:3 (NKJV)

"I cried to the Lord with my voice, And He heard me from
His holy hill. Selah" Psalm 3:4 (NKJV)

"I waited patiently for the Lord; and He inclined to me,
and heard my cry. He also brought me up out of a horrible
pit, Out of the miry clay, and set my feet upon a rock, and
established my steps. He has put a new song in my
mouth—Praise to our God; Many will see it and fear, and
will trust in the Lord. Blessed is that man who makes the
Lord his trust." Psalm 40:1–4 (NKJV)

WHEN GOD HEARS HE RESPONDS

The church doesn't have to be subject to the things that will come upon the world. For instance, Israel was safe in Goshen when the plagues hit Egypt. God is going to make a distinction between the world and His Bride. (The praying-church is establishing cities of refuge right now, at the time of this writing.) But Heaven cannot respond if we do not call. And when God does hear from heaven, it will be evident. We have to live in a different dimension: "Seek His Face **Then**…"

Psalm 91:3–4 (paraphrase) commands, "…do NOT be afraid of the terror and pestilence and destruction… I WILL deliver you from the snare of the *fowler*…" Fowlers are people who catch birds (and sometimes bats). But deliverance is how Heaven responds when it hears us. When we pray according to God's Will, He hears us, and the works of darkness are repelled and reversed.

A SNAKE IN THE POWERHOUSE

My pastor used to tell a story of a city-wide blackout that was caused because a maintenance man left the door of the power facility open, and a snake slithered in. It caused a great disturbance at the power plant. People were running, tripping, and trying to hit the snake. During the reptile chase, they damaged equipment and eventually the whole city temporarily lost power. We have to be intentional and discerning about what we allow in our life or our "powerhouse." You can be in church, but also be in sin. This negates your protection-plan, and a spiritual blackout is sure to ensue. Is there a snake in your powerhouse? 1 Corinthians 11:27–32 (NIV) says,

> *"So then, whoever eats the bread or drinks the cup of the Lord in an unworthy manner will be guilty of sinning against the body and blood of the Lord. Everyone ought to examine themselves before they eat of the bread and drink from the cup. For those who eat and drink without discerning the body of Christ eat and drink judgment on themselves.*

That is why many among you are weak and sick, and a num-ber of you have fallen asleep [die prematurely]. *But if we were more discerning with regard to ourselves, we would not come under such judgment. Nevertheless, when we are judged in this way by the Lord, we are being disciplined so that we will not be finally condemned with the world."*

PROTECTION IS NOT AUTOMATIC

Your "Goshen" alignment in the Body of Christ is not an automatic benefit. The Prophet Haggai said, "You don't think it's time to build My house… but it is! Consider your ways." Haggai 1:2–4, (my paraphrase) So let's be about it. That brings to mind a quote from one of my Bible College professors, the late Reverend Cooper Beaty, "If God can get it through ya, He will get it to ya." And with that in mind, let me go ahead and prophecy to you: There is an economic reset happening in these last days. Why? Because Jesus will build His church and He will have His harvest! So don't lay up for yourself treasure in the last days. Do like my wife says, "Spread the Happy." You can't take it with you, but you can send it on ahead. And there's plenty to use and enjoy while you do His Will.

It seems to me, that whenever God transitions His people from one dispensation to another, He always heals them and enriches them. Take Psalm 105:37 (NKJV) for example. It describes the time when God was transitioning His people from Egypt (slavery) to the Wilderness (a level of freedom),

"He brought them out with silver and gold and there was none feeble among His tribes."

This is part of God hearing from heaven, it seems.

AN ANGEL OF AWAKENING

Here's a great example of how God arouses His people. Let's look at Zechariah 4:1–7 (NKJV).

*Now the angel who talked with me came back and wakened
me, as a man who is wakened out of his sleep.*

**[An awakening angel? It seems at times God sends cer-
tain angels to wake people up. Awakening is Coming!]**

*And he said to me, "What do you see?" So I said, "I am
looking, and there is a lamp-stand of solid gold with a
bowl on top of it, and on the stand seven lamps with seven
pipes to the seven lamps. Two olive trees are by it, one at
the right of the bowl and the other at its left." So I answered and spoke to the angel who talked with me, saying,
"What are these, my lord?" Then the angel who talked
with me answered and said to me, "Do you not know what
these are?" And I said, "No, my lord." So he answered
and said to me: "This is the word of the Lord to Zerubbabel: 'Not by might nor by power, but by My Spirit,' Says
the Lord of hosts. 'Who are you, O great mountain? Before
Zerubbabel you shall become a plain! And he shall bring
forth the capstone with shouts of "Grace, grace to it!"'*

This is a picture of God awakening His prophetic voices to release
some things, by speaking them into existence. The two different "olive trees" are perhaps, among other things, a picture of the House of
God and the House of Government working together for a season before the coming of the Lord. To what end? Harvest, of course. Souls
being invited into the Kingdom of God by the Grace of God. It's always about people standing with God, isn't it? Grace is a steady current of God's divine ability flowing into us to do both God's Will and
God's Work. Or perhaps the two Olive Trees represent man's methods and systems of building the church, but God says, "It's going to
be a move of My Spirit: Grace, grace!" As God's people we must
cooperate with it, but we cannot take credit for it. But whatever the
two Olive Trees are, God will have His harvest. He waits patiently
for it. The latter days' rain is coming too, and everyone will get wet

(James 5:7)! In other words, no-one will have any excuse when they stand before God as to why they did not choose Him.

"Choose you this day whom you will serve..."

Who is your choice?

ADMINISTRATE HIS WILL

Here's another instructive verse found in Zechariah 3:7 (NKJV).

*Thus says the Lord of hosts: "If you will walk in **My ways**, and if you will keep My command, **THEN** you shall also judge My house, and likewise have charge of My courts; I will give you places to walk among these who stand here."*

I believe Apostolic Alignment is occurring in the earth today—a governing role for God's people, in addition to "positive encouragement." We've played too small for too long: let's ask God for more than our needs being met; let us ask Him for the Nations, then trust Him for the executive, administrative and creative skills and resources to influence and disciple them.

"Ask Me and I will give you the nations as your inheritance." Psalms 2:8 (NKJV)

Take heed to keep your JOY strong! You don't have to stay mad. Vengeance is God's, but His Joy is our strength. Let's be a happy people in these last days. They shall know us by our fruit. Let joy be an outstanding characteristic among us. Godliness and joyfulness are synonyms. There is no "sad anointing." If you claim to be godly, then you must also be joyful. They go hand-in-hand. Jesus was anointed with the Oil of Gladness, not sadness. Theologian and author, CS Lewis, is known to have said, "Joy is the serious business of Heaven." I agree!

Self-control is a fruit of the spirit too. By the grace of God our emotions are in our control. It was reported that President Abraham

Lincoln read Mark Twain writings and jokes in the midst of the tragic Civil War. When asked why he read comedy in the mist of national tragedy he replied, "I laugh because I must not cry." Let us intentionally move toward Joy and Love. Jesus is coming for a glorious church! Not a sick, sad, and depressed church.

The generations who have seen only the passive act of the cross have been passive themselves about a great, unprecedented outpouring of God's Spirit upon the earth. But every generation that sees the aggressive, military, victorious offensive of the cross on satan and darkness has gone on to walk in practical, effectual Resurrection Power!

> *I John 3:8 (NKJV) "For this purpose the Son of God was manifested, that He might destroy the works of the devil."*

And

> *Hebrews 3:14 (NKJV) "...that through death He might destroy him who had the power of death, that is, the devil..."*

I believe our prayers and worship arm angels and release the Holy Spirit to move in the Earth. As another theologian and church founder, John Wesley, said, "God does nothing except in response to believing prayer."

WRITE THE VISION AND MAKE IT PLAIN

Cast a vision for what revival could look like in your family and in your church and your city and your nation and beyond. Dream in God. Because when He pours out His Spirit, some of us will "see visions and dream dreams." We have no shortage of churches. But we do have a shortage of the outpouring of God's Spirit. Perhaps we have been too full of ourselves to be filled with anything else? We've gorged on entertainment and have no appetite left for Jesus. But nothing moves people in the right direction more than proper hunger.

Think of the Prodigal Son who's hunger caused him to "come to himself" and remember the good food offered back at his daddy's house. When the wandering son returned home his father met him with mercy, joy, and restoration. My hope is that you will ask God to fill you with His Spirit afresh and anew, right now. And being filled with the Holy Spirit is a constant, ongoing need that every Christ-follower has. Like the Prodigal Son, may our hunger and thirst propel us in the proper direction.

May God's goodness and mercy follow us; and may we dwell in the house of the Lord forever.

You have not because you ask not. Ask Father-God to fill you with the Holy Spirit again this very moment. You don't even fully know God's Will for your life until you have been filled with the mighty Holy Spirit! Ask. He will hear from heaven. This is your *"then He will hear from heaven"* moment. Evangelist, Smith Wigglesworth, said, "Being filled with the Spirit is not just a luxury but a command."

I invite you to pray this Prayer:

"Lord, hear me from heaven! Fill me with Your Spirit."

QUESTIONS FOR SMALL GROUPS AND PERSONAL REFLECTION:

1. What is the prayer you've been praying for some time that you feel God hasn't heard or answered? When you read about how God heard the Italian, Cornelius, does that encourage and remind you that God hears? "Call to Me, and I will answer you..." Jeremiah 33:3

2. Read Psalm 105:37 aloud. Israel cried out to God in their bondage and He heard them. When God "transitioned" His people out of Egypt He healed them and blessed them economically. We know God is no respecter of persons and He does not change. Is this something that encourages and excites you? Are you actively trusting God for physical health and the ability to be a blessing financially? How would those two things effect your life?

3. Read Psalms 2:8 aloud. Have you ever entertained the idea of asking God for a nation? Would you consider taking a nation on as a prayer project? What nation or nations are on our heart to pray for?

4. CS Lewis, is known to have said, "Joy is the serious business of Heaven." Are you perceived to be a glad person or a sad person? From this moment forward, determine to see yourself and one another as people of great joy. Verbally make this affirmation to yourself and each other now.

5. Read Acts 19:1–7. Have you received the Holy Spirit since you believed? Take a moment and ask Jesus to fill you with His Spirit. (Luke 11:9–13)

STEP EIGHT: ROYAL PARDON
"AND FORGIVE THEIR SINS…"

Now we are getting to the good stuff. There's nothing so sweet as forgiveness, whether giving it or receiving it. The Cross of Jesus is the "King's X" on our past life and deeds apart from Him. And when God releases forgiveness towards an entire community or city or people group… when people know they need forgiveness then actually receive it! Wow, what an impact on an entire region! That is a Royal Pardon and the genesis of an awakening!

What sins are we talking about being forgiven of? There could be many, like the obvious "bad" sins of lying, stealing, murder, and cheating. But perhaps the sin that so easily besets us is the one we all have in common: the sin of distraction, when Jesus is no longer our Chief Priority. But whatever your shortcoming may be, don't ignore it and allow it to cripple you any longer.

Let's see how Jesus chose to handle sin in Matthew 9:1–8 (NKJV).

> *So Jesus got into a boat, crossed over, and came to His own city. Then behold, they brought to Him a paralytic lying on a bed. When Jesus saw their faith, He said to the paralytic, "Son, be of good cheer; your sins are forgiven you." And at once some of the scribes said within themselves, 'This Man blasphemes!' But Jesus, knowing their thoughts, said, "Why do you think evil in your hearts? For which is easier, to say, 'Your sins are forgiven you, 'or to say, 'Arise and walk'? But that you may know that the Son of Man has power on earth to forgive sins"—then He said to the paralytic, "Arise, take up your bed, and go to your house." And he arose and departed to his house. Now when the multitudes saw it, they marveled and glorified God, who had given such power to men.*

Two things stand out to me in this scripture. The man was crippled by sin. And God has given power to men, not just to heal the sick, but to forgive sins. Sin is the vile root that grows the fruit of sickness. It may not be your personal sin, but when sin entered our world through the Garden of Eden, so did sickness and death. And it crippled all of mankind.

I have pastored the same church now for over twenty years at the time of this writing. And I've figured out the number one thing that cripples most people is guilt. And the number one person that people need to forgive is themselves. (That's also the person they lie to the most too.) Guilt is a horrid torturer. But confession truly is good for the soul and can shed shame in an instant. Take a look at this truth-bomb from Psalm 32:3–5 (NKJV).

> *"When I kept silent, my bones grew old through my groaning all the day long. For day and night Your hand was heavy upon me; My vitality was turned into the drought of summer. Selah I acknowledged my sin to You, and my iniquity I have not hidden. I said, 'I will confess my transgressions to the Lord,' And You forgave the iniquity of my sin."*

HOW SWEET IT IS

Man, there's something so powerful about coming clean with God and yourself. Too many people are afraid to admit their wrongs to God, but it's not like He doesn't already know! Or that you're going to freak Him out if you tell Him what you did. Can you see God grabbing His chest, as He begins to fall off His throne shouting, "Jesus Christ! Can you believe what they did?!?" No! He is God. He doesn't have any love; He is Love. And when we come to Him, instead of run from Him, He forgives. There can't be many things in life so transformative as a clean conscience. How sweet it is to be loved by Love.

1 John 1:7–9 (NKJV) explains the value of confession. (I adjusted the punctuation a wee bit in verse 7.)

"But if we walk in the light, as He is, in the light we have fellowship with one another [this is why we all need to belong to a small group]*, and the blood of Jesus Christ His Son cleanses us from all sin. If we say that we have no sin, we deceive ourselves,* [see, I told you people lie to themselves more than to anyone else] *and the truth is not in us. If we confess our sins, He is faithful and just to forgive us our sins and to cleanse us from all unrighteousness."*

ARE YOU GOOD ENOUGH?

On a scale from 1-to-100, how good of a person are you? If Jesus is a perfect 100 and 1 is a serial-killer, where you do fall on the spectrum as a human? Now, just for context, let's say that two people who ranked in the 90's were Mother Teresa and Billy Graham. If you are in the 60's or 70's, then you are a really exceptional person. Maybe better than most even. Now if you scored in the 80's you are a great human. And if you are in the 90's? Well, just put "Saint" in front of your name. Congratulations. Wow! Seriously impressive.

When you compare yourself to others, you sometimes feel better about yourself. But sometimes… you feel worse. But check out this story of two men who probably ranked somewhere in the teens at best, and let's see what we can learn from them that would be beneficial to us.

THE TALE OF TWO THIEVES

We don't know much about them… one insulted Jesus; the other asked to be remembered by Him. But we do know they were both criminals. Guilty as charged. They both deserved to be punished. But one was granted clemency by the King, Jesus. Why? Let's find out…by looking at Luke 23:32–45 (NKJV).

"There were also two others, criminals, led with Him to be put to death. And when they had come to the place called Calvary, there they crucified Him, and the criminals, one

on the right hand and the other on the left. Then Jesus said, 'Father, forgive them, for they do not know what they do.' And they divided His garments and cast lots. And the people stood looking on. But even the rulers with them sneered, saying, 'He saved others; let Him save Himself if He is the Christ, the chosen of God.' The soldiers also mocked Him, coming and offering Him sour wine, and saying, 'If You are the King of the Jews, save Yourself.' And an inscription also was written over Him in letters of Greek, Latin, and Hebrew:

THIS IS THE KING OF THE JEWS.

Then one of the criminals who were hanged blasphemed Him, saying, 'If You are the Christ, save Yourself and us.' But the other, answering, rebuked him, saying, 'Do you not even fear God, seeing you are under the same condemnation? And we indeed justly, for we receive the due reward of our deeds; but this Man has done nothing wrong.' Then he said to Jesus, 'Lord, remember me when You come into Your kingdom.' And Jesus said to him, 'Assuredly, I say to you today you will be with Me in Paradise.' Now it was about the sixth hour, and there was darkness over all the earth until the ninth hour. Then the sun was darkened, and the veil of the temple was torn in two."

Crucifixion was reserved for slaves and criminals. Additionally, it was intended to be an insult. The two thieves crucified with Jesus were bad men. Proven guilty, and they deserved what they were getting. Conversely, they could not prove any guilt in regard to Jesus. He did not deserve what He was getting. Yet one thief blasphemed Christ while the other was forgiven by the same. Why? What was the difference?

The Forgiven Thief Admits He Was Wrong

The thief that Jesus promised salvation said, "...we are getting what our deeds deserve..." That reminds me of when I was about five years old. I demolished my dad's garden in our backyard. This backyard-beauty was his agricultural pride and joy. When he came home from work, I got what I deserved: a spanking. The point I'm trying to make is that being "better than most" isn't good enough to be right with God. In-and-of ourselves we are not good, and that is our problem. Have you ever told a lie? Have you ever stolen anything? Have you ever had a lustful thought? Ever made something more important than God? Sure. We all have. So, most of us are lying, thieving, adulterating Idolators. James 2:10 (NKJV) reinforces our guilt,

"For whoever shall keep the whole law, and yet stumble in one point, he is guilty of all."

Now before you get too discouraged...

The Forgiven Thief Asks for Help

But not just any kind of help. Most people will ask God for help, but not ETERNAL help. It may go something like this: "God, if you are real, make my life better. Help me get that promotion, heal my mother, help me find my lost keys, etc."

But in this "Tale of Two Thieves," both of them were guilty and both were suffering at an unimaginable level. Both heard and saw the same thing during those six hours of torture alongside of the Christ. But only one thief was saved and forgiven. Why? Was it just God's sovereign Will to save one and allow the other to be damned? Of course not. He wills none to perish, but all to be saved (II Peter 3:9 NKJV). So, what was the life-saving difference?

We Are All Thieves

Guilty as charged. Each and every one of us. But some of us will be rescued and transformed, while someone else reading this same book

240

will remain exactly the same: guilty and condemned. You see, this tale of two thieves is our own biography. But here is the great twist in the plot. You get to choose which thief you will be. You always have a choice.

Now, How Good a Person Are You?

What was your number? On a scale from 1-to-100, what was your number? We know your number can't be a perfect 100, because Romans 3:23 (NKJV) says, *"...for ALL have sinned and fall short..."* So, you can't be a 100. Ergo is the giant dilemma: God only accepts perfection. You must be sinless; an absolutely perfect 100 to be allowed into His heaven. And therein lies the problem. Nobody is good enough to *deserve* God's mercy, love, and grace. So as my friends in India say, "What to do?"

The Coefficient of X = Y

But this is where the almost-too-good-to-be-true news kicks in: whatever your number is, Jesus makes up the difference! If you're an 82, HE makes up the missing 12. And it doesn't matter if you're a 12, He makes up your missing 82! In Christ you are a perfect 100! But you must be IN CHRIST!

"But I was born a 66," you may argue. But that is why you must be born again!

Romans 3:22–24 (NKJV) says,

> *"...even the righteousness of God, through faith in Jesus Christ, to all and on all who believe. For there is no difference; for all have sinned and fall short of the glory of God, being justified freely by His grace through the redemption that is in Christ Jesus."*

In other words, it's not about what YOU have done; it's about what HE has done *for* you, and *as* you. He was our Substitute. 2 Corinthians 5:17 (NKJV) further explains our acceptability with God in

Christ,

> *"Therefore, if anyone is in Christ, he is a new creation;*
> *old things have passed away; behold, all things have*
> *become new."*

Can you imagine when God "hears from heaven and forgives our sin" for whole communities at one time? What dramatic, divine impact that will have!

"I'LL ARRANGE IT."

I heard a well-known pastor, who I respect, share this story. After World War I, the United States of America allocated funds to orphanages in Europe because so many children had lost their parents. One day a frail man entered one of those orphanages with his young daughter in tow, asking for his precious girl to be admitted to their care.

The head of the orphanage said regrettably, "I'm so sorry sir. Resources are limited, and we can only receive children that have lost both of their parents."

The father replied, "You mean if I were also dead, like her mother, you could give my little girl food and clothing and shelter and safety?"

When the caretaker nodded in the affirmative, the father took his daughters hand, placed it in the caretaker's hand, and stated, "I'll arrange it."

And he went out and hung himself.

Jesus took my hand and yours, placed it in His Heavenly Father's hand and said, "I'll arrange it." And He hung Himself on a Cross, so we could be forgiven and taken in.

THE BOTTOM LINE

You are one of two thieves on one of two crosses. One of those thieves, at some point, changed his mind about who Jesus was. It

242

could have been when he saw Jesus endure torture with kindness. It could have been when He cried out to God, "Why have You forsaken Me?" It could've been a look of unconditional love from Jesus Himself.

But at some point, that guilty thief asked Jesus for eternal help, "Remember me when You come into Your Kingdom."

If you make the same request today, you will get the same answer: "Truly I say to you today, you will be with Me in Paradise."

You've tried to do enough good things and you hope you haven't done too many bad things. But the harsh reality is that we are all ZERO's without Jesus. But if you will ask for eternal help today, here's what's going to happen. GOD will take up residence in your heart and you will go from a ZERO to a perfect 100 the instant you yield your life to Christ.

PRAYER OF SALVATION

"Dear God, I repent of my sin. Please forgive me. I believe Jesus died for my sin and they buried Him. But on the third day, You raised Him from the dead. Raise me from the dead now too. Give me eternal help. I confess that Jesus is my Lord. Amen."

SAVED BUT STILL STRUGGLING

We've all been there. The same truth applies to struggling believers too. Ask for help.

> *"There is now therefore no condemnation for those **in Christ Jesus**." Romans 8:1 (NKJV)*

Are you "in Christ Jesus," but still feel condemned? You've got to learn to "walk not after the flesh." Don't let your *feelings* be greater than your *faith*. We are "believers" after all, not "feelers."

If you are already a Christ-Follower and having a bout with doubt (and the evil twins, guilt, and shame, have been crucifying you), peace and freedom will come and give you rest. You can't alter your past, but you can bring your past to the altar. Peace is a Person. Ask Him for forgiveness now. Freedom isn't the absence of something. Freedom is the Presence of Someone. Ask Him to step into your life right now. Ask for help—the eternal kind.

PRAYER WHEN YOU'RE STRUGGLING

"Father God, You said if I would humble myself, and pray, and seek Your face, and turn from my wicked ways, then You would hear from heaven, and would forgive my sin. I humbly admit that I need Your eternal help. I've messed up, but I'm asking You to pick me up. Would You forgive me? Remember me… Please step into my life now. By faith, I accept Your mercy and forgiveness. I don't walk in condemnation anymore, but I walk in Your Righteousness. Not because of what I have done, but what Jesus has done for me. Thank you. Amen."

SIMPLY FORGIVEN – A POEM

This grime
and the shame
are more than a stain
on my shirt
I'm running in sand
a life that doesn't work

I'm heaving
barely breathing
can't get this weight off my chest
sinking in my thinking
now I'm running out of breath

I did the crime
and now it's time
to plunge beneath the water
stop the charade
my bill must be paid
I just can't go any farther

But wait—somethings happening!
Love is wrapping
all around my soul
thought I was dying
but Peace is untying
this noose around my throat

when I emerged
I had been purged
not from the earth been ridden
clean and bright
my sin in-spite—
Simply Forgiven!

—KC

WERE YOU A SERIAL-KILLER?

Probably Not. But Saul (aka: Paul) was. Acts 26:12–19 (NKJV) shows how God reached out to even him.

"While thus occupied, as I journeyed to Damascus with authority and commission from the chief priests, at midday, O king, along the road I saw a light from heaven, brighter than the sun, shining around me and those who journeyed with me. And when we all had fallen to the ground, I heard a voice speaking to me and saying in the Hebrew language, 'Saul, Saul, why are you persecuting Me? It is hard for you to kick against the goads.' So I said, 'Who are You, Lord?' And He said, 'I am Jesus, whom you

are persecuting. But rise and stand on your feet; for I have appeared to you for this purpose, to make you a minister and a witness both of the things which you have seen and of the things which I will yet reveal to you. I will deliver you from the Jewish people, as well as from the Gentiles, to whom I now send you, to open their eyes, in order to turn them from darkness to light, and from the power of Satan to God, that they may receive forgiveness of sins and an inheritance among those who are sanctified by faith in Me.' Therefore, King Agrippa, I was not disobedient to the heavenly vision..."

And here are two scriptures that demonstrate how important Paul's (and our) actions are in the big spiritual picture.

*"He who covers his sins will not prosper,
But whoever confesses and forsakes them will have
mercy." Proverbs 28:13 (NKJV)*

*For thus says the High and Lofty One Who inhabits eternity, whose name is Holy:
"I dwell in the high and holy place, With him who has a
contrite and humble spirit,
To revive the spirit of the humble, And to revive the heart
of the contrite ones.
Isaiah 57:15 (NKJV)*

QUESTIONS FOR SMALL GROUPS AND PERSONAL REFLECTION:

1. Have you ever gotten distracted while driving or in a conversation? Spiritually the sin of distraction is especially dangerous. Is anything currently distracting you from Jesus being your chief priority? If so, what or who? Don't allow it to cripple you any longer.

2. Read I John 1:7–9 together. Now confess what's been distracting you to one another; then pray one for another that you may be healed. (James 5:16)

3. Read Luke 23:32–45 together. One thief blasphemed Christ while the other was forgiven by the same. Why? What was the difference? We are all "thieves." Which of the two thieves do you identify with and why?

4. It's not about what you have done, it's about what Jesus has done. What does this mean?

5. Discuss the story of the father and his young daughter entering the orphanage after World War I. When the father said, "I will arrange it," how did that hit you? What perspective does that give you about what Jesus did for you? Talk about it.

6. Do you identify with "saved but still struggling"? Peace is a Person. Freedom isn't the absence of something. Freedom is the Presence of Someone. Ask Him to step into that area of your life right now. Ask for help — the eternal kind. Pray now.

STEP NINE: WHAT ONLY GOD CAN DO
"AND HEAL THEIR LAND."

We have come to a special place in our journey. We have done our part and now we long for God to do what only He can do: Heal our land! But even in this special place, we see Christ's Body has a part to play. Why would "land" need to be healed? Is the Earth sick? Are there geographical regions that need their pain and anguish alleviated? Is there a wound in our nation that needs to be treated, or a division that needs to be mended? This is exactly what God promises He will do, "I will 'Rapha' (heal) your land." Sin is the disease; Jesus is the cure. And the church is Christ's body and instrument. The Church is not perfect but she is chosen.

CONTEXT FOR OUR TEXT

What does God mean, practically, when He says, "I will heal your land?" Context reveals the setting in which God proposed this formula for making revival an ongoing part of our daily life and culture. As we will see in the following passages of scripture, these people were not trying to get God to move, He was moving! Fire was literally falling from heaven upon their offerings. Revival was not something God sovereignly chose to do. It was something He did in response to His people's extravagant worship. When we draw near to Him, He promises to draw near to us! Please carefully read the following passages as they fill in some of the strategic blanks for us in this hour we are living in today. They are located in 2 Chronicles 7:1-16 (NKJV).

> *"When Solomon had finished praying, fire came down from heaven and consumed the burnt offering and the sacrifices; and the glory of the Lord filled the temple. And the priests could not enter the house of the Lord, because the glory of the Lord had filled the Lord's house. When all the children of Israel saw how the fire came down, and the glory of the*

*Lord on the temple, they bowed their faces to the ground on the pavement, and worshiped and praised the Lord, saying: '**For He is good, For His mercy endures forever.**' Then the king and all the people offered sacrifices before the Lord. King Solomon offered a sacrifice of twenty-two thousand bulls and one hundred and twenty thousand sheep. So the king and all the people dedicated the house of God. And the priests attended to their services; the Levites also with instruments of the music of the Lord, which King David had made to praise the Lord, saying, 'For His mercy endures forever,' whenever David offered praise by their ministry. The priests sounded trumpets opposite them, while all Israel stood. Furthermore Solomon consecrated the middle of the court that was in front of the house of the Lord; for there he offered burnt offerings and the fat of the peace offerings, because the bronze altar which Solomon had made was not able to receive the burnt offerings, the grain offerings, and the fat. At that time Solomon kept the feast seven days, and all Israel with him, a very great assembly from the entrance of Hamath to the Brook of Egypt. And on the eighth day they held a sacred assembly, for they observed the dedication of the altar seven days, and the feast seven days. On the twenty-third day of the seventh month he sent the people away to their tents, joyful and glad of heart for the good that the Lord had done for David, for Solomon, and for His people Israel. Thus Solomon finished the house of the Lord and the king's house; and Solomon successfully accomplished all that came into his heart to make in the house of the Lord and in his own house. Then the Lord appeared to Solomon by night, and said to him: 'I have heard your prayer, and have chosen this place for Myself as a house of sacrifice. When I shut up heaven and there is no rain, or command the locusts to devour the land, or send pestilence among My people, if*

*My people who are called by My name will humble them-
selves, and pray and seek My face, and turn from their
wicked ways, then I will hear from heaven, and will forgive
their sin and heal their land. Now My eyes will be open and
My ears attentive to prayer made in this place. For now I
have chosen and sanctified this house, that My name may be
there forever; and My eyes* [concern] *and My heart* [atten-
tion] *will be there* **perpetually.***'"*

PERPETUAL OUTPOURING

These instructions from the Lord are not just for ***obtaining*** revival,
but also for ***maintaining*** and ***sustaining*** the outpouring of God's
Spirit. Our loving Heavenly Father longs to provide us with His concern and attention constantly, so multiple times in Holy Writ He reveals how we can partake of His ongoing love, goodness, care, and
concern. Clearly, God's Will for His people is Abundant Life and
extravagant manifestations of His glorious presence.

Conversely, the very purpose of the enemy's presence in your life
is to destroy you. According to Jesus, satan only shows up for one of
three reasons: to kill you, steal from you, and to destroy you. But God
said He would heal our land, and that implies He will supply constant
provision for ongoing health and wellbeing in every area of our life.
One challenge that keeps people in bondage is they are impressed
with the devil. Jesus never was. Are you?

UNIMPRESSED

Mark 9:17–29 (NKJV) demonstrates how Jesus dealt with dark spirits. Let's learn from His example now.

*"Then one of the crowd answered and said, 'Teacher, I
brought You my son, who has a mute spirit. And wherever it
seizes him, it throws him down; he foams at the mouth,
gnashes his teeth, and becomes rigid. So I spoke to Your disciples, that they should cast it out, but they could not.' He*

answered him and said, 'O faithless generation, how long shall I be with you? How long shall I bear with you? Bring him to Me.' Then they brought him to Him. And when he saw Him, immediately the spirit convulsed him, and he fell on the ground and wallowed, foaming at the mouth."

[Demons often make a last stand when you decide that you no longer want them in your life.]

"So He asked his father, 'How long has this been happening to him?' And he said, 'From childhood.'"

[I imagine Jesus standing there while the boy foamed at the mouth manifesting a demon, calmly asking the boy's father for further details, "How long has your son been like this?" Jesus is just not impressed with Satan, so you should't be either!]

*"'And often he has thrown him both into the fire and into the water to destroy him. But **if You** can do anything, have compassion on us and help us.' Jesus said to him, '**If you** can believe, all things are possible to him who believes.' Immediately the father of the child cried out and said with tears, 'Lord, I believe; help my unbelief!'"*

[We've all prayed this prayer: "Lord, if You could just get me that job or heal my kid or get me out this trouble…"]

"'When Jesus saw that the people came running together, He rebuked the unclean spirit, saying to it, 'Deaf and dumb spirit, I command you, come out of him and enter him no more!' Then the spirit cried out, convulsed him greatly, and came out of him. And he became as one dead, so that many said, 'He is dead.' But Jesus took him by the hand and lifted him up, and he arose. And when He had come into the house, His disciples asked Him privately, 'Why could we not

cast it out?' So He said to them, 'This kind can come out by nothing but prayer and fasting.'"

WHAT ELSE DO YOU WANT GOD TO DO FOR YOU?

The question is never, "What God can do?" The question is always, "What I can believe?"

We say, "God, if You can do it…" And He says, "No, if *you* can believe it." (Forgive the redundancy you are about to experience in this paragraph.) God has already done everything for you that He's ever going to do for you. When Jesus said, "It is finished," He meant it and it really is "finished!" That's why He won't do anything else for you: He's already done everything for you that needs to be done. What else do you want Him to do for you? He has done it all. God, through Christ Jesus, has already done everything for you that He is ever going to do for you. So, the question remains, "Can you believe it?" Not, "Can He do it?" Because He already has. Can you believe what He's already done? If you can believe it, then you can access it, appropriate it, and enjoy it on an ongoing basis. You can begin to live life as God's son or daughter. We believe iniquities are handed down from generation to generation, but can we also believe revival, and blessing, and favor can be handed down generationally too? If you get a revelation that "God has already done it," then you can walk in the reality that "you've already got it." *Ah-ha!*

SUSTAINABLE. PERPETUAL. GENERATIONAL.

After Jesus cast out the demon, the crowd was excited—but not Jesus. He cast out the demon, but the boy was still torn and hurt. Jesus delivered the boy, but additionally healed him. Jesus knew His job wasn't done until all the effects of darkness had been reversed in that child. *Then* Jesus celebrated. I believe this represents a generation of young people who will experience the full measure of a true encounter with the risen Savior! And, in this day and age, Jesus does His work through His body that's here on the Earth—the local church. And our task is not done until we have reversed the works of darkness in this generation. For this, we must have a sustainable, perpetual, generational, on-going move of God. Not sensationalism or a series of special meetings, or YouTube prophets, but a people of God walking in the reality of who they are in Christ and Who Christ is in them. In other words, not only has Jesus made The Way for you to be free, but He has reversed every ill-effect of the presence of satan that was in your life. There is nothing so bad that has or can happen to you that is more powerful than what Jesus has done for you. Divorce. Debt. Depression. Addiction. Disease. Darkness. The devil can't do anything more powerful to you than what Jesus did to you: He redeemed you! Jesus took on the curse to we can take on the blessing. Jesus became poor that we might be made rich. Jesus tasted death that we may partake of life more abundantly.

Whatever your enemy meant for your harm and the harm of your descendants, God is turning it around for your good. I'm not saying we deny that something negative has happened. I'm just saying if it's not good yet, then God is not done working it out yet. You're not destined to pass down poverty or broken marriages or a crazy mind to your kids and grandkids. You are going to pass down a heritage of God-honoring, Jesus worshiping, Abundant Life!

YOUR NEW NORMAL

Ironically, at this point in our journey on the road to sustained revival, the euphoria associated with God pouring out His Spirit becomes revival's greatest enemy. You are free. Perhaps thousands are getting saved and chains of bondage are breaking; everyone feels God, so why not simply enjoy it, right? There's nothing wrong with rejoicing in the Presence of God but let us not stop assuming our responsibilities either. Historically some people have abused this excitement by missing work, letting school fall behind, and neglecting their marriages—all in the name of so-called revival. If satan can't beat revival, he'll join it by provoking us to a counterfeit emotionalism or useless activities. The great revivalist, Charles G. Finney, taught us that one of the enemies of revival is fatigue. We have to pace ourselves and not allow a scarcity mentality to tempt us into fear that God's profuse mercy and grace are limited or temporary in their expression. Stay keenly aware of the possibility that we subconsciously fear that revival may go away and, as a result of this fear, we allow ourselves to frantically pursue counterfeits. Our faith in God's character, however, must remain intact. He is our sustainer. He is good. And He desires to pour His Spirit out upon us more than we desire it to be poured!

Then we can gladly say, "Praise God, this isn't going to stop, so I'll take time to keep my body healthy and rested, and my grades up. I'll keep a healthy witness at work, and I'll take this glory into my marriage and family."

Our goal is not to just *obtain* revival. It must be *contained* and *sustained.* Let us make the new-found glory our way of life. This is who we are: The People of the Outpouring! We are alive in the last days of human history and have full expectation to experience and live in the fulfillment of Joel 2:28!

CHANGING OUR DEFINITION OF NORMAL

We no longer regard token responses to Christ as genuine progress. We no longer dilute the revolutionary transformation demanded by God to a polite invitation that people improve themselves. God's goal for you and me is not self-improvement. He wants us to be radically transformed and actually move forward as we live the Abundant Life Jesus procured for us!

Radical is our "New Normal."

In this world people are crazy. They live extreme, alternative lifestyles. They burn and loot cites, endeavor to change their gender, and legalize debauchery. May they no longer be disappointed when their hungry hearts draw them to approach the church. Instead of hearing echoes of humanism and motivational speaking, may they hear a radical call to a new life and a very real Kingdom that is coming to earth! We are supposed to be a peculiar people with an "otherworldliness" that actually manifests in our daily lives. Like the first century saints in the Book of Acts, we have been touched by a mixture of the fear of God and wonder of His love. Like the apostolic men of old, our shadow raises up the lame and we endure persecution with gladness, being counted worthy to suffer for His Name's sake! We recognize that we are actually strangers and aliens. We are not of this world, rather just passing through it. We live with eternity in view. Let us abandon what we used to call "normal." Let us abandon low-living and small thinking. We refuse to live below the standard of the Christ-Man, Jesus. We are called to live a life of radical generosity and unsurpassed obedience to the Holy Spirit… A supernatural life! Living like Jesus lived: Abundant Life! That is our New Normal now. We are The People of the Outpouring!

THE BELIEVER'S JOB DESCRIPTION

"For this purpose the Son of God was manifested, that He might destroy the works of the devil." 1 John 3:8 (NKJV)

This is our job description. Anything that doesn't produce life is not from God. Like our Master, we go about doing good, healing all who are oppressed by the devil, for God is with us (Acts 10:38 NKJV). Jesus isn't impressed with satan, and if you could see the devil—what he really is—you wouldn't be impressed either. This is the New Normal! No longer are we talking and living like a victim, but talking and walking like The Victor Himself, Christ Jesus the King! How? Because Jesus made us equal with Himself in position, therefore we are equal with Him in His possession. This is "Normal Christianity." Please don't misunderstand me. We are not God. We are not The Son of God. But we are sons and daughters of God, in Christ Jesus. We are His royal subjects whom He has elevated to the right hand of His Father. We have been "raised up together, and (God) made *us* sit together in the heavenly *places* in Christ Jesus" (Ephesians 2:6 NKJV). We've been made family with God!

INSIDE OUT

Wouldn't it be better to have a Super-Natural response to life, instead of only a natural response? I know you have emotions. I know you have a physical body. But if you can have a spiritual response to life, instead of only a physical or emotional one, then you will begin to walk in this Abundant Life and victory we have been speaking of. When the circumstances of life happen—speak life! Don't live out of fear; live out of faith. Don't live out of your feelings; live out of your spirit. Live from the inside out! Speak life from your inner man, instead of fear out of your head. Respond in faith.

APPLY THE NIKE PRINCIPLE AND JUST DO IT

What is the Holy Spirit saying to you right now? Perhaps it is to practice having spiritual responses to natural circumstances. Is there a bondage in your life? Is there a sin you continue to commit over and over again? Would you like to be free? Sure, you would. But will you do something about it? Ask God what your next step is, then take that step by faith.

> *"We walk by faith and not by sight."*
> *II Corinthians 5:7 (NKJV)*

We live from the inside out; we are not limited to live from the outside in.

When I was first starting off in ministry, the Holy Spirit spoke this to my heart: *"The Shadows of Time are Gathering on the Horizon. The final grains of time are slipping through the hour-glass of History. The Son of Righteousness is Rising with Healing in His Wings. And the Days of Nominal Christianity are becoming extinct; only those Skilled at Waling with God... Knowing God and His Word and are Led by His Spirit will be those that Thrive in the Last-Days!"* I believe He was preparing me for the time we are stepping into now.

How Do I Practically Change My Life?

When you tell a lie long enough, eventually it will become true to you. Even if you've been lying to yourself. What if some things you have believed all your life weren't actually reality? 2 Corinthians 10:3–5 (NKJV) lets us know how to combat what is not Truth.

"For though we walk in the flesh, we do not war according to the flesh. For the weapons of our warfare are not carnal but mighty in God for pulling down strongholds, casting down arguments and every high thing that exalts itself against the knowledge of God, bringing every thought into captivity to the obedience of Christ."

When Paul discusses strongholds, he's not talking about demons. He's talking about wrong patterns of thought or faulty ways of thinking.

If a FERRARI has no engine or is up on blocks, can it take you anywhere? I once heard a well-known preacher say, "**Resolutions** without **routines** are like a Ferraris without fuel: it's cool to look at, but can't take you anywhere. **Resolve** can't change what **routine** created. **Determination** alone can't change what your **decisions** created. You can't **believe** your way out of problems that were created by patterns of **behavior**."

Change Your Pattern Solve Your Problem

Good news! You're not hopelessly dysfunctional. You just have wrong routines and patterns. John 15:1–7 (NKJV) lets us know that the best plan is to stick to God's plan.

"I am the true vine, and My Father is the vinedresser. Every branch in Me that does not bear fruit He takes away; and every branch that bears fruit He prunes, that it may bear more fruit. You are already clean because of the word which I have spoken to you. Abide in Me, and I in

*you. As the branch cannot bear fruit of itself, unless it
abides in the vine, neither can you, unless you abide in Me.
I am the vine, you are the branches. He who abides in Me,
and I in him, bears much fruit; for without Me you can do
nothing. If anyone does not abide in Me, he is cast out as a
branch and is withered; and they gather them and throw
them into the fire, and they are burned. If you abide in Me,
and My words abide in you, you will ask what you desire,
and it shall be done for you."*

You can't **reach** unless you **remain.** A tree can't reach up without
remaining planted. The FAITH to step out is worthless without the
FAITHFULNESS to stick it out. So don't alter your pattern for a limited time. Remember, this is your New Normal. The key to your success is found in your daily routine. I know it hurts! It's uncomfortable. But if you know there's a purpose to the pain you can stick it out.
Pain is not pointless if you remain. **We are the People of the Outpouring!** If you stick it out fruit will grow. Be like a postage stamp:
stick to it until you get there. Stick and stay; it's bound to pay. The
pain of regret is always greater than the pain of discipline. And once
you've decided your priorities you can establish the appropriate routine.

Romans 5:14 (NKJV) lets us know what happens when we don't
stick.

*"Nevertheless death reigned from Adam to Moses, even
over those who had not sinned according to the likeness of
the transgression of Adam, who is a type of Him who was
to come."*

Adam was a bad pattern. And truthfully, babies are born with a sinful
pattern. If there's a problem, then there's a problem in the original
pattern. Some people are fighting demons and generational patterns
that their great, great grandfather fought! You can break the patterns.
Disrupt it. **Adam was our pattern.** And that was our problem. But

God sent His Son, Jesus, to break the old, sinful pattern, and to become a New Pattern. Don't forget 2 Corinthians 5:17 (NKJV),

> *"If any man be in Christ, he is a new creature. Old things have passed away; all things are become new."*

PRAY THIS PATTERN DISRUPTING PRAYER OF DEDICATION AND CONSECRATION:

> "Wherever You want me to go Lord, I will go. Whatever You want me to do, I will do. Whatever You want me to say, I will say. And wherever You want me to stay, I will stay. My life is not my own. It belongs to you, for I have been bought with a price. I belong to You. Here I am. Send me. I am Yours to command. Use me for Your glory in these last days. We are the People of Your Outpouring! Amen."

FINAL THOUGHTS

God's chosen people, Israel, were slaves in Egypt for over 400 years, but the Lord sent them a deliverer, Moses. And through a series of supernatural events, these slaves were set free and departed the land of bondage in route to their "Promise Land." However, they spent four decades in the wilderness wandering about! Why? They had been taken out of slavery, but slavery had to also be taken out of them.

In like manner, Christ, our Deliver, has liberated us from the slavery of sin and self. And yet some still wander in the wilderness of mediocrity. But you have initiated your exit from the desert and your entrance into your divine destiny of abundant life in Christ.

The Israelites were a freed folk but not yet a free folk. Freedom is a journey. And you have begun it. This book can serve as a guide to help you expedite your journey. But whatever happens, do not adapt to the wilderness. It may be progress, but it is not your destiny. Total liberty and freedom is your "Promised Land." Keep moving until you get there. Read this book again if you need too. Join a small group that digests these truths together. Healing seems to happen faster in community.

Finally, always remember: The enemy has done nothing *to* you that is greater than what Christ has done *for* you. Wholeness is part of your inheritance in Christ. Abundant Life has been paid for in full and belongs to you. You already have it. It is your new normal. Now share it, and keep learning to enjoy it.

— K.C.

QUESTIONS FOR SMALL GROUPS AND PERSONAL REFLECTION:

1. Please read 2 Chronicles 7:1–16. What stood out to you or what did you notice about this passage that perhaps escaped your attention previously?

2. Iniquities are handed down from generation to generation, but revival, and blessing, and favor can be handed down generationally too. What are some ways you can "hand down" these precious, spiritual realities to your children and grandchildren?

3. Jesus was our substitute. He died FOR us, and He died AS us. Discuss what the implications of this are for Christ-followers?

4. Our goal is not to just *obtain* revival. It must be *contained* and *sustained.* What are some practical things we can do to make this renewal and refreshing a part of our everyday life?

5. We are supposed to be a peculiar people with an "otherworldliness" that actually manifests in our daily lives. Like the first century saints in the Book of Acts, we have been touched by a mixture of the fear of God and wonder of His love. What kind of things should we begin to expect on a regular basis with God pouring His Spirit out upon us? What does our "new normal" look and feel and sound like? In our churches and in our homes? In our neighborhoods, schools and cities?

6. What patterns or habits may be producing either your problems or your promises? Can you identify the 10 most powerful habits in your life right now? Write them down. Then ask The Lord if He would like to change any thing.

FOR YOUR REFERENCE

FIFTY EVENTS THAT CAN LEAD TO A STRONGHOLD

Study this list of sins which can lead to curses. Please circle those which apply to your life, then apply the five-step process located in the Introduction: Recognize, Repent, Renounce, Replace, and Return.

1. Forsaking divine order (Genesis 3:17).
2. Cursing and mistreating the Jews (Genesis 12:3).
3. Willfully deceiving others (Genesis 27:12).
4. Practicing paganistic idolatry (Exodus 20:5).
5. Murder (Exodus 21:12).
6. Striking one's parents (Exodus 21:15).
7. Kidnapping (Exodus 21:16).
8. Cursing one's parents (Exodus 21:17).
9. Causing the unborn to die (Exodus 21:22–23).
10. Practicing witchcraft (Exodus 22:18).
11. Not preventing death through irresponsibility (Exodus 21:29).
12. Sacrificing humans (Exodus 21:29).
13. Sacrificing to false gods (Exodus 22:18).
14. Partaking in séances and fortunetelling (Leviticus 20:6–27).
15. Practicing homosexuality and lesbianism (Leviticus 20:13).
16. Fornicating with animals (Lev. 20:15–16 / (Deuteronomy 27:21).
17. Keeping or owning cursed objects (Deuteronomy 7:25).
18. Practicing astrology (Deuteronomy 17:2–5).
19. Rebellion against spiritual leaders (Deuteronomy 17:12).
20. False prophets (Deuteronomy 18:19–22).
21. Unrepentant, rebellious children (Deuteronomy 21:18–21).

22. Not staying pure in body until marriage (Deuteronomy 22:13–21).
23. Adultery and rape (Deuteronomy 22:22–27).
24. Practicing idolatry (Deuteronomy 27:15).
25. Lightly esteeming one's parents (Deuteronomy 27:16).
26. Dishonestly cheating people (Deuteronomy 27:17).
27. Taking advantage of other's handicaps (Deuteronomy 27:18).
28. Oppressing strangers, widows, and the fatherless (Deuteronomy 27:19).
29. Practicing incest (Deuteronomy 27:20–22).
30. Secretly afflicting one's neighbors (Deuteronomy 27:24).
31. Killing the innocent for money (Deuteronomy 27:25).
32. Compromising God's word (Deuteronomy 27:26).
33. Attempting to turn others away from God (Deuteronomy 13:6–9).
34. The curse of the Lord is on the house of wickedness (Proverbs 3:33).
35. Not giving to the poor (Proverbs 28:27).
36. Rewarding evil for good (Proverbs 17:13, 15; Psalm 109).
37. Proudly erring from the word of God (Psalm 109:21).
38. Resorting to the arm of the flesh instead of God (Jeremiah 17:5).
39. Doing the will of the Lord neglectfully and deceitfully (Jeremiah 48:10).
40. Refusing to warn others of sin (Ezekiel 3:18–21).
41. Failing to give glory to God (Malachi 2:2).
42. Refusing to financially support the work of the Lord (Malachi 3:8–9).
43. Anyone who does not love the Lord is considered accursed (1 Corinthians 16:22).
44. The goats presenting themselves as sheep will be cursed (Matthew 25:41)
45. Preaching a false gospel (Galatians 1:8).
46. Being brought back under the law (Galatians 3:10).

47. False prophets and teachers are accursed (2 Peter 2:14).
48. Those who sin willfully after knowing better (Hebrews 10:26–30).
49. Ungodly use of the tongue (James 3:10).
50. Adding to or taking away from scripture or the Book of Revelation (Revelations 22:18–20).

ABOUT THE AUTHOR

KEVIN COOLEY enjoys ministering to and inspiring people to fulfill their Divine destiny. His ministry has spanned more than thirty years. Jesus told him as a young boy to "go to the other side of the world and tell them about My love." Today the scope of his ministry is literally on the "other side of the world" as he oversees Embassy of Hope, a non-profit missions organization.

E.O.H. is currently working in India, Nepal, and Bhutan. Kevin is the overseer of "Domata India" —a training center established to educate nationals on how to minister the Gospel in the context of their own language and culture.

Hundreds of churches have been planted so far.

Kevin is also the Lead Pastor of Harvest Church in Mobile, Alabama.

Kevin is a Rhema Bible College graduate and sat under Dr. Kenneth E. Hagin. He has served on the youth staff at Church on the Move, under Pastor Willie George. He is a native of Jackson, Mississippi and grew up at Word of Life Church.

Kevin is a visionary and a leader. His passion is igniting destiny on the inside of others and equipping them to fulfill it.

*"If you don't do more than you can possibly do,
then you will never be all that you can possibly be."*

Kevin has been happily married to his wife, Adrienne, for over thirty years. They have two great sons, Gavin and Garrison.

Pastor Cooley welcomes your thoughts and comments, both about this book or if you'd like to share any successes that occur as a result of reading it. He can be reached by email at:

kcooley@harvestmobile.com

Made in the USA
Monee, IL
13 September 2023

42673528R00166